Access to Power

MODERN SOUTH ASIA

Ashutosh Varshney, Series Editor
Pradeep Chhibber, Associate Series Editor

The Other One Percent
Sanjoy Chakravorty, Devesh Kapur, and Nirvikar Singh

Social Justice through Inclusion
Francesca R. Jensenius

Dispossession without Development
Michael Levien

The Man Who Remade India
Vinay Sitapati

Business and Politics in India
Edited by Christophe Jaffrelot, Atul Kohli, and Kanta Murali

Clients and Constituents
Jennifer Bussell

Gambling with Violence
Yelena Biberman

Mobilizing the Marginalized
Amit Ahuja

The Absent Dialogue
Anit Mukherjee

When Nehru Looked East
Francine Frankel

Capable Women, Incapable States
Poulami Roychowdhury

Farewell to Arms
Rumela Sen

Negotiating Democracy and Religious Pluralism
Karen Barkey, Sudipta Kaviraj, and Vatsal Naresh

Cultivating Democracy
Mukulika Banerjee

Patching Development
Rajesh Veeraraghavan

The Difficult Politics of Peace
Christopher Clary

Access to Power
Ijlal Naqvi

Access to Power

Electricity and the Infrastructural State in Pakistan

IJLAL NAQVI

OXFORD
UNIVERSITY PRESS

OXFORD
UNIVERSITY PRESS

Oxford University Press is a department of the University of Oxford. It furthers the University's objective of excellence in research, scholarship, and education by publishing worldwide. Oxford is a registered trade mark of Oxford University Press in the UK and certain other countries.

Published in the United States of America by Oxford University Press
198 Madison Avenue, New York, NY 10016, United States of America.

Library of Congress Cataloging-in-Publication Data
Names: Naqvi, Ijlal, author.
Title: Access to power : electricity and the infrastructural state in Pakistan / Ijlal Naqvi.
Description: New York : Oxford University Press, [2022] |
Series: Modern South Asia series | Includes bibliographical references and index.
Identifiers: LCCN 2022018790 (print) | LCCN 2022018791 (ebook) |
ISBN 9780197540954 (hardback) | ISBN 9780197540978 (epub) |
ISBN 9780197540961 | ISBN 9780197540985
Subjects: LCSH: Electric industries—Pakistan. | Electric power—Pakistan. |
Power resources—Pakistan. | Infrastructure (Economics)—Pakistan.
Classification: LCC HD9685.P182 N36 2022 (print) | LCC HD9685.P182 (ebook) |
DDC 333.79095491—dc23/eng/20220610
LC record available at https://lccn.loc.gov/2022018790
LC ebook record available at https://lccn.loc.gov/2022018791

DOI: 10.1093/oso/9780197540954.001.0001

1 3 5 7 9 8 6 4 2

Printed by Integrated Books International, United States of America

CONTENTS

ACKNOWLEDGMENTS

I couldn't have written this book alone. Charlie Kurzman shepherded me through my dissertation fieldwork and the difficult process of writing up without returning to the University of North Carolina (UNC). Charlie's generosity of spirit and mind is such that I can't imagine a better adviser. Andy Perrin, Margarita Mooney, and John Stephens took a leap of faith on a project that was little more than a hunting license in its early stages. Ayesha Jalal's razor-sharp insights on Pakistan and continued enthusiasm for the project always provided a boost. Needless to say, all errors remain my responsibility alone.

The fieldwork I did in Islamabad lies at the heart of this book. Employees of the Islamabad Electric Supply Company (IESCO) and the Lahore Electric Supply Company (LESCO) taught me how their system works, sharing their time and wisdom and tea with humor and an open spirit—all with no reward to themselves. I am especially grateful to the staff of the subdivisions who tolerated my repeated intrusions into their working lives as well as the *katchi abadi* residents of Islamabad who helped me try to see things from their perspective. I am grateful to all who shared their time and views with me.

In Pakistan, I was very lucky to stumble into a professional community with extensive experience in the Pakistani power sector when I joined the Energy Policy Program, a United States Agency for International Development (USAID)–funded consulting effort that supported the Ministry of Water and Power in its governance reform program. I learned a great deal from Mian Shahid Ahmed, Charley Moseley, Salahuddin Rifai, Manzoor Shaikh, Michael Gembol, Mary Webster, Shahid Sattar, and others. Munir Ahmed's camaraderie and support in navigating the madness of the ministry and USAID's contractor politics was essential to keeping a sense of perspective and humor. Munir was an early reader of my dissertation whose feedback I relied on. More broadly, my colleagues had a depth of power sector knowledge which they generously shared with me. Saleem Arif and Ashfaq Mahmood offered crucial support and guidance based on their tremendous experience and knowledge.

Singapore Management University (SMU) has been my intellectual home for the past ten years, and sometimes a sad one. Too many friends and colleagues departed the School of Social Sciences (SOSS), but many more have joined, and I am happy to see this environment changing into one that is more supportive for junior scholars. Chandran Kukathas has led this transformation, and I am grateful to him for his faith in my work. Christine Henderson and Chandran have jointly set the tone by opening their home to myself and colleagues with generosity and joie de vivre. The academic writing group at SOSS has been a wonderfully supportive peer-learning environment. I'm particularly thankful to Nick Harrigan, Serena Wee, Jake Ricks, and Gao Yang for their inputs to this book (and other projects), but most especially for their friendship. Ulas Ince and Hiro Saito gave constructive comments to unpolished drafts. Rebecca Maniates at the SMU library solved my problems with handling citations across multiple formats in unwieldy files. I also need to thank the students of my development class who learned more about electricity in Pakistan than they perhaps wanted to! The SMU School of Social Sciences and the Lee Kong Chian Fellowship both provided funding for this book. Part of the research for Chapter 4 was supported by the Singapore Ministry of Education Academic Research Fund Tier 1 grant C242/MSS13S004.

Parts of this book have been published in the *Journal of Development Studies, Current Sociology, and Urban Studies*. Developing these sections for publication was an essential step toward improving the argument in those chapters, and also in developing the overall framework of the book. I thank the editors and the anonymous referees for their comments. I also benefited from the collective effort entailed in the *Current Sociology* publication, which was guided by Diane Davis and Julie-Anne Boudreau.

In no particular order, I have many debts of gratitude to acknowledge for people and institutions who have helped me develop this work (directly or indirectly). Aasim Sajjad Akhtar helped me get started on serious fieldwork in Islamabad. Tariq Rahman at Quaid-e-Azam University's National Institute for Pakistan Studies generously provided me with a temporary academic home away from UNC. I benefited from a seminar at Oxford organized by Indrajit Roy. I thank Miguel Loureiro and Shandana Mohmand Khan for hosting me for a talk at the Institute of Development Studies. Majed Akhtar very kindly arranged for me to give a talk at School of Oriental and African Studies (SOAS), where Ed Simpson and Liz Chatterjee provided insightful comments. Audiences at Northwestern and Brown turned up for online talks and gave comments that helped me refine the argument. Kamran Asdar Ali, Shahnaz Rouse, and Itty Abraham have all offered sage advice and warm support at different times.

Federico Rossi provided theoretical sophistication and friendship in large doses. Seth Schindler brought me to Manchester's Global Development Institute for a workshop on the Belt and Road Initiative, which helped me see the significance of Sahiwal for my argument. Subadevan has been an extraordinarily capable research assistant over several years and is now well on his way toward developing his own scholarly agenda. Ate Poorthuis and Anirudh Govind helped me immensely with the models and charts in Chapter 4. Anirudh also contributed to almost every figure in the book, giving each a little more style and purpose than they might otherwise have had. Syed Zahoor Hassan opened doors at LESCO for me at just the right time. Waqas bin Najib has been an invaluable interlocutor. Ejaz Haider tried to mitigate the damage I was doing in translation and transliteration. I am grateful to Libby Beri for casting a professional editor's eye on the entire book in her role as development editor. The book's cover is based on a photo taken by the very talented Omer Rana.

I owe a great deal to the salty sharks for keeping me current with developments in Pakistan and allowing me to learn from their incisive commentaries. I hope this is reflected in the quality of this work, and if not, I will certainly hear about it!

The two weeks in 2015 that I spent at Brown's Watson Institute for the program on Governance and Development in the Global South have had a very broad influence on this project. Nitsan Chorev, Andy Schrank, Prerna Singh, and Michael Kennedy, among others, helped me see a larger intellectual landscape. On an unrelated but equally important note, I also learned at Brown that Latin Americans are simply more ready to have fun than anyone else! Patrick Heller gave valuable feedback on the development of the book at the proposal stage. He and Ashutosh Varshney opened the door for me at OUP's Modern South Asia series.

I have more reason than most to thank my editor at OUP, Dave McBride, as well as the anonymous reviewers. The reviewers understood this book and captured its strengths in better ways than I have often managed. Their generous praise and constructive critiques were a delight to receive and have given me a chance to improve the book. There are few joys in academic life better than having your work read, critiqued with care and skill, and returned with encouragement. My thanks to Dave for shepherding this process through in a timely manner, not least in securing the vital second review the week that SMU was to decide on my tenure case. He and the delegates who endorsed the manuscript have my sincere gratitude.

In Matthew and Tom I have two friends as loyal and true as one could wish for. They, and the FC crew, have also forced me to stay much healther than I otherwise would have done. To help me finish on time, Tom and Kate even threw me a party to celebrate the completion of my book manuscript!

Sofi is the best kid a dad could ask for; enough said. Leylac saw this book develop through many iterations of dissertation chapters, articles, and talks. We traveled a long way together. Thank you.

My wonderful siblings are a testament to all the love that is possible in a big family. We live so far apart, but they have always managed to be there for me. I can't wait to join them and all of the 37-D gang at our next raucous celebration.

This book is dedicated to my parents, whose love, encouragement, and support have been such a powerful constant in my life.

1

Introduction

Pakistan would desperately like to produce enough electricity, but it usually doesn't. This is the rare issue on which government and private sector can unite, and it is the cause of suffering for rich and poor alike across the entirety of the country. For most of the last two decades, urban residents in Pakistan may have been without power for 8 hours on any given day, and rural residents for 12 or more. Electricity shortages are one of the many poor governance outcomes characteristic of the South Asian state. Standard development thinking points to a lack or absence of institutions in comparison with an idealized and distant other country, such as Denmark, with governance reform programs formulated accordingly. The orientation toward what Pakistan is not takes us away from how it actually functions and to whose benefit. Electricity governance reinforces relations of power between provinces and the federal center, contributes to the marginalization of subordinate groups in the city, and orients citizens toward a patronage-based relationship with the state through encounters with street-level bureaucrats.[1]

Pakistan's power sector's woes are less mystery than tragedy,[2] but to conclude simply that a weak state produces poor governance outcomes misses the manner in which these arrangements are important for reproducing existing relations of domination and are resistant to change. The question this book addresses, therefore, isn't just about why Pakistan doesn't produce enough power. There is no lack of political will to address the power sector's challenges, and the sector has received relentless attention from bilateral donors and multilateral development institutions over many years—yet reforms have failed and Pakistanis still suffer. Why?

This book seeks to unpack our understanding of how states in the Global South, with their complex colonial histories and regional tensions, actually work. The argument builds on the literatures on good governance and class-centric analyses of power relations while remaining focused on solving real-world problems. An adequate electricity supply is a necessity for all states. In addition,

Access to Power. Ijlal Naqvi, Oxford University Press. © Oxford University Press 2022.
DOI: 10.1093/oso/9780197540954.003.0001

the challenges of state-formation entailed therein, including constructing the infrastructure and extracting the related stream of payments, are general tasks with broad relevance to other infrastructures and public goods across the Global South. In many senses, Pakistan's electricity problems are neither unique nor even surprising given that public service failures are commonplace in the Global South. This book moves beyond the diagnosis of a lack of Weberian state capacity and looks instead at the relationships of power and processes of governance that produce these poor outcomes and why they are resistant to change.

The Pakistani power sector is bedeviled by operational and financial troubles. The rolling blackouts known as loadshedding have become a regular feature of daily life in Pakistan with huge consequences. Loadshedding disrupts business and deters investment,[3] and it is estimated to reduce economic growth in Pakistan by 2%.[4] The federal government's subsidy to power consumers for the three fiscal years between 2008 and 2011 exceeded one trillion rupees ($117 billion) and added 10% to the total national debt; this subsidy was greater than the entire public sector development budget over that same period (Ministry of Finance, 2011). Since then, residential electricity subsidies were found to be 0.8% of GDP in 2015, a comparable amount to total public health spending (World Bank, 2017, p. 1). Unpaid electricity bills contribute to the crippling accumulation of debts owed from one government entity to another—known as circular debt—which both arise from and contribute to this budgetary stress.

The scale and importance of the electricity crisis have escaped nobody's attention. In his 2008 inaugural address to the National Assembly, Prime Minister Yousaf Raza Gillani promised to address the electricity shortage.[5] However, loadshedding worsened during his tenure, and the government's promise to end the shortages in 2009 brought them ridicule both when the plan was announced and when the government failed to meet it. The Pakistan Muslim League-Nawaz (PML-N) government of 2013–2018 was committed to ending loadshedding as its signature policy initiative and campaign issue.[6] Although the PML-N government did add more capacity, cash flow problems coinciding with a change of government meant that any respite from loadshedding was temporary. The issue received international attention as well: addressing the electricity shortages was also near the top of the United States Agency for International Development's plan for spending $7.5 billion in aid to Pakistan under the Kerry-Lugar-Berman Act. Unfortunately, the governance reforms and capacity additions pursued under United States Agency for International Development (USAID) also had limited success. More recently, the China–Pakistan Economic Corridor (CPEC) was launched with $37 billion worth of energy projects intended to address Pakistan's power sector woes by replacing expensive power with cheaper alternatives.[7] National policy concerns are regularly in the headlines, but the personal experience of loadshedding is more directly disruptive to everyday life.

The idea for this research project started in the summer of 2005 when I was part of a disgruntled mob of middle- and upper-class Pakistani men that had gathered in front of the local office of the electrical utility in a residential neighborhood in Lahore. We had been without power for most of the night, and in the hundred-plus-degree heat many people could not sleep or be comfortable when deprived of fans and air conditioners. The assembled group had come to the office to find out why their power was out and when it might be restored. My father had made me come down to the office. I had resisted—what was the point?—but I finally relented. I was familiar with Pakistanis maneuvering their way through government bureaucracies armed with introductions and references from some important third party (*sifarish*), and perhaps even supplementing these requests with a payment (*rishwat*). But until that night, when I first encountered ordinary Pakistanis demanding that their state provide them with a service they needed and wanted, I had never seen such a vociferous expression of demands on the state that hinted at citizenship rights.

Armed with little more than their frustration, these otherwise-stolid burghers fumed in the heat but got no satisfaction from the employees of the electrical utility who were on duty that night. Eventually, one person who had gotten into the office (the majority of us stayed outside) informed the rest of the crowd that the phone line had been deliberately disconnected so that the employees on duty would no longer have to listen to our complaints. People started to make bold claims about what they would do to resolve the situation. One man claimed that he would march to the house of the utility's chief executive, to which another responded, "I'll follow you, lead the way." After someone suggested going to the house of the *nazim* of Lahore, a group of about 30 people gathered to walk or drive the quarter-mile to his house.[8] I left for home, having no confidence that the *nazim* would achieve anything if anyone was even able to contact him.

Several hours later that morning the electricity came back on, without any indication of why it had gone or why it returned when it did. Over the years I lived in Islamabad from 2008 to 2011, I was to become very familiar with this characteristic lack of transparency and accountability as I researched the power sector across government departments, city neighborhoods, and the offices of the Islamabad Electric Supply Company (IESCO). The eventual choice of appealing to the *nazim* was probably influenced by his proximity. The *nazim* has absolutely no authority over the electrical utility, and—if he were to do anything—it would be to call someone at the utility and request that they address the problem. Petitioning an elected representative to help in redressing a grievance is a staple of democracy, but the appeal to the *nazim* also reflects a patron–client mode of supplicating a notable member of society to put pressure on state officials.

National, City, and Individual Levels of Analysis

The book uses a three-part narrative structure to explore how the relationships around electricity carry different meanings and sustain distinct debates at different levels of analysis: national, city, and individual. At each level, I treat the unevenness of electricity governance as a product of state-building and an integral part of the system of rule rather than an absence or erosion of governance. Meanwhile, the material properties of electricity require the entire nation to be synchronized in its production and consumption of electrical power.[9] At the national level, the federal government must balance the rival claims and contributions of each province, wherein ethnic differences and the legacy of past disputes become entangled with political economy. At the city level, squatter settlements seek legal access to electricity as an acknowledgment of their occupancy, while industrialists and the middle class are increasingly aggravated by the poor quality of service. At the individual level, people encounter street-level bureaucrats with whom they negotiate using a blend of personalistic appeals, bribery, and threats of violence or intervention by influential individuals. The bureaucrats themselves carefully shade the moral valences of the shortcuts they take against the constraints of sustaining an underfunded system that pays them poorly.

Each level of analysis has its own dynamics and is typically the domain of different academic disciplines. By knitting these levels together through the theoretical framework of the "infrastructural state" (which will be advanced in this Introduction), we are able to see why it is so difficult to reform the governance of Pakistan's electricity sector. The different disciplinary approaches typically speak past each other, but deploying them together helps to show how Pakistan's power sector troubles manifest at different levels of analysis in interrelated ways. National policy concerns emerge from the consequences of dynamic processes at multiple levels. From above, policy decisions are driven by a commitment to a unitary vision of national identity governed through a strong federal center. From below, the rules of street-level bureaucracies are embedded in practices of patronage and rents, culture, and interpersonal connections. In the absence of an established interdisciplinary approach to knit these different levels of analysis together, the most influential school of thought for addressing governance reform has come from economics.[10]

Critique of the Dominant Governance Paradigm

The message that governance reform requires attention to more than the formal rules of governance is now well entrenched in development thinking.

Governance reforms that concentrated on formal rules and excluded the informal realities of country context have been a failure. Despite spending in excess of US$10 billion per year, aid from countries in the Organization for Economic Co-operation and Development (OECD) that targets governance as a set of formal rules has had "limited impact" (Institute of Development Studies, 2010). However, the dominant theorization of governance for development is drawn from new institutionalist economics, which—in practice, at least—largely restricts itself to formal rules. There are historical and sociological strains of new institutionalism that are much more attuned to how institutions develop and evolve (Hall & Taylor, 1996), but these are nowhere near as influential in development thinking.

The seminal statement of new institutionalism in economics is Douglass North's (1990, p. 3) formulation that "Institutions are the rules of the game in a society or, more formally, are the humanly devised constraints that shape human interaction." These rules can be formal—codified by human beings—or informal, "such as conventions and codes of behavior." That the new institutionalist economics framework includes informal rules is a major step beyond neoclassical economics, in which treatment of the Global South relied on "social arrangements that economists usually take for granted, but which are conspicuous by their absence in poor countries" (Rodrik, 2007, p. 153). Northian informal institutions are conceptually cluttered in that they contain everything from *panchayats* (village councils) in South Asia to the Protestant ethic.[11] The critiques of new institutionalist economics come from too many sources to be able to cover them all. Mushtaq Khan's (2018) political settlements approach draws attention to the social context from which institutions emerge as a key point in understanding their relative effectiveness (or lack thereof). In turn, political settlements analysis can be critiqued for being insufficiently attentive to the role of ideas in bringing together elite cohesion. Moreover, the developmental outcomes of political settlements are mediated by a meso-level field specific to the policy domain in question (Kelsall & vom Hau, 2020). Relatedly, the developmental state literature examines the evolution of industrial policy through the back and forth between state actors and key industries.[12] Two recent examples from political science point to the broad deficiencies in new institutionalist economics using the cases of road building in Indonesia and in the economic rise of China. Jamie Davidson (2015) proposes a political sociology of infrastructure development in which he uses a study of toll roads in Indonesia to speak to shortcomings in new institutionalist economics. The three main deficiencies are a neglect of close ties between state and business, the importance of regulations and ordinances other than parliamentary legislation, and the local power struggles revealed in contests over eminent domain. Ang Yuen Yuen (2016) argues that China's development involved a coevolution of institutions and markets from a starting point of weak institutions. Ang contrasts her dynamic view of institutional development to Acemoglu and Robinson (2012), whose explanation of why nations fail focuses on the absence of strong institutions due to some unspecified historical conditions.[13] Power and politics are all too often absent from new institutional economics (Bates, 1997), and the emphasis on formal institutions—rather than power or politics—invites further tweaks to institutional design when the subsequent reforms don't pan out as expected (Radaelli, Dente, & Dossi, 2012). Indeterminacy in causal claims and an emphasis on top-down interventions concentrating on formal rules are significant limitations of governance reform based on the new institutionalist economics. Where my work can build on these literatures is to trace state policy down to the everyday state, in its citizen-facing rather than industrially oriented stance, and to explore the unevenness of state capacity across its territory.

Many sociologists and political scientists engage with state capacity as an alternative framing to the literature on good governance and institutions. In a recent programmatic statement, Centeno et al. (2017) define state capacity as "the organizational and bureaucratic ability to implement governing projects." Arguing that state capacity is based on "a constellation of organizational qualities" whose interactions are complex, they consider the "pursuit of parsimonious theories and linear methods unproductive" (pp. 26–27). Unpacking the state to examine state capacity also lends itself to problem-solving sociology (Prasad, 2021), in which the analyst seeks to solve rather than just critique problems, and to bridge the distance between victims of social problems and those who cause (and benefit) from them.

The theoretical framework for this book focuses on state capacity with an eye toward problem-solving as well as critique. The framework is based on three elements that I draw from existing literatures. The first element is to approach the state as a set of nested fields. The second element is to study the state by tracing the material connections across society and territory that constitute the electrical power network. The third element is to approach the unevenness of state capacity as a result of deliberate action, rather than a lack or absence of the state. Building on these three elements, I call the theoretical framework of this book "the infrastructural state."

Using the three elements of the infrastructural state framework and a methodological blend of ethnography, statistics, and comparative political economy, this book uses Pakistan's chronic shortages of electricity as an entry point for making more general claims about the state in Pakistan:

1) Pakistan's inability to meet its power supply requirements is nested within dynamics of governance and power relations that cannot simply be reduced to a lack of Weberian state capacity;

2) Pakistan is neither a weak nor a failed state, but state capacity in Pakistan is chronically uneven and marked by profound inequalities;
3) Moreover, the unevenness of the Pakistani state works in specific ways to suit and benefit regions and groups that hold power, and the resulting "inequality by design" is the product of many layers of conscious strategic decision-making;
4) The everyday state is bound up in the personal and the informal rather than departing from the Weberian ideal. These informalities pervade relationships at all levels of governance, making governance—understood as an emergent compromise—especially resistant to top-down interventions privileging formal institutions.

Theoretical Framework of the Infrastructural State

The State as a Set of Nested Fields

The first element is to approach the state as a set of nested fields, where each field is an arena of conflict over the distribution of valued resources—in this case electrical power. An institutions-based approach privileges codified rules, whereas a field-based approach is above all else relational—and thus about power—and informed more by culture and habit than strategic decision-making. Moreover, conceptualizing the state as a set of nested fields allows us to establish how national-level issues emerge organically from the underlying behaviors of interest at the city and individual levels.

Fields are arenas of struggle in which actors with varying capacities vie for advantage. Actors in a field share an understanding of what is at stake and how the positions of different actors are related (i.e., their relative power), and they understand the rules of the game that shape the permissible and feasible modes of behavior. The field is a well-established sociological concept most strongly associated with Pierre Bourdieu (Bourdieu, 1999), but that has been interpreted by other leading theorists more recently as well (Fligstein & McAdam, 2012; J. L. Martin, 2003).[14] This book draws from each of these theorists but extends them into domains less traveled rather than seeking to specifically intervene in the theorization of fields themselves. For example, the approach to individual action taken here is more in line with a Bourdieusian field rather than the strategic action fields of Fligstein and McAdam, in that I conceive of action as more tacit and practically informed than shaped by conscious strategizing (Swartz, 2014). Regardless, the empirical material this book engages with does not have the kind of episodes of strategic contention in which fields are reshaped that would lend themselves toward the strategic action fields approach.

Within this broad theoretical approach, one aspect in which I do follow Fligstein and McAdam (2012) is in the formulation of treating states as a dense network of fields. The different levels of the Pakistani electrical power sector are vertically nested fields. Each has its own players and dynamics, but the city and local fields are dependent on the national field in that crucial decisions of policy—such as the content of governance reforms—are decided at the national level and implemented (ideally) at all levels. At the same time, the consequences of lower-level contests over electricity filter upward to shape the emergent properties of the system. Each level has differing patterns of coordination and regulation as well as different ways in which power is brought to bear.

Emergence is the idea that systemic characteristics arise organically from the interaction of a system's parts. Emergent properties (which belong to the system, not the individuals) cannot be determined in advance. It is a central concept in sociology because we are studying not just aggregations of individuals but also the organizations and institutions that arise out of social life.[15] The dynamism with which people and their social environments adapt to each other is a key part of what makes social life so difficult to model or predict.

Emergence is one example of the type of nonlinear system dynamics associated with complexity science that are becoming more established in social sciences and specifically in development studies.[16] Through a complexity lens, human societies are nonlinear systems with multiple, independent actors who coevolve with their environment. Referencing complex adaptive systems in the context of development is useful because complexity science has become associated with policy approaches that are themselves decentralized, dynamic, and adaptive, in contrast to the Washington Consensus suite of policies, which align better with a focus on formal institutions and top-down prescriptions.[17] Chapter 3 will discuss complexity and its application to policy in some more detail, but at this stage it is important to contrast the approach being taken in this book to the dominant paradigm of development thinking.

A field-based approach is quite different from an institutions-based approach because of the emphasis on relationality and power. The conceptual apparatus of the field entails more work for the analyst, but that effort brings attention to questions of relative power and position, as well as the many informal ways that these dynamics play out. The approach of treating the state as a set of nested fields can also be contrasted to the development and policy literature that focuses on configurations of classes and political parties as well as anthropological approaches, which often look for "the universe in a grain of sand" and generalize from one case or locality to the larger whole.

My approach of conceptualizing the state as a set of nested fields is also aligned with Neil Brenner's (2004, p. 8) approach to "the scale question." Each nested field reflects a different scale, allowing for the integration of distinct vantage points across them, with attention to how the relationships of social processes across these scales influence each other. However, Brenner's more geographical approach—strongly influenced by Henri Lefebvre's work on state and space (see, e.g., 2009)—also underscores the need for attention to the hierarchy of scales and their spatiality, meaning that these spaces are ordered within vertical and hierarchical relations of domination that reproduce themselves through the social processes of governance. The second element describes how this book uses the material infrastructure of electricity in Pakistan as its entry point for tracing the connections within and across scales, and the third element of studying the infrastructural state discusses this spatial unevenness in more detail.

Material Infrastructure as a Point of Entry for Studying the State

The second element of this book's theoretical framework is the use of the material infrastructure of electricity as an entry point for studying the state. By following the infrastructure of electricity from national issues down to the behaviors of real people, we dive deeply into the challenges of state-making in the Global South and build an understanding of governance grounded in its material manifestations rather than its paper representations. An institutions approach to governance struggles to penetrate below the national level. Taking the approach of a comparison among provinces or states does offer sub-national insights, but tracing the material infrastructure reveals a direct connection between national-level policy and the home or firm, as well as the interrelatedness and integration of sub-national regions into an uneven, unequal whole.

The link between infrastructure and the state is well established. Henri Lefebvre points repeatedly to the centrality of infrastructure to the establishment of state or political space:

> With its technostructure controlling energy questions, the state gradually becomes the master of them, not only because it controls the units of production, but because it partitions space under the double surveillance of its technicians and police. The production of energy is closely tied to the production of political space, i.e. state space. (Lefebvre, 2009, pp. 237–238)

Infrastructure in general, but especially energy, is a mechanism for the state's control of both territory and population, and in the ongoing social processes around access to that infrastructure the state further sets out the terms for this dimension of citizenship. In a historical study of road building in 17th- and

18th-century Britain, Jo Guldi (2012, p. 3) examines "the politics of an infrastructure state" arising around conflicts to do with changes to infrastructure (and access to it). As Guldi identifies, infrastructure is both expensive and necessary for a people to flourish in the modern world, and thus the construction of infrastructure begets conflict over inclusion in its benefits: "only a government that reflects [the people's] interests equally can design a form of infrastructure that serves them all" (p. 23). Guldi positions the British state squarely at the heart of these new developments and highlights the state making that accompanied British road building, ranging from the establishment of the legal principle of eminent domain to acquire lands for public use, to the various financing arrangements put in place by parliament to pay for infrastructure. State-building of this kind is more typically associated with the preparation for—and the conduct of—armed conflict rather than infrastructure (Brewer, 1989; Tilly, 1985).

Historians of technology and students of science and technology studies (STS) will be familiar with electrical power systems due to Thomas Hughes' (1983) *Networks of Power*,[18] which observes that "power systems are cultural artifacts":

> Electrical power systems embody the physical, intellectual, and symbolic resources of the society that construct them. . . . In a sense, electrical power systems, like so much other technology, are both causes and effects of social change. (Hughes, 1983, p. 2)

Hughes illustrates this point through examples such as the development of the first electrical power distribution company by Thomas Edison and General Electric. Edison didn't just invent an improved light bulb; he implemented a system for generating and distributing electricity for lighting. Central to his concern was the commercial viability of such a system that depended on beating the cost of natural gas. It was an "inseparably technical and economic" problem (p. 29). Edison chose downtown New York City for the density of consumers and for the possibility of influencing financiers. It was no accident that the first consumer connection was to the offices of the financial services firm Drexel, Morgan & Co at 23 Wall Street. As Hughes so elegantly demonstrated, the distribution and administration of electrical power is never solely a technical matter but, rather, a tussle between the influence of the social and political on the technical—and vice versa.

The infrastructure of electrical power has an irreducible materiality that is distinct from other infrastructures such as those for rail or water. Electrical power operates at a speed that "does not so much flow . . . as flash, annihilating the space between the consumption and production in both the immediacy and the constancy of its usage" (Needham, 2014, p. 17). Due to this speed, the social and territorial distances spanned by the electricity network are easily ignored. Railroads also connect people and goods over space, but they enable the transportation of individuals at a speed and in a style that expose them to each other and their surroundings.[19] Water infrastructures also share a resource across distances, but unlike electricity, water cannot readily be generated, only tapped from existing sources such as rivers and aquifers.[20] While electricity can be generated, it cannot stored for delayed release in a manner that is efficient or viable at scale with current battery technologies.

Electrical power generation and consumption have to be synchronized, not only in their timing, but also in the operation of the grid across the entirety of the territory they serve. An excess of supply or demand will result in a cascading failure across the entire grid. Thus, the generation and consumption of electricity has to be coordinated across the territory that the grid serves. For Pakistani electrical power, this paramount goal of maintaining the operation of the grid is manifested in the National Power Control Center in Islamabad, where a large digital display shows the frequency at which the grid is currently operating. This frequency should be kept at 50 Hz, although in practice the frequency routinely dips lower (with 49.5 Hz representing a lower bound beyond which catastrophic failures are possible). These material qualities of electricity, distinct from those of other infrastructures, sustain meanings and social relations as well.

Infrastructures operate at multiple levels simultaneously (Larkin, 2013), sustaining a "poetics and politics" in addition to their technical operations (which are never solely technical). Electrical power is an avatar of modernization. In practical terms, it is an essential component of contemporary life that is as integral to the steel mill as it is to the convenience of a modern washing machine. The experience of electrification in the Global North was not a singular modernizing monolith. Alongside Benjamin Franklin's scientific experimentation with electricity, there were many exuberant, irrational, and intimate experiences of electricity as the modern sublime (Delbourgo, 2006). Decisions such as adopting a DC or AC current and a system of pricing are contingent historical decisions influenced by societal factors (Yakubovich, Granovetter, & McGuire, 2005). The spread of electric power shaped and was shaped by social transformation in early 20th century America (Nye, 1990). Far from being purely technical decisions, the rollout of the electrical grid and its distribution networks were cultural artifacts shaped by their social context (Hughes, 1983). Even in the context of electrification, the expression of modernization that was built into the infrastructure and its associated policies was always shaped by context and culture. The changes wrought by the forces of modernization were never predetermined in their outcomes but always contingent on circumstance. As modernizing states seek to build out and operate their electrical grid, the ability to do so effectively is a valuable indicator of state capacity.

A state's capacity to act over its territory is known as its "infrastructural power" (following Michael Mann, 1986). Mann illustrated the concept with reference to the Red Queen's pursuit of Alice in Lewis Carroll's *Alice in Wonderland*. Ordering her soldiers to cut off Alice's head indicates despotic power, a form of tyranny, whereas it would reflect infrastructural power if the soldiers actually pursued and implemented the order while out of the Queen's sight. More precisely, Mann defined infrastructural power as the "the capacity of the state to actually penetrate civil society, and to implement logistically political decisions through the realm" (Mann, 1984, p. 189). In other words, can the state actually do what it says it will? Since infrastructural power is multifaceted, Mann—and scholars after him—identifies multiple dimensions of infrastructural power such as the state's control of space and society, its legitimacy, and its territorial reach.[21] A multidimensional approach to infrastructural power is helpful in that it encourages us to think beyond bureaucratic capacity or state autonomy, but it shares with O'Donnell's (1993) approach to sub-national state capacity the implication that the state is present and functional in some areas while absent or dysfunctional in others.[22]

States of the Global South often have an uneven state capacity across their territory. Adnan Naseemullah (2016) describes state capacity in India as being suffused by contestation and conflict. Due to the unavoidable limits to state capacity (which are especially pertinent in postcolonial states of the Global South), unevenness is produced, as states must always choose how and where to deploy their limited resources. Hence, Naseemullah sees the state itself as an arena, rather than the neutral agent of its political leadership. Similarly, for the case of Pakistan, I will argue that that this unevenness is not simply an absence or a lack of state capacity, but a product of ongoing processes of state formation and contestation.

Somewhat counterintuitively, Mann's infrastructural power doesn't explicitly engage with infrastructure itself, although other scholars often use infrastructure-based indicators as a way to measure the concept (e.g., Herbst, 2000). Mann's emphasis (per the definition above) is the state's capacity to penetrate the society logistically. Chandra Mukerji's (2009) study of the building of the Canal du Midi in 17th-century France offers us a linkage between infrastructure projects and infrastructural power, through the logistics entailed in project construction as an act of state formation that can succeed on multiple levels. Indeed, the canal project was sold to Louis XIV and his court, who sought to establish a new Rome for the King's greater glory. Despite this focus on the Sun King himself, and the punishments meted out to the canal's champions—who were chastised for seeking to valorize their own roles in its construction—the canal served to establish an impersonal logistical rule in service of a stewardship of the land.

Impersonal rule was "born at an intersection of social, moral and material worlds" (p. 206). Mukerji's historical account points to how the logistics of the canal's construction furthered the state's infrastructural power, as impersonal rule began to supplant patronage relations and the all-encompassing sovereignty of the French king. The analogous processes in the Pakistani electrical power sector, however, have not built an equivalent degree of infrastructural power.

My approach to studying the state through how its accoutrements have been built out was influenced by James Ferguson's (1990) *Anti-Politics Machine*. Ferguson saw the state in Foucauldian terms, as the "knotting and congealing" of power through bureaucratic practices rather than the "name of an actor" (p. 273).[23] Importantly, where others saw failure in a development project that was intended to improve land management productivity, Ferguson saw an exercise in state-building that established the influence of the central government of Lesotho more forcefully in a region that had a history of resistance. In similar vein, I study the expansion and development of the Pakistani power sector as an exercise in state-building. Further, rather than accepting the usual verdict of failure and inefficiency, I seek to examine exactly how the state that has been built out in no small part through the electricity infrastructure actually works, and to whose benefit.

Pakistan "Works," but for Whom?

The third element is that Pakistan "works," despite the frequent descriptions of it as a failing or fragile state, although this is not to say that it works well or in the interest of ordinary people. By saying that Pakistan "works," I am drawing on Chabal and Daloz's (1999) analysis of how "Africa works," wherein disorder is a political instrument that reinforces patrimonial relations in postcolonial societies. Similarly, the governance of electricity in Pakistan serves existing relations of power and patronage. Building on Catherine Boone's *Property and Political Order in Africa* (Boone, 2014), I argue that the inequality and unevenness of electricity governance in Pakistan is by design. This is not to say that it follows a master plan, but that it is the result of a series of conscious decisions concerning who gets what, when, and where.

Recent books on Pakistan have moved away from harping on state fragility or failure to recognize that there is a logic to its continued survival.[24] This sense in which the phrase "Pakistan works" is deployed can be extended and deepened with reference to Africanist academic literature because Pakistan clearly doesn't work equally well for all its citizens, nor across all its territory. Lieven (2012), for example, is somewhat guilty of giving too much credit to the army's response to Baloch militancy without recognizing the degree to which the army denies Baloch voices while cementing in place a power structure where the Pakistani army itself sits at the apex.[25]

In *Africa Works*, Patrick Chabal and Jean-Francois Daloz (1999) argue that the state in sub-Saharan Africa serves as a vehicle for patrimonial exercises of power. "Big men" use "disorder as a political instrument" in the conduct of what Jean-Francois Bayart calls the "politics of the belly," where "weak states and weak civil societies enable the domination of machines which function on the basis of the logics of factionalism, patronage and regionalism" (Bayart, 1993, p. 60). According to Bayart, the postcolonial African state is one that has been indigenously refashioned and thus reflects local attitudes toward power. Achille Mbembe (2000, p. 45) sees the foundations of the authoritarian postcolonial state in a "trinity of violence, transfers and allocations" through which the state manages inequality. Reflecting on the insights of this Africanist literature invites a careful consideration of who the Pakistani state's own disorder most benefits.

By looking within Pakistan to see who the state works for—and who it doesn't work for as well—we are able to move beyond a methodological nationalism that takes the nation-state as an ontologically given unit of analysis. The dominant approach to governance—exemplified in the World Bank's World Governance Indicators (*World Governance Indicators*, 2017)—uses a single figure to represent a country's score on various sub-indicators, despite the fact that great disparities exist within countries. For example, Erin-Metz McDonnell (2017) examines how pockets of excellence emerge at the interstices of Ghanaian government institutions; national-level indicators are not able to capture the possibility of sub-national excellence. In Eastern Europe, Marina Zaloznaya (2017) finds variation in bureaucratic corruption among health and education facilities in Byelorussia and Ukraine. With a focus on sub-national variation, Zeloznaya's findings can usefully inform reform programs that are tailored to both regions and organizations.[26]

A seminal statement on uneven stateness is Guillermo O'Donnell's (1993) framework for looking at uneven democratization in Latin America, which maps areas in blue, green, or brown to denote a decreasing degree of stateness. Richard Snyder (2001) usefully extends O'Donnell's work to set out an approach for sub-national comparisons. However, the emphasis in this book's analysis is not on sub-national comparisons but on the way in which the parts fit into the whole. As both O'Donnell and Snyder observe, there is a danger in sub-national comparisons of overlooking the relationship of the subunit to its surroundings, as these can be an important component of national politics.

The spatial unevenness of the state is a key theme for Lefebvre, who argues that it serves "*the reproduction of the relations of domination*":

> Places are arranged unequally in relation to the centers, which are themselves unequal—from commercial centers to administrative centers. State action exacerbates this situation: spaces form extreme hierarchies, from the centers of domination to the peripheries that are impoverished but still all the more strongly controlled. (Lefebvre, 2009, pp. 243–244, italics in original)

The unevenness of state space stems from and is part of the reproduction of a hierarchized and unequal set of relations, with the city at its core. As alluded to in the discussion of the state as a set of nested fields, this unevenness and inequality is both horizontal, in terms of the core and periphery of a territory, and vertical in terms of relationships across scales (Brenner, 2004, p. 10).

Catherine Boone develops the concept of "inequality by design" through a study of land institutions in sub-Saharan Africa (Boone, 2014). Boone's starting point is that the built state is an outcome that calls for explanation; state infrastructural power is "the product of negotiation and conflict between central and local actors" (Boone, 2012, p. 627). The center has options in terms of putting effort and resources toward the integration of territories and may strategically choose to do so, or to effectively abandon certain state functions, as part of a strategy of staying in power and ruling effectively. The resultant inequality is to be expected. The plurality of possible relationships makes the hinterlands governable and imposes a political order. Because the state produced this unevenness in order to govern through it, the resulting inequality is "by design." Boone's work builds on Mahmood Mamdani's (1996) framing of a postcolonial "bifurcated citizenship" wherein local political arenas are dislocated from a national citizenship regime that is chiefly urban. A core difference, though, is in stressing that the unevenness speaks to the political contest over the state's incorporation of these territories and is strategically chosen (or negotiated) as part of a larger regime. Boone contrasts the practices of customary tenure and statutory tenure to "see political logics encoded in existing land regimes, and how rulers may use land rules strategically to gather and maintain power" (Boone, 2014, p. 16). The focus of this book instead takes us to the institutions governing electricity generation and distribution, particularly the extent to which consumers pay for the electricity they consume as a proxy for their degree of incorporation into the national state.

Methodology

Every ethnographer has to gain access to the setting they choose to study. In many senses, Islamabad was not only my field site but where I actually lived.

I had also lived there before, from 2001 to 2002, am a citizen of Pakistan, and had both immediate and extended family members living in Islamabad, Rawalpindi, and Lahore during the period of my own residence in Islamabad from 2008 to 2011. This claim to authenticity of residence, however, meant little in terms of gaining access to my target organizations. Finding, getting to speak to, and observing my respondents involved regular reprisals of this process of gaining access. Getting "in" was not accomplished at a single stroke, nor the result of any dramatic events, but always a matter of degree and subject to ebbs and flows.

My approach to gaining access was based on securing introductions to my field sites and a non-threatening presentation of myself as a student. I faced the challenge of recruiting respondents by identifying areas I wanted to access and using the networks of my existing contacts to gain access to them. Once I had established some relevant contacts, I used their networks to introduce me to new field sites and to recruit new respondents. By and large, this strategy was successful.

The most difficult entrée was at the subdivision level at IESCO. Through a former colleague from my work in the federal government in 2001–2002, I met a serving power sector official in Lahore. This senior official found my project interesting and agreed to support me by introducing me at IESCO headquarters, from where I was referred to an executive engineer (a mid-level manager, abbreviated XEN). The XEN was chosen as an appropriate person for me to talk to by IESCO leadership, who described him as a good and competent officer. The XEN, in turn, introduced me to the subdivision officer (SDO), Farid sahib,[27] in whose office I did much of my field research. This initial introductions to a specific division and then subdivision were made for me by IESCO leadership. My expectation that I had been led to sites that made IESCO look good was borne out in the fieldwork and distribution company data. However, rather than a shortcoming, this site selection helped me meet my objective of studying the best service delivery environment. Even then, the service area of a subdivision (some 25,000 households) or division (often six or 10 subdivisions) has ample variation to explore in terms of the urban social fabric.

The primary challenge in gaining cooperation from my respondents was to show that I was not a threat. Being a student helped in this regard, as I could position myself in terms of conducting a study without a profit motive or corruption-exposing agenda. The digital voice recorder that I had intended to use in my interviews was completely unwelcome, and I only used it in one interview—that of a retired federal secretary in his own home. I did, however, keep my notepad out and visibly take notes during and after conversations as a reminder of the informed consent my respondents provided verbally. Without a written record of their participation, there is nothing concrete to link quotes and actions to particular individuals, thus protecting the anonymity of my respondents. No IESCO employee or location has been identified in this work, as was promised to my respondents. Farid sahib, the subdivision officer who headed the office where I did much of my fieldwork, actually wanted to be identified along with his location, but I felt unable to honor that request because the anonymity of too many other individuals (who did not so consent) would be compromised by doing so.

Much later in my fieldwork I realized that my respondents' networks had certain characteristics. At one stage, several of my respondents turned out to be members of the *tablighi-jamaat*, a nonviolent proselytizing movement. At another, I had a sequence of *shi'a* respondents who were particularly helpful to me—perhaps because I have a recognizably *shi'a* last name. Tapping these networks was unintentional, though it does echo what I observed in terms of the pathways and connections used by Pakistanis to navigate the state (see Chapter 7). Otherwise, I tried to be as indiscriminate as possible and meet with whoever would talk to me.

I supplement the place-based ethnography at the heart of this book with statistical analysis of the distribution company serving Lahore (LESCO). Although it was always my intention to include this methodological approach in the project, the data was not made available to me until years after my fieldwork had concluded. The statistical analysis offers a synoptic perspective across a larger geographic area than my ethnographic work could address. While the ethnographic work was fundamental in terms of revealing the processes that inform the dynamics of electricity governance, the statistics at both the city and national level help expand the argument regarding the unevenness of state capacity that is central to the book's argument.

Both Islamabad and Lahore represent something of the best-case scenario when considering governance in Pakistan. Islamabad, the federal capital, is a planned city, home to the offices of the federal government and their many employees. Farid sahib's subdivision is even a "model subdivision" with reduced staff (33% less) and increased wages (33% more). Islamabad is the most formal and best-administered setting one can find in Pakistan. One well-worn joke describes Islamabad as being located only 20 minutes from Pakistan. As for Lahore, Punjabi chauvinists proclaim that if you haven't seen Lahore you haven't been born (*Jinnay Lahore naeeN vekhya o jammya naeeN*). Lahore is the cultural, political, and economic heart of Pakistan's largest province. While one would never mistake Lahore's thrumming energy for Islamabad's orderly suburban calm, they are both loci of power, well populated by Pakistani elites accustomed to making things work in their favor. These are the places where the state is present and—ostensibly—works, or at least where Pakistanis expect it to be present and work.

Outline of the Book

This Introduction establishes the overarching theoretical framework for the book. It conceptualizes the governance of the Pakistani power sector as a series of nested and interdependent fields of strategic action at the national, city, and individual levels. This theorization is a sociological take on governance challenges that are typically considered at distinct levels of analysis. By combining the different levels of analysis, I reveal how Pakistan's national problems of power sector governance emerge from sub-national and even local-level dynamics.

Part I (Chapters 2 and 3) focuses on the national level. Chapter 2 is primarily concerned with the unevenness of electricity governance across the territory of the Pakistani state. I explore how this unevenness has been produced over time by studying government plans and some specific power generation projects that illustrate the way that provincial (and thus identity) politics play a role. The unevenness of electricity governance is most visible in the varied performance of the distribution companies, and in their (in)ability to collect payment for the electricity they deliver. There is an interprovincial political economy of power based on generating and consuming electrical power, and the policies that balance power generation and payment for power consumption across the country are central to maintaining the delicate balance in this fractious federation's political order.

Chapter 3 focuses on questions of governance reform as a component of the development agenda, incorporating both the national perspective and the role of international development actors such as bilateral aid agencies (e.g., USAID) and multilateral donors (the World Bank and the Asian Development Bank in particular). Development actors are regularly aware of the shortcomings of governance interventions before, during, and after development assistance is introduced, yet those programs continue and are even revisited. Why? I examine the Pakistani experience with power sector reforms to illustrate how the donor-led reform agenda had readily apparent shortcomings. A new wave of development thinking attempts to respond to such failures by drawing on complexity theory and moving toward more local, iterative, and experimental approaches. However, the awareness of problems with reforms is not sufficient to avoid them; there is a higher order of obstacles inherent in the structure of development assistance that limit the potential for governance reforms to reshape the workings of the state at the city or individual level.

Part II (Chapters 4 and 5) addresses the unevenness of urban citizenship in South Asia by connecting the individual experience to the neighborhood and city they live in. Chapter 4 looks at different levels of electricity governance in Lahore through a quantitative analysis of consumption and loss data at the feeder level (each feeder serves some 2,000 households). Through a statistical analysis using hierarchical linear modeling, I argue that more variation in losses is explained at the feeder level than at the subdivision level, thus reinforcing the view that local power relations matter more than administrative rules in influencing state capacity.

Chapter 5 examines a common challenge in the rapidly growing cities of South Asia—the quest of squatter settlement (*katchi abadi*) residents to formalize and document their claim on urban citizenship. The experience of *katchi abadi* residents in Islamabad who succeed in formalizing their claims for individual electricity meters has an unexpected outcome. I draw on ethnographic fieldwork to show how some *katchi abadi* residents struggle to navigate the process of making formal claims on the state for individual electricity meters, thereby exposing themselves to new forms of predation. These formal claims are individual, as opposed to the communal negotiations that are conducted by a committee on behalf of all residents sharing a communal meter. The experience of the *katchi abadi*'s bourgeois neighbors also shows that making formal claims on the state is as negotiated and contested as the process of making informal claims. Rich and poor alike describe a pervasive expectation of predation that allows them to put little credence in formality.

Part III (Chapters 6 and 7) is concerned with the individual level of analysis and particularly the citizen's encounter with the local state. Both chapters draw heavily on semi-structured interviews and ethnographic observations at the offices of IESCO to present how this government bureaucracy actually works under real-life constraints. The extent and manner to which institutions of governance are embedded in local relations of domination are crucial to understanding both the unevenness of the state's capacity and the serial failure of reform programs, as discussed in parts I and II. In Chapter 6, I show how "the rules of the game" are only partly constituted by codified rules, which is completely contrary to the conceptualization of governance underlying the reform programs described in Chapter 3. Codified rules exist, and they certainly matter, but access to them is wrapped in layers of social negotiations and contestations. Rather, governance is a compromise between formality and informality, with street-level bureaucrats exercising a great degree of flexibility and discretion in service of the organization's goals and the public good. However, the social and organizational constraints on the discretion of bureaucrats often fall short of preventing an abuse of office.

In Chapter 7, the focus remains on the individual level but shifts more directly toward patronage and power. At the heart of the relationship between citizen and state lies an encounter between electricity consumer and street-level bureaucrat that is usually conducted face to face. The parameters of this encounter are shaped by power in the form of money and personal connections, with an underlying (and usually hidden) threat of violence. In the final vignette in this chapter, the conflict between the protagonists reveals an overt collision between abstract and more immediate claims to power. The bureaucrat tries to draw legitimate authority from the rules, and the English in which they are expressed, but is quickly forced to submit to local power dynamics.

Chapter 8 concludes with a summary of the argument that governance of the Pakistani electrical power sector is shaped by lower-level dynamics. I synthesize the insights at the national, city, and individual levels from parts I, II, and III, respectively, and draw out the linkages between the different levels that are so important to influencing the overall system. I then summarize the book's contribution to the sociology of development and its implications outside Pakistan. I also take a more forward-looking view toward some policy approaches in Pakistan that can build on this book's argument by encouraging local adaption and bureaucratic entrepreneurship in a framework of permissible variation and administrative oversight. The last part of the Conclusion addresses the massive Chinese energy investments in Pakistan as part of the China–Pakistan Economic Corridor and their potential to solve Pakistan's electricity sector problems.

PART I

THE NATIONAL LEVEL OF ANALYSIS

The chapters in this section approach the question of Pakistan's perennial power problems at the national scale, exploring the unevenness of the interprovincial political economy of power, and how successive generations of power plans have instituted this inequality by design. Further, structures of international development assistance hinder the planning process from addressing these political compromises, as the attempt to achieve a Weberian dream state through the manipulation of formal institutions is repeatedly compromised. The dynamics that link cash flows from distribution to payments for power generation capture lie at the heart of these challenges.

The national level of analysis is closest to the perspective of policymakers, which is why the book starts from here and later moves down to the city and individual levels of analysis to show how macro challenges have their roots in behaviors from below. Even so, by approaching the national level as a field the book takes an explicitly political perspective that foregrounds power and the compromises made by parties in relative positions of centrality. Both chapters look to the kind of compromises that characterize electricity governance, but in acknowledgment of the political work that is done through such compromises rather than only seeing them as a lack or deficit in comparison with technocratic ideals.

The two chapters in this section engage with the history of the power sector to show how the recurrent crises of the power sector have deep roots. The cost and cash flow demands of producing electricity are heavily influenced by the presence and relative weightage of imported fuels in the overall fuel mix, which is itself tied to the political accessibility of domestic fuel sources. Adding sufficient capacity at affordable prices has been a persistent challenge. High losses are an established feature of the system, and generally resistant to change. These challenges can easily reinforce each other and have done so at regular periods in the past. Unfortunately, while many of these interlinked challenges in the power sector are more tragedy than mystery, the proposed solutions tend to follow established technocratic paradigms that haven't solved the problem. Moreover, international development assistance is constrained by the nature of its organizational practices: projects with limited time frames and scope, hiring of international experts without local knowledge or connections, accountability to foreign governments wary of misspent taxpayer money, and adherence to terms of reference written prior to the project's commencement and typically on the basis of decontextualized expertise.

The ideas for electricity governance reform proposed through international governance assistance favor Washington Consensus principles (market-based competition, eliminating subsidies) while overlooking the important political relationships entailed in the existing policy and institutional frameworks. The chief dynamic at the national level is the core–periphery contest between the federal center and Punjab against the smaller provinces. However, the same policy instruments that go some way to keeping the interprovincial peace also create budgetary risks by seeding the circular debt that burdens the federal center.

Historical Background

Electrical power in Pakistan prior to 1958 was within the purview of private regional utilities without any national integration or planning. The era of national planning begins in 1955 with the First Five-Year Plan but truly kicks off with the founding of the Water and Power Development Authority (WAPDA) in 1958. Through WAPDA, the Government of Pakistan constructed three large dams (Mangla in 1967, Warsak in 1960, and Tarbela in 1974) and integrated the previously distinct islands of generation and distribution through a national transmission backbone. WAPDA coexisted with private utilities until 1972, when the government of Zulfiqar Ali Bhutto's Pakistan People's Party nationalized the private power utilities as part of its program to eliminate the "exploitation" and "evil" it considered inherent in the capitalist system (Pakistan People's Party 1970). The intent to reintroduce private capital to the power sector was indicated under the military regime of General Zia ul Haq (1977–1988), although it was not until the mid-1990s that private participation in the power sector returned in force with private power producers contracting to sell power to the national transmission and distribution companies. WAPDA's power generation, transmission, and distribution functions were separated into distinct entities with the aim of eventually privatizing many of them. A regulatory body, the National Electric Power Regulatory Authority (NEPRA), was established in 1997 to oversee the sector in its new form. Pakistan's then-largest thermal generation plan at Kot Addu was privatized in 1996, and Karachi's vertically integrated utility (with its own generation capability) was privatized in 2005. The current state of the power sector is a hybrid of private and public sector components. Transmission is entirely in the public sector. All distribution with the exception of Karachi is in the public sector. There are both private and public power generation companies.

2

The Interprovincial Unevenness of the Infrastructural State

Loadshedding and power outages are a national issue in Pakistan, but one whose genesis is more complex than there simply being an inadequate quantity of power to meet the nation's demand. The argument presented in this chapter identifies loadshedding and circular debt as directly resulting from strategic choices that are integral to Pakistan's infrastructural state. The grid that has been built out—and the ordering of citizen–state relations entailed therein—reflects Pakistan's strategic choices regarding the relationship of the provinces to the federal center and citizens to their state. And, as much as national authorities (political, administrative, military) might want different outcomes, a large part of the reason why loadshedding and circular debt persisted through so many years is that national authorities are unwilling to revisit these underlying strategic choices. China–Pakistan Economic Corridor (CPEC) investments have expanded power supply sufficiently to largely eliminate loadshedding—subject to the caveat that cash flow requirements must be met, which is frequently not the case —but this does not reflect any change in the state's strategic priorities, nor does it reflect increased state capacity.

Thus, our understanding of Pakistan's bouts with crippling loadshedding and circular debt must be both historically and socio-spatially informed. It must be historically informed because where we are is the direct result of past state-making practices in the power sector. Our understanding must also be socio-spatially informed because there is substantial sub-national variation in terms of the state's capacity across the country. What the state can do is shaped by its established practices, and that capacity to act is inconsistent across its territory. Nonetheless, this unevenness across the territory is part of a coherent whole, an infrastructural state, in which the inequalities fit together in the rough bargain binding together this sometimes fractious federation.

Access to Power. Ijlal Naqvi, Oxford University Press. © Oxford University Press 2022.
DOI: 10.1093/oso/9780197540954.003.0002

This chapter examines how loadshedding and circular debt in Pakistan emerge from strategic choices at the national level of analysis. The starting point for this argument is in the national power sector cash flows that link generation and distribution in a perpetual (albeit fluctuating and crisis-prone) cycle. Disaggregating these cash flows reveals a profoundly infrastructural state. Non-Punjabi electricity consumption is both subsidized and the site of higher losses, but power generation facilities have also been built out in a manner that reflects the uneven incorporation of the non-Punjabi provinces into the state. The grand bargain that mitigates conflict in the interprovincial political economy of the power sector is one that preserves the ideological commitments of a unitary state at the expense of excessive burdens on the federal exchequer. Crucially, the expansion of power supply under CPEC does not reflect state capacity to marshal domestic resources or enforce payments. While the core issues in Pakistan's electrical power sector have been clearly articulated in planning documents for decades, the many national and international plans to address the power sector's woes have repeatedly come up short.

The Cash Flows at the Heart of Pakistan's National Electricity Challenges

The crucial relationships that shape the national-level issues of electricity provision are illustrated in Figure 2.1, and these relationships link electricity generation, transmission, and distribution to the cash flows that sustain the system. The foundations of chronic undersupply and loadshedding can be seen in this diagram. The fuel mix (i.e., which fuel sources are used and in what proportion)

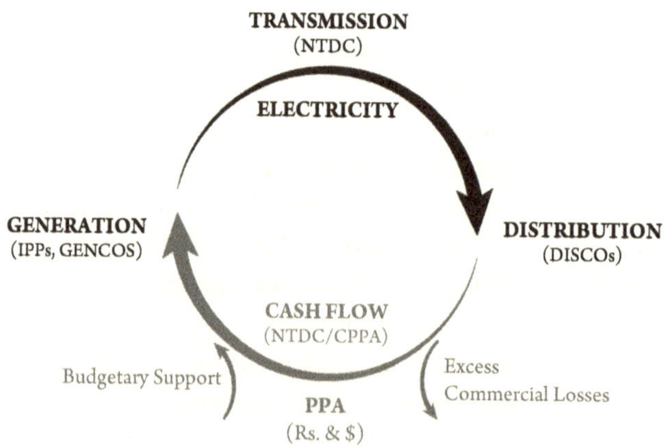

Figure 2.1 Cash Flows of National Electricity Supply

in generation is the key driver of cost, but also of exposure to international fuel markets, their volatility, and pressures to make payments in a timely manner. These costs must be recovered through distribution, which requires getting consumers to pay their bills in full and on time. Some degree of losses is factored into pricing, but if the distribution company[1] (or DISCO) suffers losses above this level, then there will be a shortfall in cash flow. Strictly speaking, fuel costs are also factored into the costs of production, but—just like excess commercial losses—higher prices for fuel put a burden on the central government. Increasing fuel costs are passed through to the government by the independent power producers (IPPs) due to the terms of their power purchasing agreements (PPAs). Similarly, any foreign exchange fluctuations are also passed through by IPPs.

In practice, revenues from electricity distribution are less than the costs of generation, and the central government must ensure that power producers and fuel suppliers are paid in order to provide adequate supply. The budgetary support from the central government to cover subsidies and excess losses is mitigated through reducing supply, that is, loadshedding. By reducing the quantum of electricity supplied through loadshedding, the government reduces its financial exposure. This is of course an incredibly damaging policy response because the knock-on effect in terms of economic and human harm is substantial, but raising electricity prices for consumers would have its own human, political, and economic costs, while the preferred option of reforms that address the systemic weaknesses of governance have proven to be beyond the capacity of successive governments. If commitments for subsidies are unpaid, or losses exceed targets by too much, the pinch must eventually be felt somewhere. To the extent that the system is also exposed to international oil markets for securing fuel supplies, the need to ensure adequate and timely cash flows becomes more pressing due to the reduced tolerance of market operators for any delay in payment (as compared with domestic contracts, which are softer constraints). Pakistan's fuel mix and capacity to extract timely and complete payments are thus tightly linked to the adequate provision of electricity in the country. Increasing prices and cutting subsidies—much favored prescriptions of the IMF—are one possible response, but these options would have political repercussions.[2]

The cash flow diagram in Figure 2.1 also serves as a map to the structure of this chapter's argument. Starting with losses, the chapter moves to a discussion of subsidies and then power generation capacity, with attention to selected examples of power generation projects to illustrate the tensions of state making present in Pakistan's electrical power sector. Within each section I engage with historical and socio-spatial dimensions of state making to show that the uneven state capacity visible at the national level reflects inequality by design.

Electricity Losses as an Indicator of State Capacity

Using transmission and distribution losses as a proxy indicator for state capacity reveals a lot about the unevenness of state capacity at the sub-national level in Pakistan.[3] That we can use losses in this manner follows from an understanding of state capacity as a matter of the state's ability to penetrate society and implement projects across its territory. Given that electricity losses measure the extent to which consumers are billed for the electricity supplied to them, varying degrees of losses indicate the extent to which a territory is incorporated into the state as part of a larger regime of inequality by design. Figure 2.2 below has two panels that show losses by distribution company, with bold lines indicating provincial boundaries. Moving clockwise from the northwest, the four provinces are Khyber Pukhtunkhwa (KPK), Punjab, Sindh, and Baluchistan. The panel on the left is shaded according to transmission and distribution losses, and it shows that losses are lowest in the Punjab. Punjab is the richest and most industrialized province and has historically been the dominant province in domestic politics. DISCO losses range from 38% in the Sukkur Electric Power Company (SEPCO) service area of interior Sindh to under 10% in the Islamabad Electric Supply Company (IESCO), serving northern Punjab and the Islamabad Capital Territory.

There is also great variation within each of these distribution companies. Even within IESCO, which has the best overall statistics, and even within the Islamabad circle, which serves the capital region itself and has the best performance within the Islamabad distribution company, 23 out of 234 11-kV feeders had system losses of over 50%.[4] Chapter 4 examines the losses of one distribution company—the Lahore Electric Supply Company (LESCO), serving the Lahore area of central Punjab—in more detail, and explores the extent to which high- and low-loss feeders can even coexist within the same subdivision.

Total commercial losses (the right panel of Figure 2.2) are the product of transmission and distribution losses multiplied by the proportion of bills that are actually paid. Commercial losses give a better view of the cash flow implications of the distribution company's operations, but the data is not available historically for Pakistan, nor are they as widely reported or used by analysts. The commercial losses panel reveals the same broad pattern where Punjabi consumers pay their bills to a greater extent than the rest of the country. However, Balochistan and interior Sindh are particularly noticeable for the extent to which the electricity supplied is simply not paid for at rates of 75% and 64%, respectively. The budgetary consequences at the national level are muted because per capita consumption is so much lower in those regions, but the inability of distribution companies to bill for their supply, and to collect on the bills that are distributed,

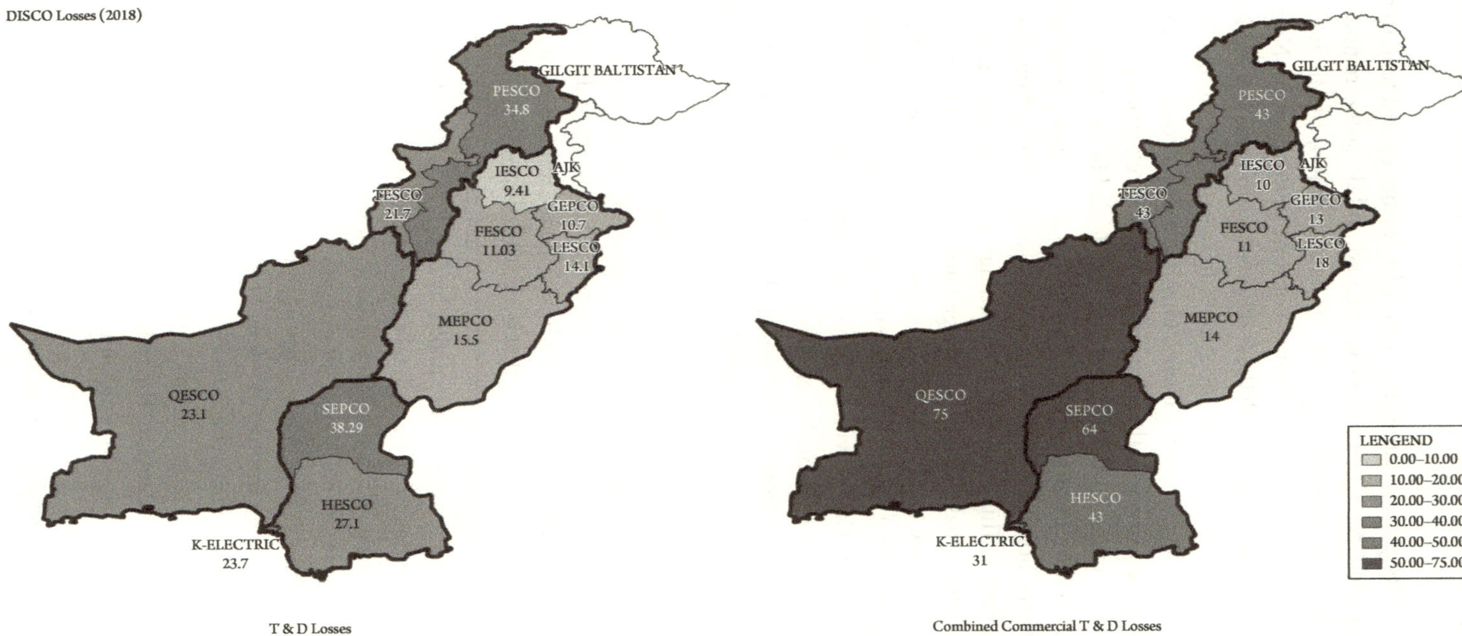

Figure 2.2 Losses by Distribution Company, 2018

is a striking marker of the limitations of formal governance in these peripheral state spaces.

Broadly speaking, those same areas where losses are highest tend to be those regions where electricity generation is situated. While some regions pay for electricity consumption, others provide for its generation, and there is a rough balance to be found across them in terms of their contributions. Nonetheless, the state's presence and capacity in these different regions are not equivalent: in the electricity-generating regions the state utilizes natural resources to produce electricity that the wealthier and more industrial regions consume, yet it is the electricity-consuming regions that also implicitly pay for electricity consumption in the high-loss regions. This grand bargain is reflected in two key policies: the Common Generation Pool, whereby all provinces share their power generation, and the Universal Standard Tariff, whereby consumers throughout the country pay the same prices. This commitment to a single price for electricity gives rise to the Tariff Differential Subsidy, whose gargantuan size is a threat to national finances. The interprovincial political economy of power informs other such institutional bargains that reflect the differential state capacity across the country and the interests of the provinces. While this unevenness of state capacity is of huge concern in present-day electricity policy, this unevenness has been produced by past generations of electricity policy. It is easier to see this historical production of uneven state capacity in the discussion of constructing different types of power generation facilities that accumulate in the stock of the nation's built infrastructure, whereas transmission and distribution losses are a part of a repeating cyclical flow that sustains the operation of this built infrastructure.

From the governance reform perspective evident in the plans discussed in this chapter and the next, losses are a flaw to be eliminated and a perfect example of governance conceptualized as a lack, that is, the distribution company's inability to enforce payment discipline on electricity consumers. Instead, the conception of losses proposed here is one of "inequality by design," in which losses represent the strategic choices taken by the federal center to accommodate the realities of Pakistani state making. Thus, the high degree of losses in parts of the country can be understood in the context of interprovincial relations as part of the balance of power relations. One might even push this analysis further in terms of representing governance through the lens of electricity: high losses persist in interior Sindh and Baluchistan because these frontier and unsettled regions (terminology evident in state documents dating back to the colonial era) are not deemed amenable to settlement. The federal center chooses not to expend the necessary effort—military, economic, ideological—to subdue and integrate resistance in these regions. For contrast, one can consider the enormous efforts seen in the former Federally Administered Tribal Areas (FATA), such as with the suppression of militancy in Waziristan during the Pakistani army's operation *zarb-e-azb* in 2014–2016 and the constitutional integration of FATA into KPK. The task is daunting, as demonstrated by the multiple and continuing Baluch insurgencies. Nor is it perhaps deemed worthwhile in the calculus of the federal center to expend such effort, given Baluchistan's small population and relative poverty,[5] and its peripherality to the idea of Pakistan. Hence, the continuation of the colonial model of cantonments and co-opting local notables continues. The benefits to the federal center of the common generation pool require some limited integration of these peripheries, and the cost is the budgetary burden of prices that don't meet operating costs (not with current levels of state capacity with billing and payments) and the heavy subsidies that offset electricity costs of wealthy landlords. While versions of this argument are well traveled for Baluchistan, later chapters explore the unevenness of state capacity even within the core areas of Pakistan.

Electricity Losses: A Stubborn Problem

High transmission and distribution losses have plagued the Pakistani power sector since its earliest days. Figure 2.3[6] shows these losses since 1960.

Average system losses peak at 35.7% in 1977. National losses exceeded 30% in the years 1969 and 1973–1980. Losses were below 20% in 1960 and returned below that level in 2014. The prevalence of high system losses across the country and over time has resulted in annual losses averaging 25% from 1960 to 2018, which means that, on average, consumers were not billed for a quarter of all electricity supplied.

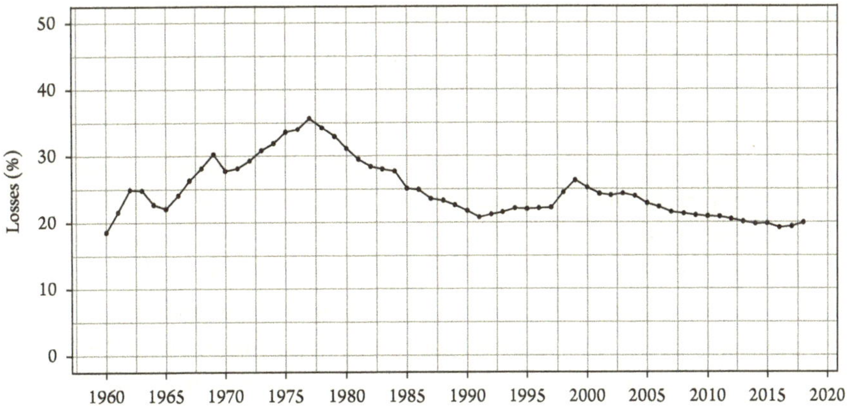

Figure 2.3 Percent Transmission and Distribution Losses, 1960–2018

The pattern of losses in Figure 2.3 doesn't immediately accord with the conventional discussion of state strength in Pakistan, which sees the decline of the central administrative services starting with the PPP under Zulfiqar Ali Bhutto, and largely continuing unabated since then.[7] It may be the case that expansion into new service areas and the number of new connections during the 1970s was a driver for losses. Another possibility is that the earlier strength of the state (if that view is accepted) was itself uneven and did not actually entail much institutional power outside the major urban areas and the Punjab, so that expansion into new areas added consumers who were less likely to be amenable to state control. Unfortunately, neither materials in the Water and Power Development Authority (WAPDA) House library in Lahore nor elsewhere had much to say on electricity governance in earlier periods, nor are they a feature of the five-year plans.

The first mention of high transmission and distribution losses as a serious problem comes in the *Fourth Five Year Plan*—issued in 1970—which states that "During the Third Plan, the service was marred by loadshedding and abnormally high system losses" (425). The concerns about theft and system losses are prompted by the observation that "Deficits appeared for the first time in the revenue accounts of WAPDA" (422). This newfound concern notwithstanding, losses remained higher than their 1970 levels (27.8%) until 1984.

None of the plans since 1970 that discuss the problem of high system losses engage with the causes of losses and offer more than a cursory glance at how to address the problem. The plans refer to combatting losses through "concerted action" involving an "independent inspection squad" (*Fourth Plan*), or a "major effort" (*Seventh Plan*), though the outcome by 1993 was judged to be "pathetic" (*Eighth Plan*). Planning documents have spent much more time addressing concerns on the generation side rather than the transmission side, with fuel costs and capacity being the focus of much attention. Coherent plans to address losses are conspicuous by their absence, perhaps in tacit recognition that addressing electricity theft is a very local governance issue and thus not amenable to central planning.[8]

Although the recorded levels of losses are already high, industry observers fear that they might understate actual losses. The technical audit of the Islamabad distribution company conducted by the United States Agency for International Development (USAID) in 2010–2011 concluded that the official figure of 9.8% losses for FY 2009–2010 was "inconsistent with the findings of both of IESCO and [USAID] loss analysis," suggesting that a higher rate of 13.7% was more accurate (MWP-USAID Power Distribution Improvement Program, 2011, p. 39).[9] In India, "more realistic estimates" increased the recorded losses of Area Electricity Boards (Kale, 2004, pp. 470–471), and a similar situation is almost definitely the case in Pakistan, where "overbilling" is an established phenomenon. In 2012, LESCO's own audit department investigated accounts of overbilling and found that inflated bills were being issued to reduce recorded line losses. Officials at all levels were found to be complicit.[10]

All these losses must be paid for, and that burden falls invariably on the Government of Pakistan due to the sovereign guarantees that undergird the power purchasing agreements (PPAs) with IPPs. When losses exceed National Electric Power Regulatory Authority (NEPRA) targets for any given distribution company (DISCO), there is no other place for that obligation other than the federal government. Higher losses in any given DISCO mean that the tariff differential subsidy will increase. These are the relationships illustrated in Figure 2.1, and they are described in more detail in the next section.

The Burden of Electricity Subsidies

The tariff differential subsidy is by far the biggest type of subsidy in the pricing of electricity.[11] The term "tariff" is used in policy discussions for the price of electricity to consumers. The differential involved is the difference between what the regulator, NEPRA, determines that the DISCO should charge, and what the Government of Pakistan notifies as the official tariff (i.e., what the consumer pays). In 2010, blending all categories and weighting by consumption, the NEPRA average tariff was Rs. 10.17 per kWh, while the Government of Pakistan's average notified tariff was Rs. 7.12 per kWh.[12] This gap of 3.05 per kWh is the loss per unit sale of electricity that must be covered by the federal government. In FY 2007–2008 the tariff differential subsidy was Rs. 87 billion, in 2008–2009 it was Rs. 133 billion, in 2009–2010 it was Rs. 226 billion, and in FY 2010–2011 it was estimated at Rs. 145 billion (FODP, 2010). To appreciate the scale of the subsidy, the 2010 figure is close to 10% of total government revenues.[13] In 2014–2015 the subsidy was Rs. 144 billion, approximately 0.8% of GDP, which is comparable in size to total public health expenditures (World Bank, 2017). In 2019–2020 the tariff differential subsidy was Rs. 162 billion (Government of Pakistan, 2020, p. 15).

All DISCO consumers are charged the same prices—a uniform national tariff notified by the government—even though NEPRA determines a different tariff for each DISCO. NEPRA's process is intended to reflect the cost of service for each DISCO, though it is not based on a true cost of service study but an assessment of the revenue each DISCO requires to run its operations. NEPRA's goal is that the DISCO's consumer revenues balance the cost of purchasing power.

The determination that DISCOs need different levels of revenue per consumer can in part be justified by the different social and physical characteristics of the territories served by each DISCO as described in below.

Line losses tend to increase with the area of service and decrease with customer density. Losses also decrease with a greater proportion of industrial and bulk consumers, as these are the easiest to monitor.[14] DISCO management even refers to these as "zero loss" consumers. The distribution companies with the best performance in terms of line losses are Gujranwala Electric Power Company (GEPCO), Faisalabad Electric Supply Company (FESCO), and IESCO. These have relatively small service areas with a higher density of consumers and more industrial and bulk consumers. The worst-performing distribution companies are Hyderabad Electric Supply Company (HESCO) and Peshawar Electric Supply Company (PESCO), which have very large service areas, dispersed consumers, and fewer industrial connections. This basic analysis applies broadly but not to all cases. Multan Electric Supply Company (MEPCO) has a larger service area than PESCO, lower consumer density, and a lower proportion of unit sales to industrial and bulk consumers, but line losses of only 19% against 37% for PESCO.

Table 2.1 **Distribution Company Profiles**

DISCO	*Customers per KM of 11 kV Line (2010)*	*Area of Service (km²) (2010)*	*Industrial & Bulk Consumers (% of unit sales) (2015)*	*Line Losses (2015)*	*Recovery (2015)*	*Commercial Operations, Losses × Recovery (2015)*	*TDS per Unit in Rs. (2012)*
IESCO	101	23,160	42%	9.41%	99.8%	90.4%	1.02
LESCO	147	19,064	41%	14.1%	95.9%	82.4%	1.78
FESCO	89	36,122	37%	11.0%	100.1%	89.1%	2.59
GEPCO	131	17,207	31%	10.7%	97.0%	86.6%	2.91
PESCO	89	74,521	29%	34.8%	88.0%	57.4%	5.09
HESCO	36	126,758	26%	27.1%	78.2%	57%	4.30
MEPCO	72	105,505	23%	15.5%	102.3%	86.5%	3.27
SEPCO	30	56,300	23%	38.3%	57.8%	35.7%	4.65
QESCO	17	334,616	5%	23.1%	32.6%	25.1%	4.48
TESCO	60	27,220	4%	21.7%	73%	57.2%	

Sources: DISCO Performance Profile 2009–2010, prepared by the Power Distribution Improvement Program of USAID, NEPRA 2015 State of the Industry Report, Fatima and Nasim (2013).

Table 2.1 above is ordered in terms of decreasing proportion of industrial and commercial consumers. This single dimension mostly orders the DISCOs in terms of increasing losses, decreasing recovery, and higher subsidies. All the DISCOs with losses over 20% are outside the Punjab, and all those with losses under 20% are in the Punjab. On the distribution side, the DISCOs outside the Punjab substantially underperform those inside it.

As with many utilities, urban areas are easier to serve because consumers are densely clustered. In rural areas, dispersed populations impose additional service costs. Typically, the length of the feeder lines that serve consumers must be longer, and DISCO staff will have to cover more of an area to serve their consumers. The physical length of a line adds to technical losses because the resistance of a conductor increases with its length. Population density and length of feeder line alone cannot, however, justify the much higher line losses of the worst-performing DISCOs.

Line losses come in technical and nontechnical varieties.[15] Technical line losses represent leakages due to the fundamentals of conductor materials and system design. The nontechnical line losses—which are often referred to as "electricity theft"—make up the difference between the technical losses and actual losses of up to 30%–40%. Theft frequently occurs with the collusion of WAPDA employees who are paid or coerced to look the other way or doctor the books. As discussed in Chapter 6, enabling theft is a team effort rather than an individual one. All kinds of consumers steal electricity from the roughest Karachi neighborhood to the swankiest F-6 mansion in Islamabad.

Losses contribute to the sector's liquidity problems because the distribution company is responsible for the electricity they distribute, regardless of whether they bill for it or not. NEPRA tries to accommodate the reality of losses by setting targets for losses that are close to the actual losses, but still demanding improved performance. If the DISCOs achieved NEPRA's targets, the federal government would only be liable for the level of subsidy and support that it has officially committed to. Although this is substantial, and frequently has not been paid on time, the fact that DISCOs exceed their targets for losses means that the federal government has to contribute even more than it budgets for. Ultimately, a large portion of the revenue shortfall from the distribution companies due to losses and non-payments must be borne by the federal government through taxation and borrowing, just as it must do for the tariff differential subsidy.

The tariff differential subsidy is an enormous fiscal burden for Pakistan. In the Eleventh Plan, there is an open recognition of this challenge:

> Furthermore, the power sector continues to be affected by the circular debt as revenues collected do not fully cover the cost of production due to high Tariff Differential Subsidy (TDS). The debt at the end

> of 2011 was Rs. 532 Billion, which rose to Rs. 872 Billion in 2012, representing about four per cent of the GDP. The issue has not yet been addressed fully, and it will continue to constrain the sector. (Planning Commission, 2013, p. 209)

For the Pakistani government to bear this fiscal burden, it would have to raise tax revenues, which the Pakistani government has usually shown little capacity to do effectively.[16] The Eleventh Plan acknowledges the government's inability to afford the subsidy in its reference to the government's "limited fiscal space" (p. 209). Understanding the political economy of electricity subsidies is crucial to explaining their persistence, particularly in the face of sustained IMF pressure to eliminate them at times when successive governments have been driven back to the IMF as a result of an inability to achieve growth targets and manage the budget. Bardhan's (1984) analysis of Indian subsidies was that they served the interests of the dominant groups exerting influence over the state, and that the subsidies served a political purpose in knitting together a heterogeneous class coalition across the country. While the state's facilitation of rents for economic elites are certainly a feature of Pakistan's political economy, electricity subsidies have been criticized in the past for being insufficiently targeted to the poor (Friends of Democratic Pakistan, 2010). The argument to be advanced in this chapter is that in Pakistan the role of electricity subsidies is less about knitting together a class coalition (per Bardhan's analysis of India) than tying together divergent provincial interests.

What the tariff differential subsidy represents is a loss on each unit of electricity sold. Beyond the theft and other losses, even when electricity is legally sold and paid for on time, the federal government must pay a portion of the bill. The power sector as a whole does not achieve cost recovery and cannot do so under the current setup. Generating more power will only compound the problem by increasing the size of the subsidy.

While individual government employees may steal their electricity, government institutions are much more likely to simply not pay their bills. In Islamabad, only 20% of electricity consumption is in the public sector, but they owe some 80% of the arrears.[17] The reasons are various. Government institutions habitually don't often enforce rules on one another, as their employees are much more used to exchanging favors from which they personally benefit. Moreover, without powerful organizational backing, a low-ranking officer of the distribution company will not directly challenge powerful government organizations. Nonpayment of bills by public sector agencies limits the ability of the distribution companies to make timely payments to their suppliers, who pass the problem up the supply chain of electricity until it reaches fuel importers.

By relying on imported fuels for non-gas thermal power generation, Pakistan introduces two pressure points into the energy sector. The first is that international fuel suppliers require immediate payment and impose a hard constraint that domestic power sector entities do not impose on the Pakistani government. The second is that when oil prices go up Pakistani power producers pass on that cost to the government (in its capacity as the sole power purchaser) per their tariff agreement.

Inter-corporate debt and loadshedding link together when there is no money to import fuel, be it fuel oil or LNG or coal. Without sufficient imported fuel, thermal generation is reduced, and loadshedding increases to balance supply and demand of power. In the near term, these two are enough to choke the economy and keep the power sector mired in its dysfunctional state. The thrust of the Eleventh Plan was to shift the reliance of the power sector from fuel oil to other sources, particularly coal. While coal is also imported (domestic coal from Thar only powers 1466 MW of 8000 MW coal-fired plants in total as of this writing), it is substantially cheaper than fuel oil. Despite the reduction in production costs during the Eleventh Plan, circular debt remains high (National Electric Power Regulatory Authority, 2016).

Inter-corporate debt is crippling for the long-term prospects of the power sector because it drives investment out of the power sector. Private capital has avoided the Pakistani power sector even when investing in telecommunications (IGI Securities, 2010). That the state's power sector managers make irregular payments while expecting continued operations is a surefire way to deter investment. In June 2015, circular debt was Rs. 648 billion. Due to Covid-19, Rs. 538 billions in arrears were accumulated during FY 2020, significantly higher than projected under the IMF's first Extended Fund Facility (EFF) review, and bringing the total stock of arrears to Rs. 2,150 billion at end of June 2020. The stock of arrears had grown to 5.2% of GDP at end-FY 2020.

Multilateral investment in the sector is deterred by the tariff differential subsidy. So long as the federal government cannot afford this subsidy—and it cannot—Pakistan must look to its international allies and donor partners to save Pakistan from financial collapse. In Pakistan's repeated engagements with the IMF, raising prices and cutting electricity subsidies have been high on the list of austerity measures required as part of the conditionalities attached to its loans.[18] But, because losses are a component of the balance of power relations across the provinces, there is a great degree of political resistance toward following through on these commitments and plans.

Persistent Capacity Constraints

Since its earliest days the managers of Pakistan's power sector have had to struggle with the lack of adequate power generation capacity. The race to eliminate power shortages by adding new capacity has been a regular feature of five-year plans, with the *Sixth Five Year Plan* describing a difficult recurring situation:

> The Sixth Plan faces formidable tasks. It has to overcome the shortages which have already acquired disturbing proportions. It must provide adequately for augmenting supplies to support economic growth and new investment during the Sixth Plan. Simultaneously, there should be initiation of long range planning for the Seventh Plan and beyond to avoid shortages re-emerging at a later date. (Planning Commission, 1983, p. 252)

Depressingly, this view reoccurs because the failure to meet the targets for increases in installed capacity is a persistent theme.

Installed capacity is the ubiquitous measure of how much electricity can be produced in the Pakistani power sector. It is derived from nameplate capacity, which is the capacity at which a power plant is rated at the time of its installation, and usually "derated" to reflect performance deterioration over time (typically to some 75%[19] of the original installed capacity for thermal plants).[20]

Figure 2.4[21] illustrates the divergence between actual and planned growth in installed generation capacity. The continuous line plots actual growth in installed capacity over time in the PEPCO system, that is, excluding the Karachi Electric system as well as captive power plants for industrial facilities. The graph of installed capacity over time shows an increase in Pakistan's total power generation capacity from 268 MW in 1955 to 32,525 MW in 2015, which represents a compound annual growth rate of 7.9% over that period.

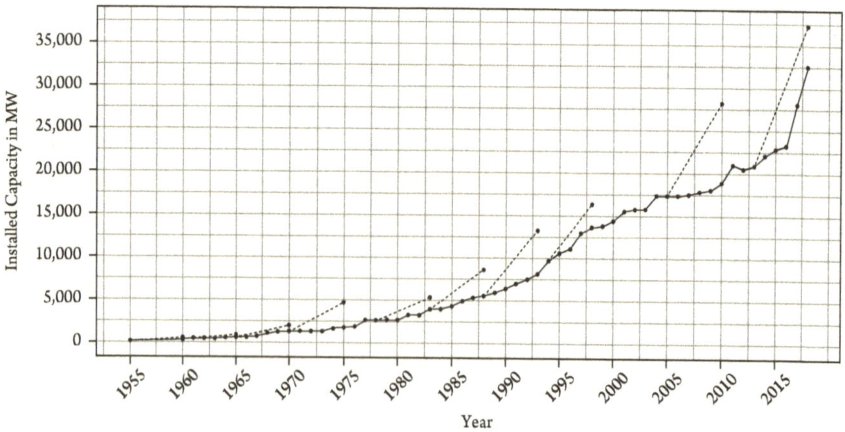

Figure 2.4 Actual and Planned Growth in Installed Generation Capacity, 1955–2018

The shorter line segments are planned growth targets from five-year plans that grow increasingly inaccurate over time. After the independence of Bangladesh in 1971, the planned growth curves resemble a series of hockey sticks sitting on the steadily increasing installed capacity line, each representing a mythical takeoff that is never achieved.

The extent to which the targets of the five-year plans for installed capacity have been achieved mostly followed a steady decline during the 20th century. The Fourth Plan period is an exception in that only 51% of the planned gain was achieved, down from 78% in the Third Plan and 73% in the Fifth Plan. The Fourth Plan period is marked by the independence of Bangladesh and is referred to as the "non-plan years" due to the seven-year interregnum from 1971 to 1978 during which Zulfiqar Ali Bhutto's supposedly socialist-leaning government dispensed with medium-term planning.[22]

In terms of achieving the targeted increase in capacity, the plans after the First that came closest to achieving their capacity addition targets were the Eighth Plan of 1993–1998 and the Eleventh Plan of 2013–2018. The Eighth Plan was notable for the induction of IPPs in 1997 and 1998 totaling 2,188 MW, or 39% of the total gains during the plan period. The public sector did not add the capacity it was supposed to, in part because the oversubscription of IPPs was already leading to a surplus of generation capacity and reduced the need for public sector additions. The induction of IPPs under the 1994 policy is discussed in Chapter 3. The addition of new capacity came at a significant cost, which has had a long-term impact on the financial sustainability of the power sector.

The period covered by the Eleventh Five Year Plan has concluded, but it will take more time for its impact to be fully understood. This plan heralded the arrival of CPEC power plants such as the Sahiwal coal-fired power plant. The absolute amount of generation capacity added was 11,675 MW, an addition of 56% to the installed capacity in PEPCO. However, the plan indicated that some 16,000 MW would be added, which means that in percentage terms the Eleventh Five Year Plan didn't quite meet its target despite the substantial new generation capacity added. Further, much like the Eighth Plan when the first wave of IPPs were introduced, the financial impact of this additional capacity has the potential to be actually quite damaging. While the new power plants are being dispatched and are rated as having a lower per-unit cost than those they replaced, circular debt is increasing, and questions remain regarding the relative expense of the plants in question.

The *Medium Term Development Framework* (MTDF) of 2005–2010 is the plan that was furthest from achieving its targets. The period of 2005–2010 saw reductions in private sector hydroelectric and thermal generation capacities of 19 and 5 MW, respectively. The only gain was in the addition of new IPPs. Between the commissioning of the 1,450 MW Ghazi Barotha dam in 2004 and

72 MW Khan Khwar hydroelectric project in 2010, not a single megawatt of capacity was added in the public sector. However, 1440 MW were added to the sector through IPPs. The *Medium Term Development Framework*'s power sector component is the worst example from Pakistani planning history of a plan without implementation.

Although the *Medium Term Development Framework* was produced under a military regime, the government's failure to achieve its targets from 2005 to 2010 (or with prior plans, for that matter) can't really be attributed to regime type. The long planning and construction time of power sector projects means that they typically span many governments. The Ghazi Barotha dam, for example, was completed in 2004 and counts as the most significant addition in generation capacity of the Musharraf era. However, bid documents for the civil works at Ghazi Barotha were issued in August 1994 (Asian Development Bank, 2005), during Benazir Bhutto's second government. Either of these two regimes could claim credit for the addition of Ghazi Barotha's generation capacity, as well as the intervening Nawaz Sharif Government (1996–1999). Moreover, at no stage has the Pakistani military not been hugely influential in Pakistan's political economy. For these reasons, coding years as authoritarian and democratic in order to test statistically any difference in the power capacity added would be potentially misleading.

Similarly, blame for the three-year delay in the completion of the Ghazi Barotha project must be shared around:

> Project implementation was delayed by 3 years, due to (i) late handover of land for the power channel and the power complex, which caused resettlement delays; (ii) various contract delays for the main components, mainly due to WAPDA's financial shortfall in counterpart funding; (iii) some difficulties arising from labor unions and various contractors not having been paid for several months; and (iv) necessary repatriation of foreign consultants from the site, owing to the events of 11 September 2001 in the United States. (Asian Development Bank, 2005, p. 5)

The difficulty in land acquisition stretched from 1995 to 1999, thus implicating the same governments that would take credit for the project's origination. In 2001, the National Accountability Bureau started investigations into the World Bank–sponsored land acquisition process. The World Bank responded by threatening to suspend disbursements to the Government of Pakistan because it felt the investigation wasn't recognizing the Bank's legally mandated role (World Bank, 2004, p. 14). Further, the project appraisal expected the government to introduce a 30% tariff increase in 1998 to meet the increased payment demands of the IPPs. Such an increase was completely untenable—a fact recognized by the World Bank as an error for which it bore some culpability (World Bank, 2004, p. 13)—and without a tariff increase WAPDA was unable to meet its contributions to the project's financing, thus further delaying the acquisition of land. For good measure, the September 11, 2001, attacks and subsequent invasion of Afghanistan delayed the project in a manner for which no party to the project can be considered responsible. With blame for delays and credit for its completion to be shared out, the process of planning and constructing the Ghazi Barotha project is illustrative of the challenges of meeting the power sector's capacity constraints. A lack of political will is one possible explanation, but the following section presents ample evidence to the contrary.

Consistent High-Level Recognition of the Problem

Every single power sector plan and assessment since the First Five-Year Plan was published in 1955 has recognized the importance of an adequate and reliable supply of electricity to the performance of Pakistan's economy. Any suggestion that Pakistan's past failure with governance reforms stems from a lack of political will has to contest with the repeated and very public declarations of commitment to addressing the country's electricity problems by its highest leadership. The *First Five Year Plan* published in 1955 points to "the crucial significance of developments in the water and power field for the success of the entire process of economic development" (Planning Commission, 1955, p. 336). In 1965 the *Third Five Year Plan* warned that "The importance of water and power facilities, therefore, cannot be overstressed" and identified electrical power as both cause and effect of economic growth (Planning Commission, 1965, pp. 289, 303). The *Fourth Five Year Plan* gave electrical power "top priority":

> . . . availability of cheap and abundant supply of power is of paramount importance not only to create physical infrastructure for economic development particularly in East Pakistan but also to spread the social benefits of power supply to a larger section of the population. Within the limited financial resources, therefore, top priority has been given in the plan to generation transmission and distribution throughout the country. (Planning Commission, 1970, p. 421)

The *Sixth Five Year Plan* (1983–1988) reflected on global energy scarcity and the oil price shocks of 1973 and 1979 in stating that "No developing country can, therefore, expect to maintain a reasonable rate of growth in the economy without a forceful and comprehensive energy policy" (Planning Commission, 1983, p. 256). The *Seventh Five Year Plan* (1988–1993) opens the chapter on energy with the view that "The prosperity and future welfare of Pakistan largely depends on our commitment to support rapid economic growth with adequate and assured inputs of energy" (Planning Commission, 1988, p. 193). Almost 20 years later, the *Medium Term Development Framework* for 2005–2010[23] baldly opens the "Energy Security" chapter with the statement that "Energy is the life-line of economic development" (Planning Commission, 2005). Every single economic plan of the Government of Pakistan gives an extremely high priority to electrical power. There is no point in the history of Pakistani energy planning when this recognition was absent or that the role of electrical power was seen as anything other than central to the economic future of the country.

The most recent plan, the Eleventh,[24] which covers the period of 2013–2018, coincides with the bold election promises of the Pakistan Muslim League-Nawaz (PML-N) government to end loadshedding during its period in charge of national government (Planning Commission, 2013). In his budget speech of 2018, Finance Minister Miftah Ismail stated that "The biggest promise we made during the last election to the nation was to eliminate electricity loadshedding which stands fulfilled today."[25] Although the fulfillment of that promise was only intermittently sustained by the next government, the Finance Minister's statement underlines the continuing centrality of the power sector as the main promises of the previous electoral cycle were brought up in preparation for the 2018 electoral season.

A State of Perpetual Crisis

The poor record of meeting planning goals helps produce power shortages and loadshedding that have periodically grown to crisis proportions. In response to these crises the political leaders of Pakistan have made ambitious claims that the crisis will be resolved within a few years. One such example comes from the power crisis of the mid-1980s. In 1986 WAPDA was charged by the prime minister with developing a plan to end loadshedding by 1990. The plan to achieve this goal is outlined in WAPDA's 1986 *Power Development Plan for Elimination of Loadshedding by January 1990*, which opens with a description of the power crisis and a statement of intent:

> For the past few years, the country has been in the throes of a power crisis, the like of which has never been experienced before. This imbalance between power demand and supply has emerged as the major bottleneck in the growth and development of country's economy, and has adversely affected the investment climate. If due cognizance of the worsening situation is not taken and the power shortage is allowed

> to extend into the next decade, this will seriously hamper the rate of industrial growth in the future. It is therefore imperative that a comprehensive accelerated programme be launched immediately with the objective of improvement of the efficiency of the power system, and elimination of load shedding.
>
> The Government of Pakistan is fully cognizant of this need and stands committed to the goal of autarky in electrical energy for the country and extension of reliable electrical supply to the entire population. Accordingly, the Prime Minister has issued directions to WAPDA to prepare a comprehensive plan for eliminating load shedding completely by January 1990, and to ensure that ninety percent (90%) of all villages in the country are electrified by June 1990. This report presents the plan prepared by WAPDA in response to the Prime Minister's directive, and identifies the capital outlay that is required for the implementation of these plans. (Water and Power Development Authority, 1986, p. 1)

The challenges in meeting this aggressive schedule were apparent to the authors. They worked backward from a deadline of January 1, 1990—a date that appears to have no significance beyond being a convenient future marker—and identified possible projects to meet the target. Their complete disbelief in the validity of the plan is implied in the numerous caveats they include regarding the plan's incompatibility with reality. The scale of the investment required was completely unprecedented, as investment in the sector would need to rise to Rs. 27.4 billion per year from Rs. 4 billion. The tight time frame allowed no room for delays. For good measure, the authors note that incorporating thermal power generation using imported fuel would be a great risk as the price of oil could increase—perhaps as high as $25 per barrel! The plan also relies on energy conservation and reducing theft, although there are no details as to how this will be achieved. Through the inclusion of multiple caveats, each indicating that the plan called for results beyond anything previously achieved, the authors implied that the plan was both untenable and perhaps undesirable in its current format and likely to have been formulated to meet demands imposed from above that a plan be proposed to eliminate loadshedding within a few years.

Almost 25 years later, some similar characteristics can be noted in a report produced by a The Friends of Democratic Pakistan (FODP), a coalition of largely Western European and North American nations supporting governance reforms as part of Pakistan's transition to democracy. The FODP report issued in 2010 also works backward from a target date, planning to end loadshedding in three years. The authors knew the date to be aggressive and even unreasonable but used it to demonstrate both what needed to be done and what they considered to be possible.[26] The *Prime Minister's Vision Statement for Accelerated Development of Pakistan's Power Sector for Sustained Economic Growth* issued on May 24, 2010 (Government of Pakistan, 2010) works on the goal of adding 20,000 MW by 2020, effectively doubling Pakistan's generation capacity in 10 years. This ambitious goal was based on substantial additional private investment and support from multilateral lenders, as Pakistan could not generate such investment domestically (IGI Securities, 2010). The fund to be created for these investments never materialized, and interviewees involved in electricity policy suggested that this was because multilateral support and possible government financing were instead being diverted to cover the sector's subsidies.

The *Prime Minister's Vision Statement* acknowledges that the key policy action required for its success is

> restoring financial sustainability of the power sector (tariffs policy and financial discipline), reduction of transmission and distribution losses, introduction of suitable private-public participation structures, streamlining the institutional framework and industry's structure, and establishment of the Energy Development Fund. (Government of Pakistan, 2010, p. 9)

The vision statement contains no plan to address these issues even though it acknowledges them as the key action required.

The elimination or reduction of subsidies is a good example of a precondition to the success of reform that is unlikely to happen. Both the *Prime Minister's Vision Statement* and the FODP report identify electricity subsidies as undermining the financial sustainability of the power sector, and the Pakistani state. Few observers could disagree: the federal government paid Rs. 259 billion ($3 billion) out of the 2010–2011 budget to support the power sector, which is over 10% of the entire federal budget (Ministry of Finance, 2011). The federal government's subsidy to power consumers for the three fiscal years up to June 2010 exceeded one trillion rupees (US$117 billion at the time) and added 10% to the total national debt; this subsidy is more than the entire public sector development budget over that same period. The subsidy is simply too large to be affordable, yet the PPP government balked at implementing tariff increases that would reduce the subsidy by raising prices to consumers. The history of such efforts to increase consumer prices substantially in Pakistan is a cautionary tale. In January of 2011, a petrol price increase of 9% was reversed after the ruling coalition briefly lost its majority in parliament when a key coalition partner withdrew its support due to the price increase.[27] Increasing electricity prices is a politically loaded issue that cannot be taken for granted.

Relegating the removal of electricity subsidies to a precondition for reform removes policy from the political sphere. In this way, the citizen and the political process are written out of policymaking. This depoliticization expands the claim of the bureaucratic apparatus of the state to power by referring power relations through bureaucratic channels (J. Ferguson, 1990, p. 274). Even if the development discourse is depoliticized, decision-making in the Pakistani power sector is not—as shown with the experience of fuel price increases in 2011 and again in 2021. The inevitable failure of policy reform in the event of preconditions remaining unfulfilled allows the planners and policymakers to point to politicians as the source of the failure. Responsibility for the gap between planning and implementation has no takers. The depoliticized approach taken in governance reforms is a particular obstacle when dealing with Pakistan's infrastructural state because the politicization of decision-making isn't simply an obstacle—it is how state capacity is enabled at all. The unevenness of state capacity isn't just a lack of governance capacity but reflects the choices taken along the way in a federal system that espouses a unitary national identity and gives short shrift to individual rights or provincial claims for autonomy. The structure of the federation and the concentration of power in the federal center in Pakistan is not the proximate cause of its inability to implement reform plans, but it conditions what is politically possible in ways that limit the federation's ability to act. The refusal to listen to ethnicized political claims on matters of, for example, language or human rights abuses, is why there is little headway toward the demands the federal center might make regarding eliminating electricity losses.

Building Out State Space through Energy Infrastructures

The Politics of Provincial Identity

Although the principle of exploiting domestic resources before internationally sourced fuels is well established in the five-year plans, in practice there are numerous complications that stem from the location of the resources, interprovincial politics, and security issues, none of which can be entirely disentangled from the other.

The national political field in Pakistan is characterized by relations of power that pit the federal center against the provinces:

> Pakistan's history shows one primary axis of political conflict—the state (or the centre) versus peripheral regions. These regions represent politicised ethnic collectivities, and thus the central question in political

> contestation has been over the distribution of resources, rights, and authority for these regions / ethnic groups. (Javed, 2019)

This is not only true for the resources that contribute to power generation, but it has also been true since Pakistan's founding that the resources of subordinate provinces have been utilized for the benefit on the federal center. After 1947, Pakistan's export earnings were largely reliant on jute from East Pakistan (now Bangladesh), but these export earnings were primarily used to import military supplies (Jalal, 1990). Chief among the East Pakistani complaints against the West Pakistani administration was the use of resources from East Pakistan for the benefit of West Pakistan, as well as a broader exclusion from full and equal participation in the civil and military apparatus that ruled Pakistan for almost the entirety of the 1947–1971 period (Rahman, 2006). The Bengali Language Movement captured the spirit of this demand for recognition, and its martyrs served as symbols of Pakistani oppression long past the 1954 vote of the Constituent Assembly recognizing Bengali as an official language. The demand to have Bengali as an official language was forcefully opposed by Liaqat Ali Khan and Mohammad Ali Jinnah, who were the leaders of the Pakistan movement and whose deaths in the first few years after Pakistan's founding are often considered to have undermined a stable path to statehood. Both Jinnah and Liaqat Ali Khan spoke strongly against the recognition of Bengali as a state language of Pakistan or its use for communication between provinces, while supporting the use of Bengali for all official and administrative business within the province. Jinnah characterized the demand for Bengali as a state language as a form of "provincialism" that was a "poison" in his 1948 Dacca address, invoking the specter of Indian interference behind the Bengali language movement (Jinnah, 1948). Liaqat Ali Khan and Jinnah both described Urdu in terms of a unifying force for Pakistan and the hundred million Muslims of South Asia. Both considered the Bengali Language Movement as a threat to the unity of Pakistan, and both referred to Pakistan as a Muslim state in doing so. In Ayesha Jalal's words, "Urdu is an inevitable extension of that already loaded and untenable equation of Muslim, Islam and Pakistan ideology" (Jalal, 1995, p. 87). Although Bengali was recognized as a state language from 1954 onward, this tussle over West Pakistani domination (as it was certainly perceived by Bangladeshis) marked Pakistan's progress down the path toward the 1971 war.[28]

The current conflicts between the federal center and the provinces follow a similar pattern of becoming ethnicized, and thus pitting ethnic nationalisms against the singular Islamic national identity propagated as part of the national myth of founding. Farzana Shaikh notes this question of identity as the fundamental weakness at the heart of the Pakistani state-making project, which she expresses as "the question of whether Pakistan was intended to be an Islamic state that privileged Muslims, or a Muslim nation-state that would guarantee the equality of all its citizens" (Shaikh, 2009, p. 116). These are two opposing options, and the ideology of the unitary Pakistani national identity serves to suppress all ethnic and peripheral demands for inclusion and voice, and to mark them as threats to the state. Verkaaik notes how provincial politicians articulated a locally flavored Islam as a key part of their ethno-nationalist resistance to the federal center (Verkaaik, 2004). With questions of resource exploitation falling across provincial (and thus ethnic lines), it is no surprise that these are the vectors through which the broader conflict between center and periphery are articulated.

The army has claimed for itself the role of jealously guarding this unitary national ideology "grounded on the denial of difference due to the common bond of religion" (Jalal, 1995, p. 81). In Cohen's phrasing,

> For the foreseeable future, the army's vision of itself, its domestic role, and Pakistan's strategic environment will be the most important factors shaping Pakistan's identity.... Regardless of what may be *desirable*, the army will continue to set limits on what is *possible* in Pakistan. (Cohen, 2004, pp. 97, italics in original)

Hamza Alavi compared the army's endorsement of Pakistan's Islamic ideology to "medieval claims of a divine right to kingship" on the part of the army (Alavi, 1988, p. 64). The military dictators General Ayub Khan and General Zia-ul-Haq both summarily dismissed democratic demands for greater provincial autonomy by giving priority to a strong and unified state—strong precisely because it was unified (Butt, 2017).

In contrast to domestic resources, internationally sourced fuels are largely available to anyone who will pay, although the case of the IPPs following the 1994 policy in the next chapter illustrates the dangers of making such commitments all too well. The allure of international fuel sources that bypass interprovincial rivalries is a key contributor to the power sector's challenges. We chart a path to this position by first considering why it is that domestic fuel sources have been so difficult to exploit, and the conflicts that have arisen around them.

The various energy infrastructures used in Pakistan each contribute to the establishment of Lefebvrian state space, but the governance relations established through these infrastructures are not always conducive to social and economic inclusion or the establishment of a clear sense of the nation. In this vein, large hydroelectric dams are frequently sites of substantial conflict across the world, which is often portrayed in terms of modernizing national authorities (backed by international development and commercial actors) wielding the rhetoric and toolkit of economic development against subaltern voices allied to environmentalists and civil rights campaigners.[29] However, Majed Akhter moves us beyond this binary through his analysis of Pakistan's largest dam project at Tarbela:

> But because this attempt to produce homogenous state space was not accompanied by an inclusive vision of Pakistani nationhood, it resulted in the opposite of what its proponents intended. State-led large-scale infrastructure construction heightened regionalist consciousness, provoked the articulation of alternate visions of Pakistani nationhood, and increasingly differentiated Pakistani state space instead of homogenizing it. (Akhter, 2015, p. 850)

The absence of this inclusive national vision in the context of gas infrastructure projects that are seen to serve the Punjab rather than Balochistan limits the potential for any integrating function of the infrastructure itself. Similarly, the militarized construction site and repeated kidnappings at Gomal Zam reveal how weakly these peripheral areas are incorporated into the idea of the state. Rather than support national integration, large infrastructure projects such as big dams have had the opposite effect of exacerbating interprovincial tensions, with the Kalabagh Dam—even more than the example of Tarbela invoked by Akhter above—as the prime example.

Kalabagh Dam

The province of Sindh led the opposition to the construction of the Kalabagh Dam, where the dam was seen as "yet another insult to the long series of injuries inflicted on them by Punjab province through its appropriation of Sindh's rightful share of water" (Daanish Mustafa, Akhter, & Nasrallah, 2013, p. 15):

> It is ironic to Sindhi nationalists that they are expected to have their share of water diverted, so the upstream Punjab can build a hydropower dam, bag hundreds of billions of rupees in royalties every year, and reclaim hundreds of thousands of hectares of barren land, while Sindhis endure the consequences of diversion of millions of acre feet of water in loss of livelihoods, deprivation of marine food, and salinization of their land from sea invasion. (Niazi, 2018, p. 19)

The dam was also seen by Sindhis as an assault on the Indus River itself, whose significance is prominent in the Sindhi Sufi practices centered on shrines, particularly that of Lal Shahbaz Qalandar at Sehwan Sharif.[30] This "emotionally saturated spiritual attachment to the indus" is linked to syncretic religious traditions that are central to the Sindhi nationalism articulated by GM Syed and others (Niazi, 2018, p. 11).

The opposition by Sindh was joined by KPK and Balochistan as well. In KPK, the concern was partly for the safety of historical cities in the vicinity, but also about the royalties from the dam's hydroelectric power generation. The reservoir for Kalabagh would be in KPK, and thus the loss of land submerged under the reservoir would also be in KPK. However, the powerhouse is situated in the Mianwali district, and thus the royalties would accrue to the Punjab rather than KPK. To add insult to injury, Mianwali is a Pashtun area that was only administratively incorporated into the Punjab in 1955. The Baloch position is more straightforward in that there is little direct impact on Balochistan, but they stand with Sindh in opposition to the Punjab out of a sense of solidarity among smaller provinces (D. Mustafa, Gioli, Karner, & Khan, 2017, p. 20).

Opposition to the Kalabagh Dam is characterized by its proponents as anti-state. Niazi invokes Shams ul Mulk, former chairman of WAPDA and chief minister of KPK, as a prime spokesperson in favor of the Kalabagh Dam. Mulk denigrates opponents of the dams in public forums and on TV by invoking the specter of Indian influence and suggesting that the dam's opponents are "enemies of the country."[31] The chairman of the Lahore Chamber of Commerce and Industry declared that "All those against Kalabagh dam, I say are Traitors! Traitors! Traitors!" (D. Mustafa et al., 2017). When debate has degenerated to this level, there is little scope for reason or compromise. Mustafa et al. observe that the lack of trust between Sindh and Punjab "was admitted by all the political parties on the right and left of the political spectrum" (D. Mustafa et al., 2017, p. 20).

The proponents of the Kalabagh Dam—when not denigrating opponents as traitors—focus on technocratic arguments, while the arguments mobilized by the opponent of Kalabagh have environmental, ethnonationalist, and spiritual components to them as well as challenging the technical claims of the dam proponents (Niazi, 2018). The opponents of the dam mobilize local knowledge of hydrology and ecology. In this sense, the opponent are far more in tune with global trends that have shifted support away from the construction of large dams precisely because of the social and ecological damage they wreak (World Commission on Dams, 2000). Despite repeated attempts by elected and military governments to push ahead with the Kalabagh Dam, the resistance by the provinces has held firm.

The issue of the Kalabagh Dam doesn't just speak to the issues of hydroelectric infrastructures; it also exposes the underlying tensions of Pakistani state making as well:

> Lastly, it is possible to view the interprovincial water conflict as a political conflict masquerading as water conflict—that is, as fundamentally about competing visions of what type of polity and state Pakistan should be. Should it be a centralized developmental state? Or should it be a federated state where different ethnic differences and interests are deemed legitimate and not made subservient to visions of a unitary polity? (D. Mustafa et al., 2017, p. 22)

On the evidence from Kalabagh, as well as from Gomal Zam and the Balochistan gas fields, the centralized developmental state is continually failing to integrate the smaller provinces convincingly into its vision for the nation. Ethnicity and the challenges of national identity have bedeviled Pakistani state making since the beginning, with the independence of Bangladesh marking the voluntary secession of the numerical majority of the country at a time when their political representatives had just won the majority of seats in national parliament. Echoes of the conflict with Bangladesh can be heard in the depiction of provincial voices being derided as anti-state actors under Indian influence. In many respects, Pakistan still has not addressed some fundamental challenges of state making:

> Without sustained debate on citizenship rights, accompanied by a reapportioning of responsibility for the construction and dissemination of ideas and knowledge between state and civil society, Pakistan cannot take the elementary steps towards forging a collective ethos as a nation-state. (Jalal, 1995, p. 87)

The Natural Gas Reserves of Balochistan

Pakistan's gas resources are spread across three provinces, but 68% of its gas reserves and between 36% and 45% of its gas production is located in Balochistan.[32] The exploitation of Baloch resources by the Pakistani state is a source of long-standing grievances. Baloch nationalists argue that the province is inadequately compensated for providing these resources. Gas royalty payments to Balochistan are proportionately one-fifth of those paid to Punjab and Sindh (Wirsing, 2008). These payments were fixed at the time the gas fields were developed, and as the Baloch gas fields are the oldest, their prices are the lowest. Exclusion from the benefits of Baloch resources, such as the lack of domestic gas supply to the town of Sui (the site of Pakistan's largest and oldest gas field), also rankles. The Baloch also complain of having little involvement in the decision-making concerning mega-projects in Balochistan such as the Gwadar Port, Mirani Dam at Turbat, and the Makran Coastal Highway, and that few of the jobs generated by the projects are going to the local people (Ahmad, 2011, p. 4; Jamali, 2014). The marginalization of the Baloch from the decision-making and benefits of Balochistan's resources is a long-standing complaint.

Five separate insurgencies between Baloch nationalists and federal forces have taken place since Pakistan's founding, the most recent of which has been ongoing since 2004.[33] In 1947, the ruler of the princely state of Kalat chose independence rather than join India or Pakistan, but the Pakistani state's forcible incorporation of Balochistan against Baloch wishes triggered the first insurgency. In the 1970s, Zulfiqar Ali Bhutto's dismissal of the elected National Awami Party (NAP) government in Balochistan in favor of his chosen proxy, Nawab Akbar Bugti, was a key step toward the 1973–1977 insurgency. This sense of distance and disregard of Baloch desires by the federal Pakistani state is a continuous thread through accounts of Baloch nationalism. It is also consistent with a practice of rule by which the state empowered tribal chiefs and their patronage networks over local administration, a practice dating back to the British colonial era (Butt, 2017).

Pakistan's energy infrastructure and personnel are frequent targets of attacks by the Baloch nationalists. Quetta Electric Supply Company (QESCO) suffered a capital loss of Rs. 245 billion due to acts of sabotage from March 2003 through September 2010.[34] In January of 2015, Baloch insurgents caused Pakistan's largest-ever power outage when sabotage of a power transmission line near Guddu resulted in a mass blackout affecting over half the country. Sabotage of gas pipelines is also commonplace, with 54 incidents reported in January to September 2011 by the South Asia Terrorism Portal.[35] Accounts of earlier insurgent actions from the '70s include a similar targeting of energy infrastructure and personnel, including oil exploration teams and the transportation of coal to the Punjab (Butt, 2017).

The Pakistani state has tried to suppress the insurgency forcibly through military operations as well as the undocumented and illegal disappearances of thousands of Baloch. The missing persons cases taken up by the Supreme Court of Pakistan were part of the high-profile conflict between Chief Justice Iftikhar Chaudhry and the Musharraf regime. Prime Minister Gilani said that the number of Baloch missing persons was between 6,000 and 8,000 under the Musharraf regime. The Human Rights Commission of Pakistan (HRCP) has documented many of these cases, with neither the HRCP nor any other observers giving credence to Musharraf's claim in an April 2009 interview with Al Jazeera that these people went missing on their own (Human Rights Commission of Pakistan, 2010, pp. 104–106). Pakistan will struggle to utilize its gas resources well so long as the Baloch insurgency continues.

The question "Why aren't we [Pakistan] properly exploiting our gas?" was vigorously rejected as invalid by a Pakistani oil and gas executive. While the physical characteristics of Pakistani fields and prospects are of modest appeal to a multinational oil and gas company, the low prices allowed for Pakistani natural gas by the Oil and Gas Regulatory Authority limit the profit from operating a gas field. Most importantly, the lives of oil and gas workers are at risk. Two Pakistani employees of a Hungarian oil company were killed in January of 2011 and two others kidnapped.[36] Under these circumstances, the executive said, "you cannot expect reputable firms to operate in Pakistan."[37]

Pakistani energy policy is affected by security issues in Balochistan, and the insurgency in Balochistan is also fueled in part by Pakistani energy policy. Perceived injustices in shares of the benefits from Baloch natural resources are used by Baloch nationalists as justification for the insurgency. Insurgency in turn limits access to existing gas reserves and constrains further exploration. The Seventh National Finance Commission Award of 2009, which distributes Pakistan's taxation revenues among the federal and provincial governments, provided greater compensation to Balochistan for natural gas, but this did not translate into an immediate impact on the insurgency.

Gomal Zam Multipurpose Hydroelectric Dam

Due to the foreign exchange burden of imported fuels for power generation for the Pakistani economy, a focus on the development and exploitation of indigenous fuel resources has been a constant factor in energy planning. Along with natural gas, the most important indigenous fuel resource for Pakistan is hydroelectric power. The contribution of hydroelectric power to total power generation was 65% in 1960 and ranged between 49% in 1966 to 78.7% in 1979 after the construction and expansion of the Tarbela Dam. Since 1980, the share of hydroelectric power in Pakistan's total power generation has steadily declined to 28.5% in 2015 (National Transmission and Despatch Company, 2017).

Gomal Zam Dam is located near the Afghan border in the South Waziristan agency, one of Pakistan's seven tribal agencies and six frontier regions that constitute FATA. After 2001, FATA became the stronghold of the Taliban and the launching point for attacks on NATO troops in Afghanistan (Rashid, 2008). FATA had never been fully incorporated into Pakistan until the passage of the 25th Amendment in May 2018,[38] and up to that time it was excluded from the jurisdiction of the Pakistani Supreme Court by article 247 (7). While FATA has elected representatives to the Pakistani parliament since 1997, acts of parliament did not apply to FATA (per article 247[4] of the Pakistani constitution) unless the president deems otherwise. In the absence of legislative and judicial checks and balances, the executive branch appointed political agents to administer FATA under the 1901 Frontier Crimes Regulation. On August 12, 2011,

President Zardari amended the Frontier Crimes Regulation to allow political parties to become active in FATA and to allow FATA residents a first-ever right of appeal against decisions of the political agent. FATA exists on the margins of the Pakistani state in every sense, but the funding and security problems experienced at Gomal Zam are indicative of state formation throughout the country.[39]

The history of the Gomal Zam Dam in South Waziristan illustrates the stop–start progress of many construction projects in Pakistan. First identified as a site for water storage in the mid-19th century, it was selected as the site for a dam location by WAPDA in 1959. Construction began in 2001 but was halted in 2004 after the kidnapping of two Chinese engineers working on the site. One of these engineers returned, but the other was killed. The construction company withdrew its participation in the project in 2006 as a result of this incident. Further kidnappings occurred in subsequent years but did not delay the project as extensively. In 2012, eight WAPDA officials were kidnapped and held for almost two years before their release. In 2015, 21 laborers working on a road to the dam site were kidnapped for two weeks. The project was restarted in 2007 with an expected completion date of 2010 but ran into problems in January 2010 when the contractors stopped working due to nonpayment by the Pakistani government. USAID included Gomal Zam into its energy sector support to Pakistan in July 2010 and paid the contractors so that work could resume. The construction of the dam was completed in spring 2011, the reservoir filled over the summer, and power generation was intended to start soon after. However, the dam's power generation capacity was knocked out in 2016 and remained unavailable through 2018. The irrigation component of the dam project was originally intended to be completed at the same time as the dam, but it ran behind schedule as there was no funding for it. As a multi-use dam, Gomal Zam is expected to provide water storage, flood protection, and power generation. Flood protection was in place as soon as the main dam was constructed and significantly mitigated the impact of the 2010 floods on the downstream districts of Tank and Dera Ismail Khan. However, the cost of Rs. 10.4B (US $122 million) could never be justified based on the power generation of 17 MW alone. The irrigation component of the project—such an important part of the economic case for the dam—was only funded by USAID in 2015 with a scheduled completion date in late 2018. The lack of available funds that resulted in the 2010 (and subsequent) stoppages of work and the lack of progress on the irrigation component are not unusual. Many public sector projects in Pakistan have been announced but never started, and many have been started but not finished for a lack of funds.

The location of Gomal Zam has complicated the project significantly. Of the project's total cost of Rs. 10.4 billion, Rs. 0.348 billion have been spent on security. On a visit to the site in April 2011 when accompanying a press event, I saw over a hundred soldiers around the dam site. Automatic weapons were a common (though still disturbing) sight for me after several years in Islamabad, but I kept a wide berth from the soldier I saw carrying a rocket-propelled grenade launcher. Travel to the dam from the nearest towns is controlled by the Pakistan army. Approved visitors are escorted in a convoy to the dam, though one engineer complained to me that being part of a conspicuous military convoy made them more of a target. Short trips between the dam site, the helipad, the powerhouse, and the rest house are also done in convoys of pickup trucks and SUVs bristling with soldiers.[40]

Sahiwal Coal-Fired Power Plant

The first concrete manifestation of CPEC was the Sahiwal coal-fired power plant, a 1,320 MW coal power plant constructed by Huaneng Shandong Electricity Limited and Shandong Ruyi Technology Group in the Punjabi agricultural heartland. The Sahiwal plant is active and produces electricity for Pakistan's electrical power grid, and in some basic but enormously important ways it has to be seen as a success. The simple fact of its existence, functioning, and timely construction is no small feat considering the wild and uncompleted power capacity projections of past plans described in this chapter.[41]

As a symbolic statement, the Sahiwal coal-fired plant is not subtle. In the flatlands of the Punjabi plains, the 175m high chimney is the tallest structure for hundreds of kilometers in any direction. Within the facilities, signboards in Chinese and English proudly proclaim the project as a testament to the Pak–China friendship. One signboard inside the grounds of the power plant salutes the "Sahiwal Spirit" as "The patriotic spirit of being loyal to the party and winning glory for the country" as well as "The team spirit of cooperating closely for the same aim and pulling together in times of trouble." Built with Chinese engineering expertise, the Sahiwal coal-fired plant represents the manner in which CPEC is intended to make material and direct contributions toward Pakistan's development. In many senses it exemplifies what Ching-Kwan Lee described as Chinese state capital's "profits plus" mode of global engagement, meaning financial profit plus an integrated consideration of political goals (Lee, 2017).

Coal is a cheaper fuel source than furnace oil, so to the extent that it displaces less thermally efficient and more costly power plants, there are economic benefits to be gained. Still, there are definite question marks to be raised over its location, which requires not only importing coal from South Africa and Australia, but also then transporting the coal by rail from the Karachi port 1,000 km inland to the Sahiwal facility. Coal power plants are usually located near the source of the fuel, either a mine or a port. While generating electricity near a load center (i.e., the city of Lahore) helps reduce transmission losses, the relative inefficiency and costs of transporting the physical fuel by rail grossly exceed high-voltage transmission losses.[42]

From an environmental perspective, there are concerns about the water required for power generation being diverted from agricultural use, as Sahiwal is in the middle of the Punjab's agricultural heartland. Further, the pollution from coal emissions (notwithstanding the plant's supercritical combustion) could hurt the area's agricultural production and worsen the region's already poor air quality.

In terms of financial sustainability, the Sahiwal plant has already run into exactly the same issues that dog the existing private power plants, as it has repeatedly had to endure periods where the Pakistani government has fallen behind on its payments.[43] The fundamentals of the system have not changed. Even if one accepts the lower economic cost of coal power (and ignores the water and air quality issues), the vulnerability of the system to circular debt and loadshedding remains. China is exporting infrastructure, but not infrastructural power.

Conclusion

The problems of the Pakistani power sector are layered. Capacity constraints, the cost of imported fuel required by the type of capacity that exists, and the financial burden imposed by poor billing and collections practices all interact to produce repeated crises in the Pakistani power sector. Each aspect of the problem must be addressed in its own right, but—as the next chapter will discuss—the idea of conceiving of a static solution to a problem where the major aspects interact with each other and their environment is misleading.

The consequences of the unresolved issues in state making are as visible on the generation side of the power sector as we saw in Figure 2.2, the map of uneven losses across Pakistan's distribution companies. Those losses require state intervention in the form of the tariff differential subsidy, which serves to paper over the strains resulting from uneven state making and the provinces' thwarted claims to an equal participation in the idea of the nation.

The fixed repertoire of actions employed to meet this crisis purport to present such a comprehensive solution, but they fail where similar approaches have failed in the past by not engaging with the politics of Pakistani decision-making in the power sector. Driven by international donors and multilateral lenders, technical solutions strip away politics yet fail to achieve their objectives. Although international actors complain of a lack of political will when assessing the resistance to undertake radical institutional reforms or eliminate subsidies, this chapter has highlighted a consistent prioritization of the power sector at the highest level of Pakistan's government. It isn't political will that is lacking so much as the limitations of state making that privilege a strong central state over the demands of peripheral voices from the provinces. In this context of inter-provincial ethnicized contestation, the electricity subsidies and transfers that so weigh down Pakistan's fiscal ledger are not so much a sop to the poor as a means of keeping that national grid integrated and compensating for the uneven degree to which peripheral regions are incorporated into the national polity. Pushing technical solutions while ignoring the "design" that generated these inequalities has been a failing strategy.

By late 2020, Pakistan had added sufficient capacity to its system such that it actually had excess capacity. This does not, however, spell the end of Pakistan's power sector woes. As argued in this book, loadshedding and circular debt have never been matters of capacity addition alone, and, even though substantial power generation capacity has been added, pricing and governance concerns more generally mean that Pakistan is still adding to its circular debt and has not escaped the cycle of crises triggered by the power sector's financial unsustainability. This position of excess capacity has actually occurred once before, after the initial spurt of IPPs added under the 1994 power policy. Many of those IPPs used furnace oil and established the reliance on expensive imported fuels that lay at the heart of recurrent power crises since then. While the current spate of CPEC-funded projects use cheaper fuels (albeit still imported), the financing arrangements do put substantial burden on the federal government, which must continue to pay for this capacity whether or not those power plants are in use.

The subject of later chapters is to show how the challenges faced at the policy level are shaped by the nature of governance at lower levels, and particularly the encounter of citizens with the state's street-level bureaucrats. The next chapter explores the Pakistani state's limited governance repertoire, the obstacles to successful governance reform inherent in the structures of international development assistance, and the challenges of governance reform.

3

Pathologies of Development Practice

Introduction

International development actors are regularly aware of the shortcomings of governance interventions before, during, and after development assistance is introduced, yet those programs continue and are even revisited. Why? Why doesn't the awareness of the problems with development interventions prevent the continuation of failures, the repetition of mistakes, or more caution in essaying grand plans for institutional reform? This chapter uses the history of reforms in the Pakistani power sector to illustrate this puzzle and to suggest some partial answers that link the content of reforms (and the poor outcomes) to the structures of development assistance that drive them. Viewed through the framework of the infrastructural state, these shortcomings reflect the inability of top-down reform to penetrate below the national field, and the misrecognition of Pakistan's electricity governance as a lack or absence rather than a result of inequality by design.

The major focus of this chapter is to show how there are repeated points in Pakistan's experience with power sector reforms where the challenges and shortcomings are noted but not acted upon. The experience of failure didn't change approaches to reform despite abundant feedback channels and high-level political support. That development assistance generally—and governance reforms in particular—produce poor results is old news, but this nuance in the path to disappointment is usually overlooked in the literature. What the Pakistani power sector case shows is that key participants had well-founded reservations about the reforms. In the run up to the 1994 power policy that invited the establishment of independent power generation facilities (independent power producers, or IPPs), the preparatory work by consultants and government strategists clearly identified a necessary sequence of steps to ensure that private investment would be received by institutional arrangements conducive to it. When the preconditions weren't met, the major goal of the reforms

Access to Power. Ijlal Naqvi, Oxford University Press. © Oxford University Press 2022.
DOI: 10.1093/oso/9780197540954.003.0003

(to have investment without sovereign guarantees) was lost. The World Bank's analysis of its own role reveals the multiple ways in which the intervention's shortcomings were visible at early stages. In the 2010 plan guided by the Friends of Democratic Pakistan (FODP) and the programming of the United States Agency for International Development (USAID), development actors returned to the same agenda—with similar results. By contrast, the more recent experience of the China–Pakistan Economic Corridor (CPEC) sets itself apart for the lack of an overt governance reform element, though it, too, has lost momentum due to persistent cash flow problems inhibiting Pakistan's ability to service foreign debts. Pakistan's repeated borrowing programs with the IMF put great emphasis on the power sector and reinforced the drive to impose a technocratic top-down solution that sidestepped domestic politics. Nonetheless, the power sector remains mired in cash flow challenges.

The fact that development projects aren't effective or that governance interventions go wrong is well-trodden ground. Pritchett et al. (2013) castigate these programs for their pursuit of "development as accelerated modernization"—in which nonlocal expertise sets the agenda—and show how such reforms are undone by isomorphic mimicry (a superficial copying of foreign institutions as camouflage) and premature loading (stressing them with challenging reforms). Both isomorphic mimicry and premature loading are present in the Pakistani case and helpfully explain why the reforms have disappointed.

A new wave of development thinking advocates more systemic and complex conceptualizations of development challenges (Ramalingam, 2013). Based on this improved conceptualization of development challenges, the approaches recommended in this new wave are iterative, adaptive, and politically aware (Andrews, 2013; Booth & Unsworth, 2014). While there is sound reasoning behind this approach, its viability is challenged when we consider that past development efforts have been aware of their shortcomings but unable to correct their path. Moreover, this chapter will argue that the content of governance reforms is linked to the structure of development assistance, thus revealing a higher order of obstacles to successful governance reform.

The case of the Pakistani power sector reforms could be treated as important because Pakistan has the world's sixth largest population, or because it is one of the largest recipients of assistance from USAID and the U.K. Department for International Development (DFID) during the twenty-first century.[1] Pakistan's experience with electricity sector reforms in the 1990s was common to many others, both in terms of the design and execution of the reforms as well as the outcomes, and there are general lessons to be learned about development assistance from this case. Lastly, this is a site of ongoing and substantial donor involvement from the World Bank and USAID programs in the 1980s and 1990s, many programs of the Asian Development Bank throughout, and—particularly since the Kerry-Lugar-Berman bill of 2009—huge involvement by USAID, which approaches $500 million for the energy sector alone between 2010 and 2014. Most recently, the Chinese investment in the Pakistani power sector of $37 billion as a flagship project of the Belt and Road Initiative has raised the profile of international involvement in the sector yet further.

Following this Introduction, I identify the current arguments in development thinking that are influencing major development actors to adopt more adaptive approaches to development in light of a more complex framing of development challenges. Next, I explore the case of the Pakistani power sector with particular attention to the way in which the shortcomings of reforms were considered, but in which the development actors didn't change their course. The fourth section seeks to understand why development interventions weren't adapted in the face of this knowledge, and how the structure of the intervention contributed to that lack of adaptation. The fifth section briefly concludes.

Toward a More Complex Approach to Development

Governance reforms that concentrated on formal rules and excluded the informal realities of country context have largely failed (Disch, Vigeland, & Sundet, 2009; World Bank, 2008). OECD development aid targeting governance as a set of formal rules has had "limited impact" despite spending in excess of $10 billion per year:

> Programmes to improve the investment climate, strengthen the rule of law, or fight corruption do not fail just for lack of ownership or attention to politics. They fail because they make the wrong starting assumption: that progressive change consists in, and can be achieved through, strengthening formal, rules-based institutions that reflect a clear division between public and private spheres of life.
>
> (Institute of Development Studies, 2010)

Pritchett et al. (2013) use two explanatory mechanisms to explain the widespread failure of governance reform that seeks to change institutions: isomorphic mimicry and premature loading. Isomorphic mimicry refers to the superficial adoption of organizational forms as camouflage so that a donor recipient can "look like a state" while continuing with its existing practices. Isomorphic mimicry blends three sources of isomorphism identified in the sociology of organizations (DiMaggio & Powell, 1983); coercive (driven by concerns of power and legitimacy), mimetic (a response to uncertainty by modeling the forms of other organizations that are perceived as legitimate and successful), and normative (through increasing professionalization). All three are found in development, but while Pritchett et al. blend them for the purposes of their argument, drawing a distinction between them allows for the recognition that mimicry can be a very successful strategy in an evolutionary framework, and that the damage happens under conditions where a weak and fragmented state is pressured into adopting certain organizational forms (Krause, 2013).

Premature loading is a related idea in that the work of the organization doesn't yet fulfill its written or formal description (which may be the result of relatively recent institutional reforms). Thus, when a burden of fulfilling the obligations of its form is put on a newly reformed organization before it is mature, and it can't meet that challenge, the stress of this burden on the organization contributes to the failure of the governance reform. With both isomorphic mimicry and premature loading, the key concept is that the external form of the organization does not match how it works in practice. Of course, preserving necessary operational practices while adopting formal structures as legitimating myth or ceremony is a classic decoupling strategy (Meyer & Rowan, 1977) for seeking external approval without upsetting local stakeholders.

Isomorphic mimicry and premature loading result from the practice of "development as accelerated modernization" (Pritchett et al., 2013). In this reading, development assistance seeks to "skip to Weber" by copying the institutions of the Global North without going through the extended power struggles that produced those institutions. The essence of development assistance is thus decontextualized knowledge to be applied outside the time and space in which it was first acquired. This argument is powerfully articulated in James Ferguson's *Anti-Politics Machine* (1990), wherein the accretion of state power through development assistance relies precisely on such decontextualized development knowledge of institutional arrangements stripped from the field that generated and sustained them.

A new wave of development thinking seeks to respond to these critiques of development assistance by conceiving new ways to approach development. One prominent line of thought is that of Andrews (2013), who proposes Problem Driven Iterative Adaptation (PDIA). PDIA departs from traditional development assistance by looking from the outset to try multiple experimental approaches that allow development actors to learn from mistakes. Rather than a sequential series of reforms charting a path to a donor-determined set of institutions (an idealized Denmark or New Zealand [Pritchett & Woolcock, 2004]), reforms are approached by trying out what works within a specific context. In an alternative framing of a related approach, Booth and Unsworth (2014) argue for "locally led" and "politically smart" development assistance that puts a premium on the depth of local experience and political sensitivity of the personnel deployed by development actors.

Closely related insights for development have been generated by understanding development challenges in terms of complex adaptive systems (Ramalingam, 2013). In a complex adaptive system, agents learn from and change in response to the system they exist in (Axelrod, 1997; Miller & Page, 2007). These agents interact with each other in unforeseen ways, triggering negative and positive feedback loops (Arthur, 1990; Jervis, 1997), which can produce emergent outcomes that weren't necessarily foreseeable beforehand. The path from agent interactions to emergent outcomes of interest in a complex adaptive system is nonlinear and thus ill-suited to the types of linear causal models that underlie the power sector reform programs of the 1990s: you cannot depend on input x to produce output y (Mitchell, 2009). Complex adaptive systems are also highly context sensitive, and differing starting conditions will produce varying adaption responses from agents just as they adapt to stimuli such as reforms (Holland, 1992). Importing reform strategies from different settings would then need to be undertaken with extreme caution.

The bilateral development agencies of the United States and the United Kingdom (USAID and DFID)—two leading development actors in size and influence—have taken steps to incorporate the lessons of complexity and more systemic conceptualizations of development into their operations. USAID published "Local Systems: A Framework for Supporting Sustained Development," in which a more systemic perspective is taken on working with multiple and interconnected local actors to achieving lasting results (United States Agency for International Development, 2014). DFID undertook an end-to-end Review of Programme Management in 2013–2014 that sought to draw on some of the lessons of complexity and involved Ben Ramalingam, the author of *Aid on the Edge of Chaos* (2013).

Beyond the special case of developing countries, complexity offers a broader set of insights for public policy that follow from the distinctive framing of the problem based on principles of complexity: agents will adapt to policies and affect one another; cause and effect will only be known in hindsight; and starting conditions can be replicated, but not end states (Colander & Kupers, 2014). However, not all problems are complex; seeing complexity everywhere is as much a failing as failing to see it at all. In a simple system one can follow a recipe, and in a complicated system solutions can be engineered (Kurtz & Snowden, 2003).

While the language and concepts of complexity add something to discussions of development, there is a real danger of putting old wine in new bottles. The insight that reform strategies shouldn't be introduced from other settings without consideration of the local context is a development commonplace that is present in every primer on development written in the last 20–30 years. It is perhaps the first lesson that every veteran of the field would impart to a newcomer. And yet why does it seem so hard to avoid? Why is it that this fundamental tenet of development thinking has not been reflected in the push for electricity sector reform?

In the next section I apply the critiques of isomorphic mimicry and premature loading to the experience of governance reforms in the Pakistani power sector from the 1990s through the present day. While the authors cited in this section might agree with the application of their critiques to this specific case, neither they nor I am suggesting that the adaptive and experimental approaches to development that have evolved out of those critiques could be simplistically applied to the Pakistani power sector. Advocates of experimental and iterative approaches to development assistance want to depart from large-scale institutional reform efforts and would not advocate reforms such as those of the Pakistani power sector in the mid-1990s. The new wave of development approaches that build on the Pritchett et al. (2013) critique—such as PDIA (Andrews, 2013) and politically smart and locally led (Booth & Unsworth, 2014)—are not intended to function at that scale. The goal of this chapter is to use the lessons of Pakistan's experience with power sector reform to reveal a higher-order set of obstacles to governance reform that originate in the pathologies of development practice located within development organizations as they relate to the infrastructural state. As the next sections of the chapter will show, the repeated failure of governance reforms stems from how these reforms are divorced from the realities of state capacity. Technocratic ideals of independent corporatized utilities and an independent regulator are conceived of in a political void, neither attuned to interprovincial political economy (as described in Chapter 2) nor the everyday encounter with the state at the urban and individual levels (described in subsequent chapters). The response of development practitioners has been to insist on their technocratic ideals, push for an insulation from domestic politics, and create state organizations that are independent of democratic political pressures.

Institutional Reforms in the Pakistani Power Sector

The introduction of IPPs in Pakistan in the 1990s followed the World Bank's conceptual blueprint for electricity sector reform, and—as one of the first such efforts—the tools of this reform (such as power purchase agreements) developed in Pakistan were used in other countries where IPPs were introduced. The Pakistani power sector is a key part of the propagation of a standardized set of reforms for the electrical power sector that were pushed to developing countries by the World Bank and its allied bilateral and multilateral donors. Neither the view that Pakistan was part of this standardized reform push, nor the difficulties faced by such reforms where they were implemented, are contentious readings of history. Premature loading and isomorphic mimicry are both present here. What I seek to show here is that the reforms themselves were challenged and questioned before, during, and after they were introduced.

The World Bank and USAID provided the leadership for power sector reform in Pakistan in the early 1990s through their championing of the mammoth Hub River Company (Hubco) private power generation plant and establishment of the basic strategy for power sector reforms in Pakistan, respectively. *WAPDA's Strategic Plan for the Privatization of the Pakistan Power Sector* prepared by a USAID contractor in 1992 for the Water and Power Development Authority (WAPDA), the vertically integrated electrical utility, is much more than a caricatured import of Washington consensus principles despite being built around them. The central tenet is to "provid[e] for the greatest possible role for the private sector and the movement over time towards full competition." This approach is proposed as the solution to three "critical goals" of the Government of Pakistan:

> A. Enhance Capital Formation for the Pakistani Power Sector (PPS) outside the Government of Pakistan (GOP) Budget and without Sovereign Guarantees;
> B. Improve the Efficiency of the PPS through Competition, Accountability, Managerial Autonomy, and Profit Incentives; and
> C. Rationalize Prices and Social Subsidies, while Maintaining Certain Socially Desirable Policies such as Rural electrification and low Income "life-line" Rates.
>
> (International Resources Group, Putnam Hayes & Bartlett, & Hunton & Williams, 1992, p. i)

The 1992 strategy doesn't go into a lot of detail as to why or how private management will necessarily do a better job than public sector management. This reasoning is addressed to some extent under goal B, but the construction of this critical goal contains both a goal (efficiency, albeit undefined) and a chosen approach—private management. The long-term viability of public sector management is not considered, though the conditions and sequencing of reforms that can provide the setting for the success of private management are discussed.

The principal prerequisite for the privatization strategy is the corporatization of WAPDA: its reorganization into discrete profit centers with independent management and separate accounts. Once these corporatized subdivisions establish a commercial track record, then they will be "ripe for privatization" (International Resources Group et al., 1992). Further,

> The introduction of profit incentives and competition, if properly implemented, will ultimately improve the efficiency of the PPS. These improvements cannot be achieved, however, without fundamental changes in the PPS and the promotion of a business, regulatory, and political climate conducive to private investment. (International Resources Group et al., 1992, p. 4–1)

This sequencing puts the entire burden of reform on WAPDA and the Government of Pakistan. For WAPDA to reorganize itself and secure its commercial viability before privatization means that the hard work of ensuring timely and complete bill payments, eliminating political interference, and balancing costs and revenues will be substantially completed. Additionally, for the Pakistani state to promote a business, regulatory, and political climate suitable for private investment successfully would be a tremendous achievement at a time of political turmoil and economic uncertainty. For privatization to be undertaken after these achievements by WAPDA and the broader state suggests that the authors have limited hope for privatization to address the fundamental problems underlying poor power sector performance.

The authors of the 1992 strategy understood the limits of private sector management and were cognizant of the preconditions for the private sector to offer any advances over the public sector:

> The PPS whether privatized or not, will be able to raise private, non-guaranteed, non-concessionary financing at "reasonable" cost only when private investors have confidence in the entities and environment in which they are investing. This will require enforceable contracts for power sales and fuel purchases, predictable and fair regulation, and a stable social and political environment. This situation does not now exist in Pakistan. (International Resources Group et al., 1992, p. 2–2)

Despite their entirely valid reservations, the authors of the 1992 strategy still put out a relatively aggressive timetable to achieve decentralization, corporatization, and selected privatization by 1994, with full operation of the private and competitive Pakistan power sector from 1996 onward.

In order for the 1992 strategic plan to become reality, it needed to be worked into specific policy prescriptions. In October 1993, shortly after taking office, Prime Minister Benazir Bhutto constituted a 12-member task force to

> draw up a co-ordinated and comprehensive Energy Policy, formulating strategies for the elimination of load shedding, recommending proposals for mobilization of resources and promoting private sector investment, and making recommendations for enhancing indigenous oil and gas production. (Government of Pakistan, 1994)

The Prime Minister gave a deadline of six weeks to complete the report. Twenty-three additional members were drafted to provide specialist knowledge. The committee was headed by the prime minister's special assistant for economic affairs and included the highest ranked bureaucrats in the power sector as well as prominent industrialists in a manner suggestive of an embedded bureaucracy (Evans, 1995). The virtues of the *Report of Prime Minister's Task Force on Energy* become most apparent when contrasted with the 1994 policy that was ostensibly based on it.

There are major differences between the task force report and the 1994 policy in terms of the amount of new capacity to be added and the manner in which projects are to be identified. The task force report called for 1,500 MW by 1998, and the policy itself anticipates about 1,500 MW of new projects, but the 1994 policy set no limits on the new capacity to be added. A more serious problem, however, is that the 1994 policy was based on receiving unsolicited bids at a predetermined price.

The proposals may have been for private sector investment, but there was no price competition involved because the price was fixed in the policy. The generosity of the terms can be gauged by the massive investor response; almost 30,000 MW worth of proposals (Private Power and Infrastructure Board, 2001), 2,000% of what the task force report required. Competition on price typically involves a pre-identified project to be prepared for bidders who compete on price and other technical criteria. While such solicited bids were envisioned in the task force report, and competition is central to the efficiency gains envisioned in the 1992 strategic plan, the 1994 policy did not adopt that approach and never attempted to introduce price-based competition into the power generation market.[2]

A second manner in which the 1994 policy failed the goals of the 1992 strategic plan was in that it involved sovereign guarantees for private investors. The logic behind a sovereign guarantee for private investors is that it mitigates the risk of the investment by forcing the Government of Pakistan to back the stream of payments from the power sector. A World Bank assessment concluded that "It is doubtful whether any IPPs could have been financed in Pakistan without government guarantees since perceptions of Pakistan's risk had limited financing to terms of 18–36 months" (Fraser, 2005, p. 13). Pakistan has regularly owed substantial payments to the IPPs and even committed a sovereign default due to nonpayment in 2012 (Kiani, 2014; Rana, 2012).

International financial institutions played an integral role in financing the IPPs set up under the 1994 policy. Eleven of the 16 IPPs set up (88% of the total MW, and thus close to the same percentage of total investment) received funding from the World Bank group, and 85% of the foreign debt was from official sources (Fraser, 2005). The foreign debt was repayable in 10 years on average and backed by the Government of Pakistan's sovereign guarantee. As the primary financiers of Pakistan's IPPs, it is the World Bank and other international financial institutions whose risk perceptions were being mitigated by Pakistan's sovereign guarantees. The Government of Pakistan's sovereign guarantee notwithstanding, the debt with which 80% of the $5.3 billion total IPP investment was undertaken was owned by private investors. Pakistani consumers paid for that debt within (on average) 10 years of the plants achieving commercial operations, but ownership remained with private investors. The investments were considered untenable without sovereign guarantees, but at the same time the international financial institutions would not countenance lending the money to the Government of Pakistan itself.

The reorganization and corporatization of WAPDA was the focus of a later report entitled *Report of the Committee Constituted by the Ministry of Water and Power for Corporatization of WAPDA (Power Wing)*, dated October 3, 1997 (Ministry of Water and Power, 1997). One of the authors, Mian Shahid Ahmad, also worked for the USAID contractor preparing the 1992 strategy paper. There is a clear continuity between the 1992 strategy and the 1997 report; the later report is primarily concerned with one objective within the framework laid out by the 1992 strategy. The timetable in the 1997 plan—less aggressive than in the 1992 strategy—is for corporatization within two years and a competitive market within five years after corporatization. No mention is made of the intervening five years when no progress on these same goals was made, though there is a warning regarding the need to follow through on the government's commitments: "The committee [of authors] wishes to stress that unfaithful or half-hearted implementation will not yield the expected results, and consequently, the Policy and the very concept of corporatization and privatization will stand discredited" (p. 21) Although the distribution companies were reorganized into discrete entities in 1998, the requirements identified as necessary precursors to corporatization and privatization were never fulfilled.

The 1992 strategy and 1997 report both acknowledge that they are asking for a sea change in the principles of operation but say little or nothing to address how that change will be achieved. The 1997 report recognizes that currently, "most of the managerial decisions involve social and political considerations," yet it offers nothing regarding the transition from the status quo to a position where the "primary focus of each corporate entity will be profit" (Ministry of Water and Power, 1997, p. 11). Executive fiat alone, it would seem, was supposed to accomplish this transformation. Corporatization never happened, and the social subsidies and flawed hiring practices of the electrical utilities still make news 25 years later.

The 1992 USAID privatization strategy deserves credit for not blindly celebrating all private power schemes. In particular, it notes the inappropriate "use of imported oil at Hab [sic] River over imported coal or domestic fuels" (p. 2–4). The USAID privatization strategy also had misgivings about the role of sovereign guarantees:

> Currently, new generating capacity being developed by private interests, such as the Hub River project, are receiving such substantial GOP and World Bank guarantees and underwritings that they do not represent good examples of private investment. (International Resources Group et al., 1992, p. 3–6)

The Hubco project went ahead despite this stated opposition, however, in one of the key policy documents of Pakistan's unbundling and privatization.

Behind the scenes of the international actors promoting a private sector agenda for developing country power sectors were other cautionary voices as well. At a round table between Electricité de France and the World Bank (World Bank, 1993), several reservations were voiced by French participants. Notably, they did not see any plan to achieve the desired separation of utility management from the political establishment. Instead, they saw a generic plan and no requirement for specific analysis on a case-by-case basis, and they feared that the functioning of an efficient regulatory agency would require an "institutional maturity and a balance of power which is not necessarily the prerogative of developing countries" (p. 16). The French commentary also included a regret that the notion of public service had been discarded in this reform agenda—which can be read in terms of the differing social construction of economic rationality between France and the United States (Dobbin, 1994). In general, the round-table participants recognized that ambitious institutional transformation such as the deregulation and privatization of the power sector in a developing country would be hampered by deficiencies in state capacity, and that few examples of such reforms existed to draw upon. Similarly, a discussion paper at the World Bank Group (Glen, 1992) concluded that inducting private capital under sovereign guarantees can defeat the initial goals of adding to the investment in a country.

USAID-funded technical assistance for privatization and unbundling ended in 1994 per the Pressler Amendment, which disallowed aid to countries developing nuclear weapons. With the departure of USAID and its consultants, the Government of Pakistan lost access to much of the expertise it had relied on in developing the 1994 power policy. Several of the clearly written provisions of the policy were bypassed in the course of the induction of IPPs. Mian Shahid Ahmed believes that he and the team of USAID contractors could have shaped a better policy had they remained in place.[3] While the skepticism expressed in the 1992 strategy toward Hubco supports that view, Ahmed never had the opportunity to influence the response to the 1994 policy as USAID's involvement ended in 1994 subsequent to the Pressler Amendment.

The World Bank's involvement with Hubco failed to meet its own standards. The implementation completion report (World Bank, 2001) declared the outcome to be unsatisfactory, the World Bank's performance to be unsatisfactory, and the Government of Pakistan's performance to be unsatisfactory. It further found that the framework established for IPPs was unsustainable, and that there was negligible contribution to institutional development.

In its assessment, the World Bank notes that lending to Hubco consumed the entirety of the Private Sector Energy Development Project, one of two World Bank vehicles for private sector energy development in Pakistan, and that the project was perhaps too big as the initial IPP in Pakistan. The World Bank report notes that "High level senior management attention may have led to inadequate attention being given to dissenting views during the review process" (World Bank, 2001, p. 18). The scale of the World Bank's commitment to Hubco led to it becoming a broker in resolving issues between the Government of Pakistan and Hubco. The World Bank's "involvement went far beyond what was prudent for a development banker and exposed the Bank to conflicts of interest and reputational risk" (World Bank, 2001, p. 18).

The most grievous shortcoming of the Hubco project is visible in the period 2001–2006 when economic dispatch was implemented at the National Power Control Centre. The job of the National Power Control Centre is to organize and manage the generation of power so that demand is met. Economic dispatch is the process of prioritizing power generation plants in order of their variable costs and then using the plants in that order. When economic dispatch principles were used from 2001 to 2006, Hubco's energy production declined from 7,168 GWh in 2000–2001 to a low of 1,648 in 2003–2004, or 23% of its 2000–2001 production, because it made no sense to run this expensive power plant ahead of cheaper alternatives (Rifai, 2009).

While Hubco was uneconomical relative to other power plants (public or private), the entire IPP program was set up to be a loss-making proposition for Pakistan. The World Bank states that "the issue whereby WAPDA would lose implicitly US¢4.1/kWh bought from IPPs was acknowledged but not addressed through the loan" (World Bank, 2001). The breakdown of the loss is that the IPPs would be paid US¢6.5/kWh by WAPDA, but the prevailing rate of transmission and distribution losses meant that 24.2% of those units would never reach consumers, meaning that WAPDA's cost per unit served to a consumer was effectively US¢8.6/kWh while the average revenue in 1994 was US¢4.5/kWh. There was an assumption that consumer prices would be raised to cover this shortfall, but the World Bank review later acknowledged that it was "highly unlikely that the tariff increases of this magnitude would have been politically or socially acceptable, or even commercially sustainable" (World Bank, 2001, p. 18).

Neither the Government of Pakistan nor the World Bank managed to keep the IPP program under control. The World Bank and other lenders were paid back in 10 years, but the consequences of unaffordable power based on expensive imported fuels are very much still with Pakistan. The introduction of IPPs into Pakistan was isomorphic with the standard paradigm, but (the arguable case of Hubco aside) it wasn't coercive; Pakistani political and administrative leaders played a willing role. The basic parameters of the privatization policy, however, were shaped outside Pakistan and without respect to its institutional capacities.

Most experiences of other developing countries with the standard paradigm for electricity sector reform ended poorly (Williams & Ghanadan, 2006). Twenty-one of thirty-four such private power projects starting in the 1990s renegotiated their central agreements with the host government by 2005 (Woodhouse, 2006, p. 173). In India, the focus on expansion of generation capacity through IPPs was misplaced in a context of decaying infrastructure and mismanagement of distribution (Kale, 2004). Generous terms for IPPs across Asia attracted investments that weren't financially viable and put the burden of risk for private investments on national governments (Wells & Ahmad, 2007; Williams & Dubash, 2004). In many countries where these reforms were tried, the reforms were undone by the underlying political economy of the power sector, the exigencies of the state's fiscal needs, and patronage politics (Victor & Heller, 2007).

The reform program implemented in Pakistan in the 1990s falls squarely in line with this standard paradigm, both in terms of the approach and the disappointing outcomes. The example of the introduction of IPPs as part of a move toward a competitive market for electricity shows how policy departed from its lofty concepts, how prerequisites for reform were abandoned or ignored, and how the nascent regulatory structure could not manage the influx of capital on the scent of large profits.

Written 25 years later, the FODP report (Friends of Democratic Pakistan, 2010, p. vi) describes energy sector governance as fragmented and says that the "disequilibrium" and "disharmonious regulatory structures" generated by this fragmentation undermine the achievement of energy security. The solution it proposed was an integrated energy sector in which water, power, oil, and gas are not planned and regulated separately. A single ministry of energy that would combine the existing Ministry of Water and Power and Ministry of Petroleum and Natural Resources was the key objective. Further, the two regulatory authorities for power and oil and gas needed to be merged. As an immediate measure, a senior energy adviser position on the staff of the prime minister would monitor and push through the implementation of energy sector actions such as those laid out in the FODP plan. The report also observed that "Public sector energy companies (PSECs) should be run on good corporate governance models and have a commercial orientation with incentives for improved performance" (p. 21).

The FODP report's disengagement with Pakistan's politics and what Pakistan's rulers want is exemplified by the position of senior energy adviser. The senior energy adviser was to report directly to the Prime Minister—above the relevant ministers, in effect—and would be empowered to drive through reforms. The designers of the FODP program intended to solve the implementation problem that previous reform programs had struggled with by effectively bypassing the politicians (there was to be no "blank check"). No senior energy adviser post with these powers was created. Although the members of the FODP—including representatives of the Pakistani government—met in Brussels in October 2010 and issued a joint communiqué introducing the energy plan (Friends of Democratic Pakistan, 2010) among other items, the Pakistani minister of state for foreign affairs declined the additional aid because it would not allow decision-making regarding the spending of that aid to rest outside the Pakistani government ("Govt Agencies to Manage Flood Aid, Donors Told," 2010).

The FODP approach had significant signs of a more coercive form of isomorphism. In particular, the attempt to introduce an advisory position to control the reforms (to be filled by an FODP-approved person) was a blatant attempt to push through an externally driven agenda over local political resistance. The Pakistani government's response was to allow the report to proceed without actively participating in it, and then to withdraw its support. Despite the resistance of the Pakistani government to the FODP report, various FODP members continued to fund development projects in the Pakistani energy sector that sought to achieve the same objectives identified in the FODP report.

As a USAID contractor placed at the Ministry of Water and Power as part of the Energy Policy Project, I found little scope there for a critical perspective when the definition of the problem and its solution were dictated by the funding agency. For example, in USAID's terms of reference for a key power sector reform project, the goals include the elimination of subsidies and the adoption of a "commercial" rationality for the state-owned distribution companies (United States Agency for International Development, 2010). Any contractor engaged in this program is legally bound to work toward the achievement of these goals, irrespective of what they might consider the merits of imposing a commercial rationality on a public sector organization providing a vital state service. The terms of the project contract constrain development practitioners to those terms, bind them to evaluation on those same terms, and serve as the basis for selecting among contractor proposals. The morbidity of governance reform in the Pakistani electricity sector has its origins in the development practices through which those reforms have been approached.

Pathologies of Development Practice

The painfully circular experiences of reforms in the Pakistani power sector shed light on three different approaches to reform. Each of these approaches is undone by the pathologies of development practice—the tools of development assistance themselves. The first approach, the standard one, is the tried and trusted-to-fail approach of big development, which hammers at a predetermined set of objectives. This standard approach is undone by isomorphic mimicry and premature loading. The second approach appears only peripherally in that it represents a path toward a focus on public service excellence that was not taken. Implicit in the comments of Electricité de France on prospective World Bank electricity sector reforms is a treatment of public service that is quite distinct from the neoliberal approaches pushed through international development actors. The third approach is the newest one, informed by past governance reform failures and drawing on complexity. The prospects for each of these approaches to reform can be informed by the preceding section, which details how the Pakistani power sector reforms of the 1990s were launched on an aggressive timetable for corporatizing and commercializing the public sector as a precursor to enticing private investment. The previous section describes how this history shows isomorphic mimicry and premature loading in action. The power sector took on the external forms required by the donor-driven programs while the local political economy that shaped power sector operations remained intact. The preconditions for private investment were skipped, and the resultant investments were adjudged by the donors to have had no institutional impact. This history of repeated failures at institutional reforms exposes the contribution of the intrinsic characteristics of the instruments of development assistance themselves. These instruments and their inherent characteristics influence each of the three approaches to reform by limiting the pathways of possible action.

Although many critiques of the standard approach to development are available, this chapter has primarily used Pritchett et al.'s (2013) succinct and trenchant summation of decades of counter-narrative. One of the earliest critics of grand theories of development such as modernization theory was Albert Hirschman. Hirschman saw substantial intellectual risks in imposing simplistic order over the variegated forms of real life and instead strove to create *petites idées* that could be linked together. Hirschman saw parallels with Christopher Alexander's (1964) work in design theory—an important early influence on complexity—in which identifying "isolable subsystems" of relative order to address can be the basis for linking small efforts toward a larger goal (Hirschman, 1967, p. 24; see footnote 12). However, Hirschman understood that while the simplicity of a model makes it wrong, the absence of simplicity makes ideas unusable. The flexibility of Hirschman's intellectual scaffolding of *petites idées* in *Development Projects Observed* was poorly received by the World Bank despite their having commissioned the study (Adelman, 2013), and the imperative of imposing a bureaucratically legible order over the messy vitality of lived experience still impedes the work of development actors.

Andrew Natsios (2010) has written compellingly of USAID's operations, in which the growing use of private consultants has been matched by a "counter-bureaucracy" whose job it is to monitor and assess the bureaucracy and their projects. There is an onerous burden of reporting to fulfill the surveillance needs of the counter-bureaucracy. Navigating the reporting requirements in such a way that allows a project to function without deviating from its terms of reference or finance rules is a task best suited to accountants and lawyers, and Natsios bemoans the demise of the development professional within this context.

While international development interventions can be influential at the national level, the use of international development consultants inhibits any potential effect on the actually existing economy and society in the country. As terms of reference for consultants are written, a pre-approved field of for-profit contractors will assemble the resumes of likely personnel whose chief attribute will be related experience elsewhere, that is, technical expertise. That isomorphic mimicry is a pathological feature of development assistance is driven by the leading role of international consultants in the donor-funded technical assistance exercises that define the objectives and approach to institutional reforms. The assembled consultants bring non-local knowledge, and the terms of their hiring bind them tightly to a project written without deep knowledge of the local situation. Adapting to the local situation has to be carefully considered within the scope of the project documents so as not to alert the counter-bureaucracy, and development practitioners may have to work against the counter-bureaucracy by excluding their successful strategies from internal reporting (Eyben, 2010). For USAID projects in Pakistan, monitoring was supplemented by congressional requests for information, as elected representatives were on high alert for the prospect of spotlighting the waste of taxpayer money on an ally with whom the United States has a troubled relationship.

The U.S.–Pakistan relationship shaped when development projects were started and how long the projects continued. The USAID-funded work (which produced the 1992 strategy paper) ended due to the Pressler Amendment, which sanctioned Pakistan for its pursuit of nuclear weapons. A broadly held view is that the United States conveniently overlooked Pakistan's nuclear program so long as the war in Afghanistan meant that Pakistan was an important ally (Levy & Scott-Clark, 2007). While DFID moved in the opposite direction of distancing development interventions from politics, the United States moved USAID under the purview of the Department of State, thereby cementing the instrumental status of development assistance as a diplomatic tool. The Centre for Global Development suggests that USAID's overt politicization has worked against its development interventions (Birdsall, Elhai, & Kinder, 2010).

The fraught political backdrop to USAID's activities in Pakistan prompted extra scrutiny and underscored the need to produce results rapidly to justify the expenditure of taxpayer dollars. The amount of total aid and the context of the ongoing conflict attracted the attention of congressional representatives, which in effect provoked the counter-bureaucracy to a heightened level of surveillance that detracted from the time and energy available to actually work on the project.[4] Every development assistance project must work within a constrained timetable. Each project must spend money—the burn rate—in order to justify its existence. The pressure to spend money quickly conflicts with any inclination to take the time to assess the local situation (bearing in mind that the contractors leading the project, and especially the international staff leading the project, will typically have no local knowledge or networks), thus heightening the appeal of best practices from overseas with which the internationally sourced technical experts are familiar. Isomorphic mimicry is thus promoted by the time limitations of the development assistance project—not as a strategy to make states look legitimate but as a way for contractors to make development projects look legitimate and to meet their contractual obligations under significant time pressure.

In their criticism of the World Bank–proposed reform program for electrical power sectors across the Global South, Electricité de France highlighted how the spirit of public service was being abandoned.[5] Peter Evans' (1995) seminal formulation of embedded autonomy in developmental states draws on the importance of state bureaucracy that reinforces its capabilities through esprit-de-corps and other non-contractual forms of contract.[6] Instead, power sector governance reforms pushed by international development actors have emphasized contractual relationships in their attempts to improve governance. This doctrine of new public management has been as unsuccessful in developed countries as in developing ones (Hood & Dixon, 2015). The increase in transaction costs noted in the Electricité de France round table with the World Bank has outweighed any increases in efficiency, and the spirit of public service has been a casualty in this process. The tools of development assistance reflect this same paradigm whereby bureaucracies such as USAID have had their permanent staff reduced at the expense of using contractors and subcontractors.

That USAID was in danger of repeating past failures when it greatly expanded aid to Pakistan after 2009 was highlighted in research produced by the Centre for Global Development. In a review of the World Bank and partners' support for social spending in the 1990s, Birdsall et al. (2005) observe that, despite monitoring reports indicating poor performance of the programs, the World Bank chose to continue the program and not impose the specified penalties for the Pakistan government's failure to meet its commitments to reform. The donor bias to disbursement trumped concerns over performance, expectations were unrealistic, and more funding didn't translate to leverage in the face of local power relations and the underlying political economy below the national field. An analysis of past assistance to the energy sector was described by Kinder (2010) as "an exercise in déjà vu," with donors pushing for the same package of reforms and being similarly disappointed from 1992 onward. On the basis of their research, the Centre for Global Development wrote open letters to Ambassador Holbrooke (heading the USAID effort to Pakistan at the time) outlining their findings. Despite arguing that this same approach had failed in the past when pushed by the World Bank and Asian Development Bank, Birdsall (2010) advocated that USAID continue its support, albeit conditioning the support on the achievement of pricing reforms and institutions to support private investment. Local power relations and political economy did not feature in the recommendations. If this evidence was not sufficient to argue against more of the same programming, then there's little scope to suggest that a development actor will ever choose against providing development assistance that is politically desired.

Where CPEC Meets the IMF

Unlike the USAID- and World Bank–dominated examples of power sector reform discussed in this chapter, the CPEC energy sector projects did not come with an institutional agenda. The CPEC energy sector projects are financed and built through Chinese state-linked entities, but they largely fit into existing Pakistani energy institutions. While there is a new CPEC Authority established in 2021, its purview is more to do with ensuring the implementation of projects rather than their continuing operations. CPEC energy projects still come under the purview of National Electric Power Regulatory Authority (NEPRA) for regulatory matters and are paid for through government channels in a similar manner to earlier IPPs.

The link between CPEC's energy sector projects and overt governance reform has arisen over time, resulting from familiar issues with cash flow management. Overall, while CPEC has doubtless contributed to the goal of expanding Pakistan's available power supply—for example, as argued in Chapter 2, projects such as the Sahiwal coal-fired plant have added to Pakistan's power generation capacity—they have not added to state capacity, and the CPEC projects appear no more sustainable than the IPPs constructed under the 1994 policy in that they are unaffordable under the prevalent tariff and subsidy arrangements. The fiscal crisis of 2019—in which CPEC and the energy sector feature prominently—brought Pakistan to the IMF, and it is under the direction of the IMF and its lending conditionalities that Pakistan has returned to the familiar agenda of power sector reforms.

In turning to the IMF for a 22nd time since 1958—and 15th time since 1980—the government was obliged to implement the NEPRA Amendment Act as a precondition to resuming the lending program (the Extended Fund Facility, or EFF). The NEPRA amendment allows the Government of Pakistan to impose a 10% surcharge on base tariffs, which is a key mechanism for reducing the flow of circular debt in the Circular Debt Management Plan (CDMP). Further, The NEPRA Amendment empowers NEPRA to notify tariffs (i.e., give them legal effect) rather than only determine them. Previously, it was the government that notified tariffs, thus allowing politics to have its sway. Although elected representatives will now supposedly have no direct influence on power tariffs, it is difficult to imagine popular sentiment or political pressures being entirely ignored. Indeed, when the government announced plans to increase tariffs by over 34% in March 2021, there was a huge backlash among opposition politicians, with the Pakistan Muslim League-Nawaz's (PML-N's) official spokesperson, Marriyum Aurungzeb, likening it to "burying the people of Pakistan alive" and dropping an "electricity bomb" (Khan, 2018). Two months later, Pakistan appealed to the IMF to ease the requirement of raising tariffs.

The IMF's intervention is framed both in terms of an unprecedented crisis and a familiar challenge (International Monetary Fund, 2021):

> Turning the energy sector around requires *strong and sustained reforms* . . . [and] making a dent requires *steadfast implementation* of a comprehensive reform strategy. (p. 19, italics added)

> The authorities *remain committed* to an ambitious and sustained decline in the accumulation of power sector arrears. To this effect, they prepared—in close consultation with the World Bank, Asian Development Bank (ADB), and IMF staff—an updated CDMP, which was approved by the Cabinet in March 2021. (p. 19, italics added)

> While recent measures go into the right direction, staff reiterated the need to *rigorously follow through* with the comprehensive IFI-supported Circular Debt Management Plan (CDMP) given the power sector's soaring circular debt level and the repercussions on the financial sector, budget, and real economy. (p. 26, italics added)

The IMF program is a clear return to familiar prescriptions, with—as ever—the implication that political will on the part of Pakistani leadership is required.

The ultimate goal of this newest set of reforms is a competitive power market. This goal is reflected in the 2021 Memorandum of Understanding signed with IPPs that agrees a renegotiation of their power-purchasing agreements, which will only take effect after a competitive power market of multiple buyers and sellers has been established. The 1992 power strategy echoes forth nearly 30 years later. However, just like the 1992 strategy, the current hopes of a competitive power market require a transformation of the distribution companies, which just hasn't happened. Without fully corporatized distribution companies—companies that must operate with independent governance and balance sheets—cash flows to investors will always tap on the Government of Pakistan's sovereign guarantee to ensure payments, including the timely and complete payment of power sector subsidies. While corporatization and independent governance are at the top of the IMF wish list, there is a disconnection in this reform agenda from the capacity to act at the urban or street level, where the organizations of the Pakistani public sector meet the Pakistani public.

Conclusion

The case of the Pakistani power sector and its experience with governance reforms reveals how development actors revisit the same reform programs despite acknowledging their past failures. Awareness of the unsuitability of a reform program can be present before, during, and after an intervention, but future programming won't necessarily adapt in response. Governance reform is difficult enough, but the tools of development programming themselves are a higher-order obstacle to reform over and above the substantive challenges. The pathologies of development practice are borne by the tools themselves and interfere with the ability to bring local knowledge to the problem, adapt based on experience, or take a long-term perspective rather than focus on quick wins. The 1992 privatization strategy insisted that achieving commercial performance standards was a necessary first step to introducing private actors into the power sector. Specifically, the goal of inviting new investment without sovereign guarantees depended on achieving these commercial performance standards, which would ensure dependable cash flows to investors. In the absence of this requirement being met, the private investment that took place relied on sovereign guarantees, thus undermining a key goal of introducing private power producers.

The inability of development actors to respond when shortcomings in the program appear bodes ill for any approach that relies on rapid reassessments of development programming and responses. While an adaptive and flexible approach might sound good when considered in the abstract, it doesn't match the experience of how development actors work in practice. Moreover, the contracts through which external consultants—an increasingly large component of development assistance—are engaged are ill suited to opportunistic responses or the acknowledgment of failures. The counter-bureaucracy that handles contractual oversight acts against the adaptive and iterative approach that is being called for. When development programs begin and end for reasons of state, then the potential to take an experimental orientation to an adaptive search for successful innovation is reduced. The need to declare quick successes is increased when development programs are under a political spotlight.

The recent wave of reformed approaches to development takes on board these past shortcomings and offers intellectually compelling alternatives. The proponents of this most recent wave, however, acknowledge how higher-level obstacles block the way to reforming development itself. Booth and Unsworth (2014) conclude their case for locally led politically smart development with ways in which the recruitment and staffing of their own organizations would have to change in order to adopt this approach. They don't say how this would be achieved, and one is left with the impression that this is a truly daunting task that is unlikely to be achieved. Chapter 10 of Andrews' book applies the PDIA logic to "reforming the rules of the development game itself" and concludes that "It seems like the actors involved in authorizing and negotiating development interventions are satisfied with the status quo" (Andrews, 2013, p. 231). Practitioners might continue to "subvert the current system" rather than expend the effort to reform the development actors themselves, but none of these discussions involve the recipients and supposed beneficiaries of aid (Green, 2014).

The satisfaction of the actors structuring development interventions with the status quo is indicative of how development practices are systematically disembedded—in a Polanyian sense (Polanyi, 2001)—from development outcomes. This chapter has argued that the structure and operational procedures of development actors impede the feedback loops between decision-making around development practices and outcomes as experienced in local contexts. The move to take a more adaptive approach to development interventions is surely more promising than a less adaptive approach, but—just as with existing practice—its prospects for success will be undermined by the structure of development projects, the reliance on external contractors, the monitoring and oversight of the counter-bureaucracy, and the primacy of the donor's political objectives. By identifying where isomorphic mimicry is at its most coercive, development actors can pinpoint where the "looking like a state" phenomena are most likely to appear. In these situations, the state is likely to decouple the actual functions of its institutions from the organizational form. If a development actor cannot or will not back away from such an intervention, it indicates that the local feedback loops which inform effective policymaking have been severed and that the beneficiary of the project is no longer the local population.[7]

PART II

THE CITY LEVEL OF ANALYSIS

The city level of analysis bridges the policy-oriented set of challenges that feature at the national-level of analysis—and in Pakistani headlines—with the book's core insights derived from fieldwork about how governance in Pakistan works in practice. This section pairs a statistical analysis of the Lahore Electric Supply Company (LESCO) service area with a fieldwork-based study of access to electrical power in Islamabad, where squatter settlement residents and steel mill owners alike encounter the street-level bureaucracy of the Islamabad Electric Supply Company (IESCO). Islamabad is the location of Pakistan's governmental core, home to the apparatus of the federal government and many public servants. Lahore is a provincial rather than federal capital, but it exerts its own center of gravity as the cultural core of Pakistan's richest and most populous province.

As exemplified by the empirical data for this section, the book is primarily a study of governance processes in urban rather than rural Pakistan. Further, the data are drawn from what is unequivocally Pakistan's core, where wealth and power are the most concentrated. Rural Pakistan is largely outside of the scope of analysis for this book, which cannot speak to the experiences of people in rural and peripheral areas. Through the comments of people interviewed for this book's fieldwork, it seems evident that the unevenness shown in the governance processes operating in the core urban environment have even more severe consequences for the well-being of individuals outside the core. What the focus on urban Pakistan reveals, however, is that the uneven inclusion for service provision suggested by losses and subsidies at the national level is very much how governance processes operate at the urban core as well.

Chapter 4 continues on from Chapter 2 in the exploration of losses as an indicator of state capacity. Whereas the national picture reveals an uneven political economy of subsidies and power generation across provinces, Chapter 4 shows the considerable variation that exists across the city of Lahore and the LESCO service area. The chapter's statistical analysis shows the extent to which losses are driven from below, suggesting that the underlying urban fabric is the major determinant of the level of losses rather than formal institutional or administrative concerns. The rules, after all, are constant across this space, and there is much variation to be found within a single subdivision wherein even the staff and equipment administering the rules are the same.

Chapter 5 relates the experiences of a squatter settlement in Islamabad with securing access to electricity and compares these experiences with those of the settlement's wealthy neighbors, including businesses and state facilities. This chapter focuses on the role of formal rules as an element of state capacity and highlights the pervasiveness of informality for rich and poor alike.

Increased formality is often touted as an advance for the poor, and linked to a set of ideas made famous by Hernando de Soto (2000) and championed by the World Bank. Unfortunately, the case explored in Chapter 5 shows just how difficult it is for the poor to benefit from formality, and that even the rich need to use informal means to take advantage of formal rights. Nonetheless, it is definitely the case that the rich typically have formal relationships with the state and are able to find ways to utilize them.

Even as formality is shown not to be a panacea for households in squatter settlements, we see that a single institutional rule set across the entirety of a city (and its surrounding region) can produce drastically different outcomes in terms of the state's capacity to penetrate society and issue bills for electricity consumption. Notably, this is true even in the Lahore and Islamabad service areas that are undeniably Pakistan's core. If governance is so uneven in these core areas, there is even less reason to think that a reliance on formal written institutions—or adjustments to them—will produce the desired governance outcomes, unless they are accompanied by a broader (and necessarily political) initiative aimed at a broader sense of social inclusion.

4

The Administration of Losses

Electricity transmission and distribution losses are the portion of electricity supplied to a distribution system that are not billed to consumers. Losses are an important feature of a distribution system that can be analyzed in multiple ways related to the infrastructural state. Most straightforwardly, they are important to the cash flows of the sector for all the reasons discussed in Chapter 2. Pakistan's losses were 19.87% in the public sector (i.e., excluding Karachi Electric) in 2015 (National Transmission and Despatch Company, 2017), which means that almost one-fifth of the electricity generated is never billed to consumers. Distribution companies outside the Punjab struggle to recover even that amount which they do bill to consumers—even when dealing with public sector consumers—but recovering the electricity that is not even billed is an even thornier proposition. That amount must be billed to paying consumers, either legally (through higher rates for all) or by overbilling select consumers by falsifying their consumption records. Yet the constraints of importing fuel and maintaining a stream of payments to independent power producers (IPPs) mean that ensuring cash flow is a crucial requirement of the national electrical grid, which the distribution companies must fulfill. High losses beyond the level at which the regulator has already made an allowance put a burden on the federal government that can strain the budget. Also, as discussed at a national level in Chapter 2, losses represent a key component of infrastructural power in terms of the state's logistical capacity to penetrate social life and extract payment from its citizens.

The unevenness of the electricity sector across the entirety of Pakistan reflects a long history of uneven development as practiced by the federal government. This chapter focuses on the unevenness of the infrastructural state within four districts centered on the city of Lahore using operational data from the Lahore Electric Supply Company (LESCO).

The data analyzed in this chapter cannot speak to the variety of reasons and modalities that make up the phenomenon of electricity losses.[1] Some people

Access to Power. Ijlal Naqvi, Oxford University Press. © Oxford University Press 2022.
DOI: 10.1093/oso/9780197540954.003.0004

will hook a wire from their home to an overhead cable, as dangerous as that might be, whether out of greed, opportunity, or desperation. Some will be part of collective arrangements to avoid an official bill that are convened by a political broker. Some cannot produce official documentation of property ownership and are thus prevented from a legal individual connection. Others exploit positions of power, including elected and governmental appointments, to intimidate the electricity utility and avoid a bill. All of these possibilities (and others) are invisible to the data set examined in this chapter, which not only does not have individual-level data but also cannot look beyond the data that was entered into the system by utility staff. The qualitative evidence presented in Chapters 5, 6, and 7 grapples more explicitly with this human dimension and does speak to how and why individuals and communities engage with electricity governance. This chapter puts forward an analysis of electricity losses at a higher level of abstraction, chiefly through studying the drivers of variation in electricity losses in the LESCO distribution network.

Losses are sometimes further divided into technical and nontechnical losses, with technical losses referring to the losses that occur due to the physical infrastructure's material properties (i.e., resistance in electrical conductors). While a relatively small percentage (2.73%)[2] of electricity is lost due to resistance in the wires of the national grid's transmission system, the focus of this chapter—and of governance reform efforts—is on what managers of electrical infrastructure describe as nontechnical losses, which include theft in the distribution system as well as other issues related to billing.[3] In many countries (including Pakistan) such losses have proven themselves to be resistant to governance interventions, as the social and political relationships that shape governance at a local level are rarely amenable to top-down interventions (Brown & Mobarak, 2009; Victor & Heller, 2007).

A reader with an engineering mindset might critique the choice of focusing on nontechnical losses, but this move is both the only practical choice and a choice that is consistent with the book's theoretical framework. Analyzing technical and nontechnical losses separately is infeasible because the data set made available by LESCO does not separate out technical and nontechnical losses, leaving any virtues of pursuing this distinction in the conceptual domain. Separating out a technical component of losses can also imply the operation of this infrastructure without a human dimension, whereas a foundational position in science and technology studies is to see "science and technology as essentially and irredeemably *human* (and hence social) enterprises" (Edge, 2001, p. 5, italics in original).[4] This book's theoretical framework of the infrastructural state approaches the state through the lens of infrastructure and sees the uneven relationship of Pakistani citizens with the state through their relationships with the electrical power infrastructure. Following Thomas Hughes (1983), electricity systems are socio-technical systems. Treating losses as a composite suits the infrastructural state approach because I examine losses as a governance outcome produced by the interaction of state and other actors on the material infrastructures of electricity distribution.

A Brief Introduction to Lahore and LESCO

The data in this chapter comes from Lahore and LESCO rather than Islamabad and the Islamabad Electric Supply Company (IESCO), as is the case for the remaining chapters that draw on my ethnographic fieldwork.[5] While the core of the area covered by the data is the city of Lahore, there are rural and peri-urban areas as well. Although Lahore (like Islamabad) has its own distinctive features, Lahore, which expanded outward in the 19th and 20th centuries from its historic walled inner city, is more typical of cities in the Global South than Islamabad, with its planned construction in the 1960s as the seat of the federal government. It is this kind of city that Partha Chatterjee referred to when opening *The Politics of the Governed* with a claim that his book speaks to "most of the world," by which he means the postcolonial nations that were "not direct participants in the history of the evolution of the institutions of modern capitalist democracy" (Chatterjee, 2004, p. 3).

The South Asian city to which Lahore is most comparable is Delhi. Both are cities that came to prominence under the Mughals, and both served as the capital of the Mughal Empire at different times. Both have an inner city that was formerly walled—each even has a gate of its walled city named after the other—but the expansion first in the colonial era and then after independence stretched the geography of both cities far beyond the original core. Its faded Mughal grandeur notwithstanding, Lahore has a fundamentally provincial identity, situated first and foremost in the Punjab. This provincial identity places Lahore at the center of Punjabi political power in Pakistan.

This chapter explores the uneven distribution of electricity losses in the LESCO service area, which encompasses the administrative districts of Lahore, Kasur, Okara, and Sheikhupura. While Lahore is a city of 11.1 million people, the provincial capital, and the seat of the Punjab government, the larger service area includes a more varied spread of rural areas and peri-urban sites. The total population of these four districts is 21.1 million people.[6] I study the distribution of losses across this region with a particular interest in examining the extent to which losses are driven either by the underlying characteristics of the service area or by its administration. Based on the statistical analysis presented here, I find that it is the characteristics of the feeder itself that drive losses, with the subdivision level contributing comparatively less to the model's explanatory power. The implication of this finding is that variation in governance outcomes is heavily shaped by the social, political, and economic characteristics of the governed.

The Administration of LESCO

LESCO, like all the publicly owned distribution companies of the Pakistani electrical power system, has a very strict hierarchical structure with multiple levels. The administration of the distribution company is broken down into circles, divisions, and subdivisions. In 2015, LESCO had seven operational circles, 33 divisions, and 185 subdivisions.[7] Each of these levels of the administrative hierarchy has an officer in charge of operations at that level and a staff for that office. Changes in the number of these subunits and their boundaries do happen (and are not reflected in the cross-sectional data set analyzed here), but such changes are the exception rather than the rule. The subdivision is the level of the bureaucracy with which the average citizen has to engage for all basic functions such as billing, maintenance, new connections, and so on (see Chapter 7 for more discussion of the individual encounter with the subdivision office), with the exception of larger industrial and bulk customers, whose accounts are dealt with at a higher level. The subdivision is headed by a subdivision officer (the SDO), who has a staff of about a hundred people working for them. The SDO's cell phone number is printed on a consumer's bill, and this office is the primary public-facing site of the distribution company.

While the subdivision is the lowest level of the administrative hierarchy visible to the public, there is one lower level that has both administrative and technical consequences: the feeder. In a literal sense, the term "feeder" refers to the transmission wires that connect a service area to the main grid station. While this description is in some sense inaccurate for more sophisticated, interconnected distribution systems, the term remains in administrative use to designate a grouping of consumer accounts within a contiguous geographic area. Although it isn't strictly accurate, I often consider a feeder in terms of a neighborhood or *mohalla*. In practice, a feeder can include quite diverse social and spatial formations such as wealthy urban households, the people who are employed by those same households, and commercial plazas or markets. However, there is no commonality to the boundaries and spatial jurisdictions of other services such as water, police, health, or the municipal corporation. The typical subdivision has three to eight feeders,[8] each of which serves some 1,500–2,000 consumer accounts. A distribution company will refer to a consumer account of any type as a consumer, whether it is for a steel mill or a household.[9] For the distribution company, the feeder is the lowest level at which important operating information—notably losses, but also accidents, loadshedding, and unplanned outages—is gathered and reported. However, the operations of the distribution company are organized under the subdivision rather than a feeder, regardless of the diversity of feeders that exist within a subdivision. Everyone living and working within the same subdivision must deal with the same SDO as their neighbors, and the subdivision only has the one set of staff using the same vehicles and the same equipment.

Although feeders within a subdivision are geographically contiguous, in a dense urban area these service areas are not likely to be particularly uniform. In Chapter 5 I discuss the case of a squatter settlement in Islamabad that is served with the same electrical power infrastructure and administration that serves their more bourgeois neighbors. What the approach of this chapter allows us to do is identify broader patterns of such contrasts as revealed through losses. Following from the book's approach of taking the infrastructure of electrical power as a lens on governance at multiple levels of analysis, this chapter uses losses as a specific indicator that can reveal how those patterns of governance vary at a sub-national level, and even within a city.

Electricity Losses as a Proxy Indicator of Governance

International indicators from the World Development Indicators or the International Energy Agency only have national figures for losses. Consequently, electricity losses have been used in research studies as a proxy for overall performance of infrastructure provision by the state:

> Our proxy for industry performance in the electricity industry (line losses in transmission and distribution) was positively associated with regulatory separation, majority privatisation, and market liberalization (Henisz, Zelner, & Guillén, 2005, p. 890).

Electricity losses are also closely related to governance indicators and corruption (Joseph, 2010; Smith, 2004). Smith finds that theft is associated with instability and ineffective governments. These findings are reflected in Figure 4.1.

Of the World Governance Indicators (Kauffman, Kraay, & Mastruzzi, 2009), electricity losses are most highly correlated with Government Effectiveness (ironically, regulatory quality is not as closely correlated with losses). There is a general trend of decreasing losses as countries have higher levels of government effectiveness.[10] Pakistan has a middling performance among low- and

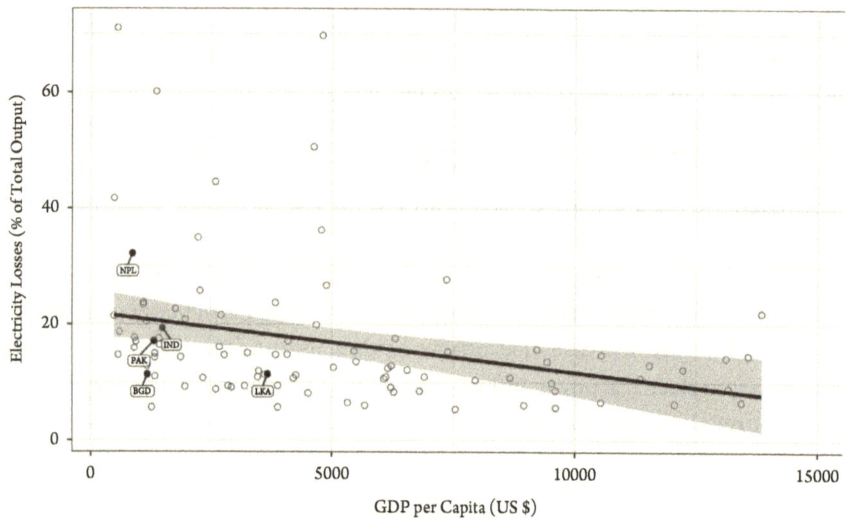

Figure 4.1 Electricity Losses against Governance Indicators for Low- and Middle-Income Countries (2014)

middle-income countries in terms of governance indicators and losses. It lies almost exactly on the line of best fit for Government Effectiveness, and within the 95% confidence interval for each of the six governance indicators taken from the World Bank. In comparisons with other South Asian countries, Pakistan has lower losses than Nepal (NPL), is similar to India (IND), but has higher losses than both Bangladesh (BGD) and Sri Lanka (LKA). India's higher governance indicators do not translate into lower losses. Nepal has generally comparable governance scores to Pakistan, but far worse losses. Bangladesh has only marginally better governance indicators (with the exception of greater political stability) but much lower losses. While the general trend is consistent with a common-sense understanding that electricity losses are a governance problem, and the South Asian comparisons give no clear pattern, these comparisons give little purchase for the analysis of either governance or losses.

The overall relationship between system losses and national income is that system losses tend to be lower in higher-income countries. Correspondingly, the line of best fit drawn on the scatter plot in Figure 4.2 slopes downward. Pakistani transmission and distribution losses are quite high at 17.4%, though other countries at Pakistan's income level have comparable losses and Pakistan lies within the 95% confidence interval around the line of best fit.[11] The South Asian comparisons show both higher (Nepal) and lower (Bangladesh) losses at a comparable level of income, similar losses at a higher level of income (India), and lower losses at a higher level of income (Sri Lanka). For both its income level and governance indicators, Pakistan's electricity losses are unexceptional among low- and middle-income countries.

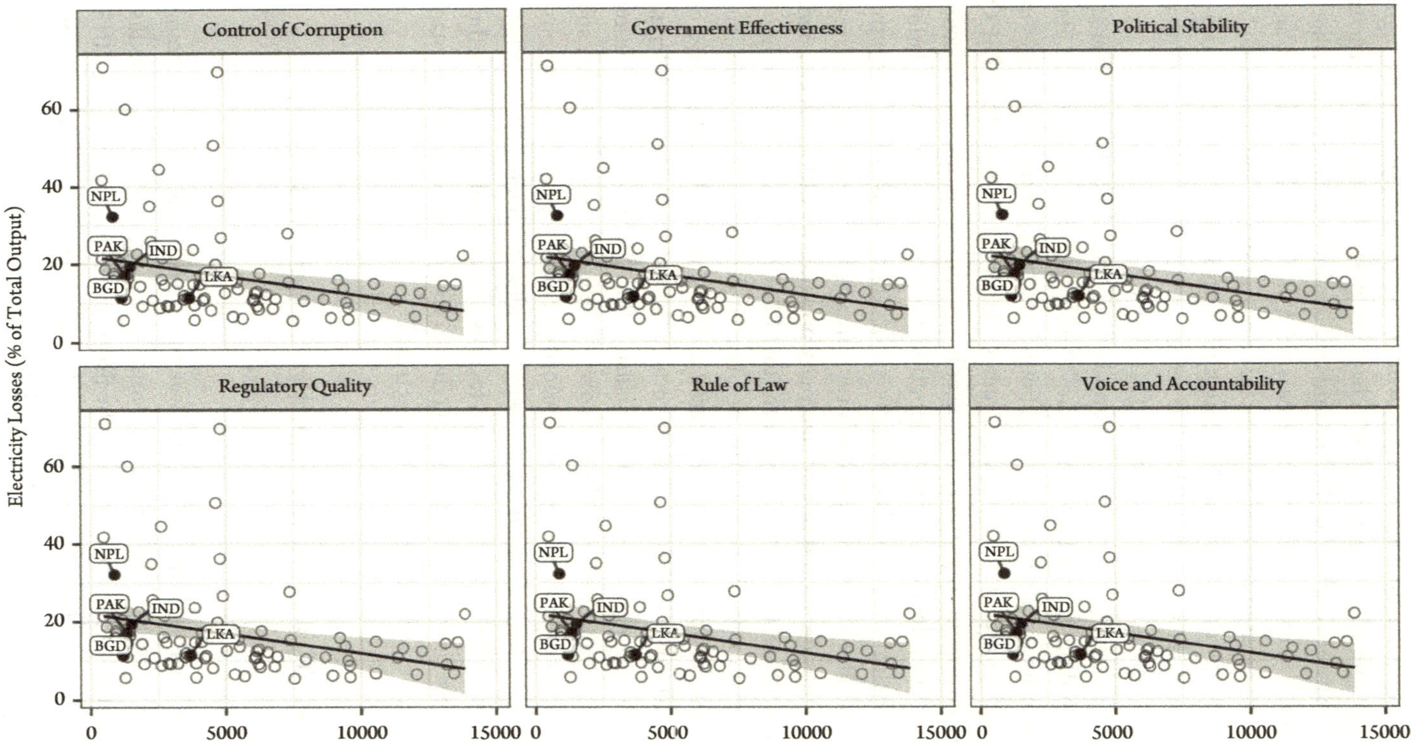

Figure 4.2 Electricity Losses against Per Capita National Income for Low- and Middle-Income Countries (2014)

A notable exception to the lack of attention to sub-national electricity losses is the work of Brian Min and coauthors, who use satellite imagery of the night sky and other sources to explore the links between party politics and electricity (Min, 2015; Min & Golden, 2014). Min and Golden find that the districts where the incumbents had greater electoral success were those with higher losses, and that losses can be used to predict electoral success in India. They conclude by arguing that their results suggest that "much line loss is not a function of technical features of electricity provision but rather an outcome of processes that benefit politicians and some consumers" (Min & Golden, 2014, p. 634).

Min and Golden aggregate their data on losses to the district level (approximately 2.7 million people for each of the 70 administrative districts of Uttar Pradesh) in order to match it to electoral boundaries because the boundaries of electricity service areas are not publicly available. Uttar Pradesh and the LESCO service area have some important differences in the administration of electricity. This chapter considers electricity distribution for a smaller total population (21 million against 190) in and around the major city of Pakistan's richest province, whereas Uttar Pradesh is a primarily rural area that is among India's poorest states. A key consideration is that all electricity provided by LESCO is metered, even for agricultural tube wells. This means that LESCO's service area might be more directly comparable to the cities of Uttar Pradesh such as Lucknow, but electricity distribution is mostly unmetered in Min and Golden's study area of Uttar Pradesh (which is 82% rural). Even though the area under study is different in these important ways, Min's broad conclusion that "Because the distribution of electricity is controlled by political actors, its benefits can be provided and taken away in accordance with political priorities and strategic considerations" (Min, 2015, p. 150) very much accords with the idea of "inequality by design." This chapter builds on Min's work, which focuses on party politics and whether electricity is provided at all, by examining the varying degree to which the state can bill consumers for the provision of electricity.

LESCO Descriptive Statistics for the 2014–2015 Fiscal Year

The data set for this chapter's analysis was provided by LESCO. It contains consumption data by type (domestic, commercial, agricultural, and industrial) aggregated to the feeder level for the fiscal year of July 2014 – June 2015. Industrial consumption is further broken down by the size of industrial unit. Consumption is measured in "units" of kilowatt-hours (kWh). Each feeder has a figure for losses for the fiscal year, total units received, and total units billed.

There are 1,468 feeders in 192 subdivisions. Each feeder and subdivision has a unique numerical code.

When cleaning the data both for the statistical analysis and the descriptive statistics, some of the feeder-level observations were excluded. While the LESCO data set had 2,109 observations, 563 feeders were mapped to multiple subdivisions. In each of these cases, the feeder's billed units were only nonzero for a single subdivision. Administratively at least, the feeder only belongs to one subdivision, and hence I summarized these instances into the one subdivision with positive billing. I also excluded 71 feeders that had either 0 units billed or received. A further seven feeders were excluded that had received less than 10,000 kWh.

It is important to analyze data for a complete fiscal year because this smoothes out the idiosyncratic features of the monthly data. Seasonality influences consumption and losses, as demand increases in the hot summer months. There are also spikes in the feeder-level data from month to month that can be smoothed out by taking into account the year as a whole. Distribution company employees warned me repeatedly of these monthly spikes, and they themselves don't look at a feeder's performance for an individual month on its own. Rather, the indicator monitored most closely in the distribution company management is progressive losses, that is, losses for the fiscal year to date, which also effectively smoothes out the month-to-month variation in performance.

Among the Pakistani distribution companies, LESCO is one of the better-performing ones. This success is often attributed to the relatively large proportion of its supply that goes to industrial consumers, who are often described by utility staff as "zero-loss" consumers. Medium and Heavy Industries make up

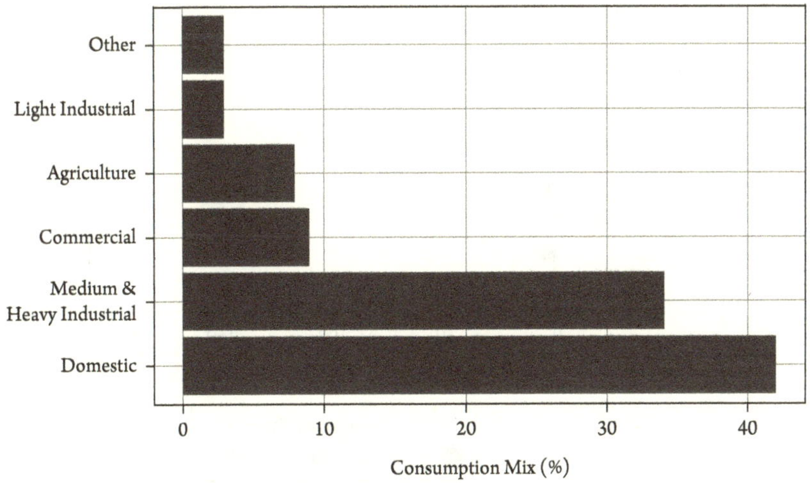

Figure 4.3 LESCO Consumption Mix for 2014–2015

39% of LESCO's total consumption, which is almost the same amount as domestic consumers at 40% of the total (Figure 4.3).[12] Although there are some agricultural areas served by LESCO, agricultural consumption is only 6% of the total. And despite the provincial capital of Lahore being a commercial hub for the region, only 8% of the total consumption is commercial. No single type of consumption dominates the LESCO mix.

Just as LESCO's overall distribution pattern is shared across different consumption types, each subdivision also tends to have a mixed profile of consumption. In Figure 4.4, the length and shading of each bar capture how many subdivisions have over 80%, 50%, or 20% of their total distribution go to a single category of consumer. Darker shading indicates a higher concentration of that consumption type, and a longer bar indicates more subdivisions having that profile. It is very rare for any subdivision to have more than 80% of its distribution go to a single type of consumer. Only six subdivisions have more than 80% medium and heavy industrial consumption, and only 16 subdivisions have more than 80% domestic consumption. Domestic consumption is the most prevalent, with almost half of the subdivisions having more than 50% of their distribution going to domestic consumers, and almost all subdivisions having at least 20% domestic consumption.

Subdivisions have on average 10% of agricultural consumption, 9% of commercial, 52% domestic, and 23% of medium and heavy industrial consumption. Medium and heavy industrial consumption is the only category that is somewhat

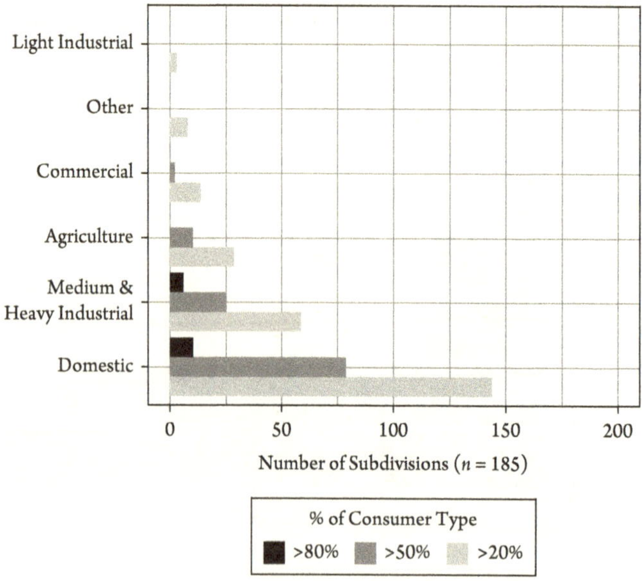

Figure 4.4 Concentration of Consumer Type in LESCO Subdivisions

concentrated; 39% of LESCO's overall consumption is in this category, but the mean for a subdivision is 23% and the median is only 6%. Although these primarily industrial subdivisions are few in number, these areas consume a lot of power to serve industrial facilities.[13] Nonetheless, there are light as well as medium and heavy industrial units scattered throughout LESCO's service area.

Unlike subdivisions, in which there is a more heterogenous mix of consumer types, feeders appear to be a little more distinctive from each other. As shown in Figure 4.5, there are many more feeders that have over 80% of consumption going to a single consumer category. Of the total 1468 feeders, 450 have over 80% of their consumption going to either domestic or medium and heavy industrial consumers. Moreover, one can see that for medium and heavy industry, it is quite concentrated in feeders where that consumption type dominates; when a feeder has some substantial level of medium and heavy industrial consumption, it tends to be dominated by medium and heavy industrial consumption. Agricultural, commercial, and domestic consumption is much less likely to be concentrated in relatively homogenous feeders.

The different levels of concentration in medium and heavy industrial consumption compared with agricultural, commercial, and domestic consumption is substantially by design. The feeders that serve medium and heavy industrial units are often reserved for that purpose, the better to facilitate the longstanding policy of having less loadshedding for industrial facilities. Although

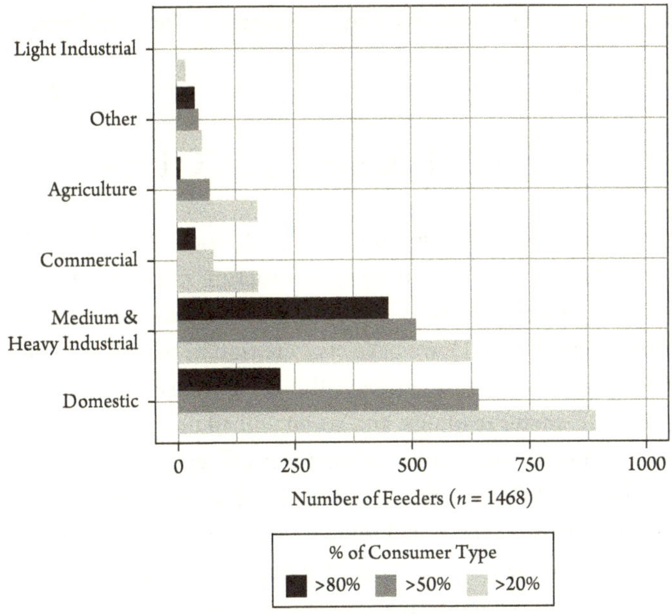

Figure 4.5 Concentration of Consumer Type in LESCO Feeders

this category is not separately identified in the data set provided by LESCO, bulk supply only exists on feeders that are dedicated to these relatively specialized purposes. Bulk supply represents a situation where a third party—such as a housing developer—has taken responsibility for last-mile distribution (and billing, if appropriate).

The heat map of LESCO losses, shown in Figure 4.6, uses the percentage of losses in each subdivision as the basis for shading that area, with darker areas presenting higher losses. The borders of each subdivision are an approximation based on the location of the subdivision office.[14] I am obliged to create this approximation because there are no better maps available of the service areas of each subdivision.

The heat map in Figure 4.6 presents no obvious clustering. The heaviest losses for a subdivision peak at 33% for the area of Sharaqpur, on the northern outskirts of Lahore. There are 13 subdivisions with losses over 25%, ranging from the aforementioned outskirts of Lahore to the rural service areas in the district of Kasur, where six of these subdivisions are located. The city of Lahore itself—shown in the right panel of Figure 4.6—has generally lower losses, reinforcing the general sentiment that billing in urban areas is generally tighter than that of rural areas.

The varying degree of losses across feeders and subdivisions across LESCO's service area tells a story of uneven state capacity in which not all residents of Lahore participate to the same degree. The public utility's ability to bill its consumers for the service it supplies is inconsistent, and—as the next section will show—influenced by the type of consumers to be found within a given feeder.

Statistical Modeling of LESCO Losses

A major question in approaching the statistical modeling of LESCO losses is how to represent LESCO's administrative structure in the model. In a similar manner to the grouping of students within schools for multilevel modeling (Raudenbush & Bryk, 2002), we have every reason to believe that a feeder's geographic and administrative location within a subdivision influence its losses. The maintenance, meter readings, and so on will all be managed by a single office under the direct control of a subdivision officer (known ubiquitously as the SDO). The subdivision office is the first and primary point of contact for all manner of consumer issues, including new connections, disconnections and reconnections, maintenance, billing, and meter reading (see Chapter 7 for a detailed examination of the individual's encounter with the subdivision office bureaucracy). Further, membership within a given subdivision is an indication of

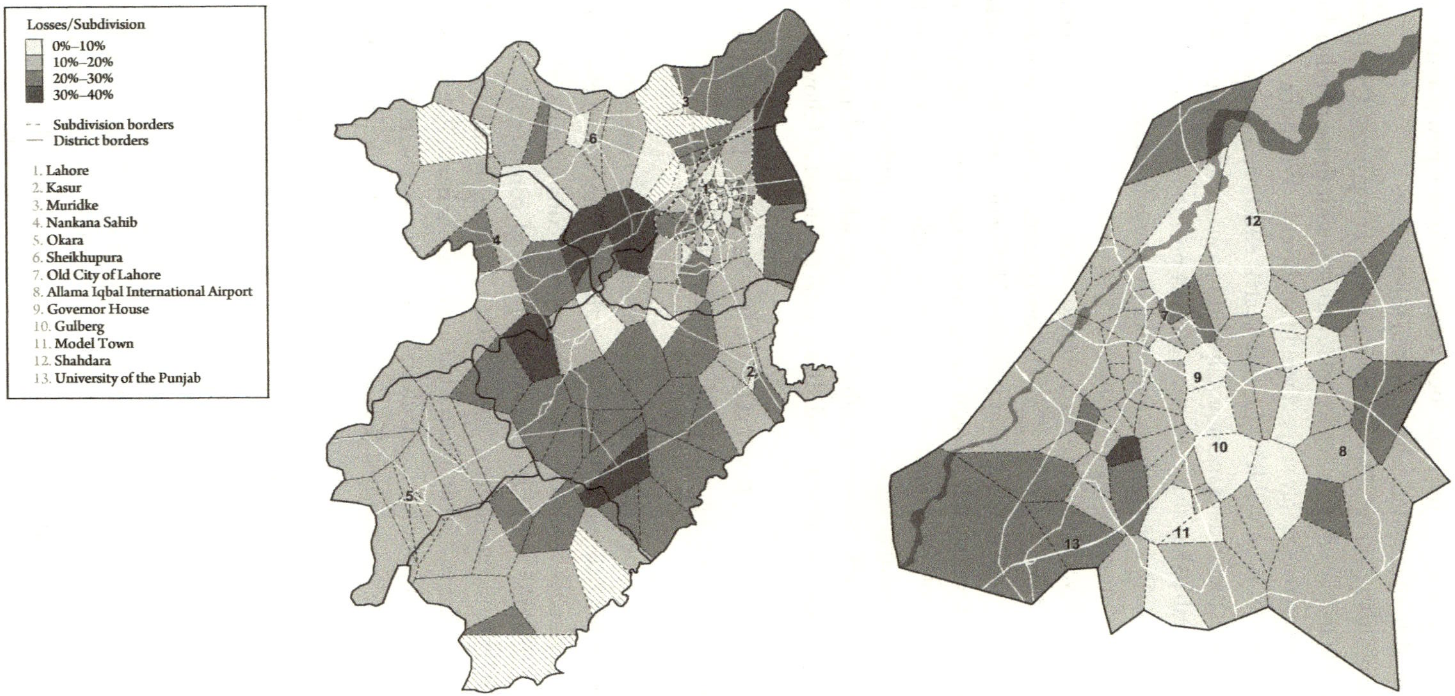

Figure 4.6 A Heat Map of LESCO Losses for the Fiscal Year 2014–2015, with Inset of Lahore

proximity, suggesting that the same local considerations of power and influence may be shared among feeders within a given subdivision.

Regrettably, this data set does not have a spatial component. Otherwise, we would be able to test whether feeder losses covary with those of other feeders close by, as we can reasonably suspect would be the case. Without a spatial component, the model is only able to capture spatial effects in a limited and indirect way through the feeder's membership within a given subdivision. However, subdivision membership also captures a distinct position in the administrative hierarchy of LESCO, which means that we cannot simply consider subdivision membership as a proxy for spatial location.[15]

The dependent variable is the percentage of losses (electricity delivered but not billed, or $1\text{-kWh}_{billed}/\text{kWh}_{supplied}$). The distribution of losses is reasonably normal, and it is treated as a continuous variable.[16] For explanatory variables, the model includes the total amount of electricity received, relative shares of electricity consumption by domestic, commercial, light, and medium and heavy industrial users, and that consumed by tube wells. The independent variables also include a fixed-effects term of subdivisions into which feeders are administratively and geographically grouped. This model is defined as follows:

$$\text{LOSSES}_{ij} = \beta_1{*}\text{RECV}_{ij} + \beta_2{*}\text{DOME}_{ij} + \beta_3{*}\text{COMM}_{ij} + \beta_4{*}\text{INDUS.LIGHT}_{ij} + \beta_5{*}\text{INDUS.HEAVY}_{ij} + \beta_6{*}\text{AGRI}_{ij} + \beta_7{*}\text{SUBDIV}_j + \varepsilon_{ij}$$

where LOSSES are the losses for feeder *i* in subdivision *j* measured as a percentage of the total consumption. RECV is the total amount of electricity received at the feeder level, DOME is the relative consumption of domestic consumers, COMM is the relative consumption of commercial consumers; INDUS.LIGHT is the relative consumption from light industry, INDUS.HEAVY is the relative consumption from medium and heavy industries, AGRI is the relative consumption for agricultural consumers, and SUBDIV is the fixed effects term of the subdivisions (i.e., a dummy variable for each subdivision). Results from these models are presented in Table 4.1.

The statistical models in Table 4.1 attempt to predict feeder losses for FY2014–2015 based on the total amount of consumption for that feeder and its relative proportions of domestic, commercial, industrial, and agricultural consumption. However, rather than try to predict the actual value of the losses for a feeder, the theoretical framework that this book has developed is concerned with electricity governance at different levels of analysis and how those different levels of analysis influence each other. Model 2 introduces a fixed-effects term in the form of a dummy variable for each subdivision. In Model 1, by contrast, we don't know where in the administrative network the feeder is located.

Table 4.1 **Losses as a Function of Feeder Characteristics**

Term	*OLS Model (1)*			*OLS Model with Fixed Effects (2)*		
	Estimate	p	*95% CI*	***Estimate***	p	*95% CI*
Intercept	0.091	0.001	0.038, 0.143	0.144	0.009	0.035, 0.253
Received	0.000	0.002	0, 0	0.000	0.007	0, 0
Domestic %	0.138	0.000	0.083, 0.193	0.061	0.038	0.003, 0.119
Commercial %	0.056	0.091	−0.009, 0.12	0.060	0.074	−0.006, 0.127
Industrial Light (B1) %	0.189	0.009	0.047, 0.33	0.175	0.060	−0.008, 0.358
Industrial Heavy (B234) %	−0.020	0.468	−0.073, 0.034	−0.090	0.003	−0.15, −0.03
Agriculture %	0.198	0.000	0.136, 0.26	0.117	0.007	0.032, 0.203
R-Squared	0.257		NA, NA	0.466		NA, NA
Adjusted *R*-Squared	0.253		NA, NA	0.366		NA, NA

The model without fixed effects (Model 1) is able to explain about a quarter of the electricity losses in Lahore (adj. *R*-squared of 0.26). The inclusion of the fixed effects term improves the model performance (adj. *R*-squared of 0.36) and explains a greater proportion of the losses. This shows us that the losses covary within administrative units to some degree, although the lack of spatial data or any other predictors at the subdivision level makes it difficult to provide a more robust explanation of this.[17]

We see through these models that the administrative regions of subdivisions are important in explaining electricity losses at this scale. The inclusion of the subdivisions as a fixed-effects term leads to an improvement in the performance of the model by about 10%. These subdivisions act as proxies for the underlying socioeconomic conditions as well as governance mechanisms, although we can reasonably expect consistency across the subdivisions in terms of administrative practices and certainly the institutional rule set. Only 8 subdivisions have significant fixed effect coefficients (7 of which are positive, i.e., higher losses, and 1 negative), which suggests that there is nothing to differentiate the vast majority of subdivisions as the average losses for subdivisions are quite similar to each other. One interpretation would be that the drivers of losses are more systemic rather than specific to a given subdivision or driven by administrative identity (i.e., a few extremely corrupt officers). Adding independent variables at the subdivision level would offer new insights, but these were not available for this data set.

For the fixed-effects model, we see that a 10% increase in the share of domestic consumption for a feeder is associated with a 6% increase in losses for that feeder. Commercial consumption appears to have a similar effect, although in both models the estimate is only significant at a reduced threshold ($p < 0.1$). The finding with respect to commercial units is somewhat surprising, as one might reasonably think that a running business would be an easy target for bill collection given that their operations would probably be vulnerable to a disruption of electricity supply. Light industrial consumption is associated with higher losses, but again the coefficient is only significant at a reduced threshold for Model 2. One could have expected that light industrial and commercial consumers would be associated with lower losses due to their putting a premium on continuous electricity supply, but perhaps what we are seeing here is that small-scale businesses with tight financial margins can find ways to evade billing. Larger industrial units with a B2 or higher tariff category, which are served by higher voltage 11 kV or 33 kV connections, are notable because they are associated with lower losses: a 10% increase in the share of heavy industrial consumption is associated with a 0.9% decrease in losses.

Discussion and Conclusions

Variance in losses is largely explained within a subdivision, not across subdivisions. With few exceptions, the specific identity of a subdivision is not significant for understanding the losses at a feeder level. The generalized result that can be based on this empirical finding is that losses are more influenced by factors operating at the feeder level rather than at the subdivision level, which is the lowest level of the state electricity bureaucracy of the distribution company.

At the feeder level, domestic, commercial, and light industry are all associated with relatively higher losses compared with heavy industry. This data set has a limited set of variables available to determine the social makeup of the population served by a given feeder and largely relies on information regarding the type of consumer served at the feeder level. Spatial locations would enable a far richer set of potentially explanatory factors to be exploited, but these don't currently exist for LESCO feeders. Additionally, there is limited availability of other governance data at a relevant level of granularity (i.e., feeders and subdivisions). Most such data is aggregated to a district level, whereas one of the contributions of this analysis is to show the extent of the variation which exists within a city that is very much at Pakistan's administrative and cultural core.

The analysis shows that state's uneven capacity at the national level is reflected at the city level, too, but with a greater degree of granularity. The state has far less capacity to penetrate residential areas or those with commercial and agricultural activity as compared with industrial areas. At the city level as with the national level, this unevenness suggests an inequality by design rather than the absence of the state, which is all too present in Lahore. The state's orientation toward the powerful and neglect of most others is consistent with the manner in which it is leaving the establishment of human settlements to private parties, a de facto neoliberalization of the state.[18]

These empirical findings suggest that the LESCO bureaucracy has a very limited capacity to penetrate social formations and enforce its rules. Lahore is the capital of the Punjab, the wealthiest province, with a very visible and substantial presence of the state through historic monuments, Governor House, offices of the state bureaucracy (including WAPDA [Water and Power Development Authority] house, a key site in the electricity bureaucracy), and the residences of elite bureaucrats in the Government Officers Residence (GOR). Lahore is a key site for actors and institutions with some of the strongest claims to national legitimacy. Even in this city, which is so central to the administrative apparatus of the state as well as its symbolic representations, there is tremendous variation in state performance and a limited effectiveness of its rules.

An important caveat for the findings in this chapter is that there is little scope to claim that the situation in other cities would be similar. Karachi in particular has a had a long-established reputation for political violence and the partisan negotiation of access to state services (Gazdar & Mallah, 2013; Hasan, 2009). These are not stories that one hears in Lahore, not least because the Pakistan Muslim League-Nawaz (PML-N) dominated all political opponents in the city in the 2013 and 2018 elections. Nonetheless, Karachi also has great variation in losses across the Karachi Electric service area, including feeders within the same administrative unit and located in close proximity, with widely varying loss profiles. A feeder-level study of electricity losses in Karachi, however, also found the underlying characteristics of feeder consumption to be the major driver of losses.[19]

A second caveat for this analysis is that it largely ignores the case of informal settlements, which often find a way to secure electricity supply despite it being officially denied to them and no official bills being issued. This topic is taken up in the next chapter.

The findings suggest various implications for governance reforms. If governance is a function of institutions, the data set reveals the degree to which the exact same institutions produce a range of governance outcomes depending on the service area and the consumer profile. Even within the same subdivision we find a range of losses for feeders. Looking within the same subdivision means that we are not just holding formal institutions constant—which is true across the entirety of the LESCO space—but also the same people who staff a specific office.

The idea that a corrupt administration is somehow the driver behind losses has to be re-examined—the characteristics of the consumer base served by a particular feeder are far more relevant than the subdivision identity. Adding the subdivision identity to the model is helpful, but the majority of subdivisions are indistinguishable by performance. The variation among feeders within a subdivision and the influence of consumption type on losses suggest that it is the consumer profile of a feeder that is the most important influence on losses. The same administrative subunits (i.e., the subdivision) are able to produce a range of governance outcomes measured in terms of feeder-level losses.

This set of analyses has strong implications for the role of institutions in shaping governance. Clearly formal institutions matter—it would be foolish to suggest that they don't—but the evidence examined here raises questions about how and where those formal institutions matter because it exposes the vast range of state performance that exists within the same formal institutional regime. These variations in state performance cannot be accounted for through formal institutions alone.

Instead, governance outcomes such as electricity losses are produced through the interaction of formal institutions and other characteristics of the social fabric of the largely urban setting we examine here. Centeno et al. (2017) define state capacity in terms of a constellation of factors involving informal norms and the relative power of actors as well as formal rule, which is a much more compelling analytical standpoint for the study of uneven governance outcomes within a city than the notion that institutions drive governance. The independent variables in the model capture the relative consumption shares of industry, commerce, agricultural, and domestic consumers. Each of these reflects a different relative positioning vis-à-vis the state. However, analysis at this level of abstraction offers an indication that there is an uneven pattern of governance but offers little insight into how that pattern emerges through the interplay of formal rules and informality among actors of varying power and relative position.

On its own, the quantitative data examined in this chapter helps establish the extent to which there is tremendous unevenness in governance outcomes within even the core areas of the Pakistani state. The variation we saw at the national level, in the interprovincial political economy of power, is also present at the city level. Combining this statistical analysis with the qualitative analyses of the following chapters supports the view that this variation is not random but, rather, indicative of inequality by design, reflecting strategic priorities of the state, and produced through the varying extent to which individuals can position themselves to best impose their own demands for access to power. It is this dynamic that is the focus of the next chapter.

5

Negotiating Formality in Islamabad's *Katchi Abadis*

Securing access to infrastructure is a central theme in the lives of the urban poor in the Global South. This is most evident in the large—and growing—squatter settlements, where the absence of property ownership is typically grounds for denying basic services such as electricity[1] to residents. The politics of squatter settlements are invariably bound up in their fight to secure those services.[2] The World Bank, Asian Development Bank, and other multilateral and bilateral development actors have embraced neoliberal approaches to poverty reduction that work from the principle that poverty reduction can be pursued by bestowing formal and secure property rights for the poor. Consequently, it is common to see programs that propose the relocation of squatters from urban centers and offer secure tenure on compensatory plots as an incentive for relocation.[3] This chapter challenges the widespread assumption that more formal rights are always and necessarily better for the urban poor.

Formality here denotes a primarily written engagement with documented official procedures. Accessing the benefits of formality is a nontrivial and risky task, and people who would champion the advantages of formal rights should also put thought toward how those benefits are realized in practice and what new difficulties may arise due to this different engagement with the state. Despite the fact that the urban upper and middle classes almost always enjoy more secure property rights than the urban poor, it does not necessarily follow that the urban poor can improve their life chances by transitioning to a formal rights-based engagement with the state. Why should we expect a state with a history of excluding and marginalizing the urban poor to graciously accede to their claims?[4]

How state organizations operate and the pattern of claims they recognize can be understood as "a congealing of networks of power":[5] it reflects the outcome of past struggles over who gets what, how, and when. There is no good reason to think that those struggles will cease if the urban poor can formalize

Access to Power. Ijlal Naqvi, Oxford University Press. © Oxford University Press 2022.
DOI: 10.1093/oso/9780197540954.003.0005

their claims to a greater degree, because formality itself represents a boundary where processes of state formation are revealed. Formality, as a status claimed by the urban poor and others when making demands of the state, is contested and negotiated rather than an objective condition. Access to Islamabad's electricity distribution infrastructure is the backdrop against which this chapter examines formal and informal claim making on the state by the urban poor and their richer neighbors.[6]

This ethnography follows several analyses of infrastructure and citizenship that highlight infrastructure's often "splintering" effects in terms of selectively excluding people from service delivery,[7] and the response of the urban poor across South Asia as they renegotiate infrastructural and property arrangements through a range of tactics for making their claims heard.[8] Much of this literature can be understood in terms of its relationship to Partha Chatterjee's (2004) seminal *Politics of the Governed* and its dichotomous framing of political and civil society. Property is "the crucial dimension along which capital overlaps with the modern state" (pp. 74–75) and the primary basis for dividing the haves and have-nots into political and civil society. Civil society is inhabited by middle- and upper-class elites and is the domain of fully equal rights-bearing citizens as conceived in the constitution of India. Political society, in contrast, is a condition of tenuous and ambiguous citizenship inhabited by the poor, including residents of squatter settlements. According to Chatterjee (2004, p. 36), "the lofty political imaginary of popular sovereignty" in civil society is contrasted against "the mundane administrative reality of governmentality" in political society. Chatterjee's clear paradigm is a convenient starting point for navigating this literature.

However, the ample South Asian ethnographic literature on the politics of urban infrastructures is often critical of Chatterjee's dichotomized division of claim making into two terrains of political and civil society, with a particularly rich and textured debate around the innovative and inventive ways that the urban poor secure their rights. Chatterjee's main example of political society is an account of how a squatter settlement in Calcutta mobilized around a collective moral claim to acquire shared electricity meters. Against Chatterjee's collective mobilization for public, moral claims, Solomon Benjamin (2008) describes a radicalized "occupancy urbanism" in which the offices of street-level bureaucracies are unruly spaces for subversive negotiation where the poor resist the imposition of capital. A much less political approach for the urban poor is Asef Bayat's (2013) "quiet encroachment," which is a silent and persistent redistribution of public goods in favor of ordinary people over the propertied. Based on an ethnography of water supply in Mumbai, Nikhil Anand (2017) describes a "hydraulic citizenship" varying in proportion to the pressure that groups can exert on a dual sociotechnical system of administrators and water infrastructure.

Malini Ranganathan (2014) presents a more subtle form of claim making with her account of how Bangalore's lower middle classes voluntarily pay for expensive but unnecessary water infrastructure in an insurgent attempt to claim greater symbolic recognition and more secure land tenure from the state. Accessing infrastructures for service delivery is an imperative for urban life, and the literature presents a wide range of strategies employed by the urban poor.

By contrast, civil society is not conveyed through empirical examples but, rather, remains more of a conceptual reference. Both in the literature and in the argument to be made in this chapter, the realm of formal rights is weakly realized at best in people's lived experience and their collective imagination. Ananya Roy (2015, p. 344) takes up this point in arguing that "paralegality is a generalized condition," and thus the distinction between formal and informal that lies at the heart of the civil and political society dichotomy must be questioned. Governance scholars have found that states of the Global South often adopt formal Weberian state structures on paper while their informal and paralegal practices continue with little change.[9] Studies of the everyday state in India and elsewhere have provided rich evidence from across the Global South on the informalities of the supposedly formal state.[10] There is very little support for the idea that formal rights are an easily accessed feature of governance in the South Asia.

Interactions with the infrastructure of electrical power present a window on urban governance that allows for the interpretation of large-scale change and seemingly disparate social developments (Angelo & Hentschel, 2015). The urban bourgeoisie's use of the same electrical power infrastructure is a necessary backdrop to understanding the experience of the urban poor. The urban poor in squatter settlements and those transitioning to formal status have to be understood as occupying the same urban world as the rich, whose own systematic informalities are so often ignored despite informality being "a routine tactic of the powerful" (Tonkiss, 2013, pp. 96–99). The informalities of the rich mirror the informalities of the poor in bringing social ties and power relations to bear on access to services (Tonkiss, 2013, pp. 105–107). The prevalence of informality among the rich brings into question the validity of any conceived improvements to the life of the poor that might be achieved by transitioning to claim making on the basis of formal rights.

Ursula Rao's careful ethnography of squatters who are resettled to an area where they have more secure formal rights attends to an important and rarely explored theme within the larger question of formality versus informality: that of the individual who successfully formalizes their previously informal existence. Rao's squatters accept a deal to move from their squatter settlement to the outskirts of Delhi, where they are given secure land title in a new housing development. Tragically, many of them fall victim to a scam and have their houses demolished; the former squatters had managed paralegality for decades but were unhoused after resettlement with a more formal set of tenure rights. Rao (2010, p. 413) notes that "Buying, selling, possessing or defending a plot is a condition of negotiation," and that the vulnerability of the resettled population was a function of their continued poverty.

The "lofty political imaginary" of civil society proposed by Chatterjee (2004, p. 36) evokes the modern social imaginaries of Charles Taylor (Taylor, 2002). Taylor argues that the production of the collective imaginary is shared broadly, unlike theory and ideology, which lie in the hands of a select few. The imaginary is "not a set of ideas; rather it is what enables, through making sense of, the practices of society" (Taylor, 2002, p. 91). The proposition that middle-class rights holders enjoy a set of practices of formal claim making that the poor are denied is at the heart of Chatterjee's dichotomization, but there is also a distinct affective component: infrastructure is not only a means of making service delivery possible, but also a material reference around which an understanding of one's own relationship to the larger society is formed.[11] In looking at the experiences of formal rights holders in engaging the Pakistani state, I seek out the imaginary that informs how Pakistanis make sense of the practices of claim making on the electrical power infrastructure.

This chapter first introduces the field site of my ethnography in Islamabad, Pakistan. It then proceeds to describe how residents of a squatter colony have historically obtained their electricity supply, as well as their orientation toward and attempts to obtain more formal rights. For comparison, the chapter then considers the experience of Islamabad residents who already have the formal rights sought by the squatter colony residents. The final two empirical sections look at the perspectives and experiences of formal rights holders, and then the experience of those few squatter colony residents who have attempted to transition to making claims based on formal rights. The chapter concludes with a discussion of claim making across the different styles and contexts and challenges the assumption that the poor can necessarily benefit from a transition to making claims based on formal rights.

Fieldwork

The research for this chapter was part of an ongoing study consisting of about 18 months of active fieldwork across four years of residence in Islamabad, from 2008 to 2011. Islamabad is a planned city, the federal capital, and markedly less violent than the major metropolis of Karachi.[12] The state, in various forms, is much more present than is the case in other Pakistani cities. State services in general are above average, electricity supply is more regular, and residents have more personal connections to the state. By studying Islamabad, one sees Pakistani state institutions at their highest level of effectiveness. If claim making based on formal rights is going to work anywhere in Pakistan, it will be in Islamabad.

The primary site for my ethnography was at multiple subdivision offices of the Islamabad Electric Supply Company (IESCO), where I followed the employees through all aspects of their work and observed their interactions with citizens who came to the office. The subdivision is the lowest level of the IESCO organizational hierarchy and fulfills most of the public-facing requirements concerning electricity supply, including new connections, billing, maintenance, and disconnections. In addition to working with the IESCO employees, I interviewed and spent time among the residents of Islamabad in their capacity as electricity consumers, including in the *katchi abadis* such as 44 Quarter in Islamabad.[13]

Islamabad has 34 *katchi abadis*, 11 of which are notified for regularization per the Punjab Katchi Abadi Act 1992.[14] Regularization leads to a formal lease of the land and access to all state services for the occupants of the *katchi abadi*, but it is not without some drawbacks. For the Capital Development Authority (CDA, the public agency that provides municipal services in Islamabad) to regularize the 44 Quarter *katchi abadi*, where I did most of the fieldwork presented in this chapter, regularization would involve planning the housing of the *katchi abadi* so that it would conform to building standards and thus contain fewer housing plots. Which households would not be accommodated and where the surplus households would be relocated are points of contention that have stalled the regularization process, since the proposed relocation site is much further from Islamabad. However, so long as 44 Quarter is not regularized, the residents are denied a document called a No Objection Certificate (NOC), which is issued by the CDA to certify that the applicant for the electricity connection is the legal owner of the land. Without an NOC, the residents of 44 Quarter cannot get legal electricity connections.

Mobilizing Collective Claims

One of my key informants in 44 Quarter is Liaqat, who, like almost all the residents of 44 Quarter, is Christian.[15] Liaqat is approximately 35–40 years old, quite short, and slightly built. The streets of 44 Quarter are uneven, sloping, and made of packed dirt. A tiny, uncovered drain a few inches wide runs in front of the houses on Liaqat's street. I can touch both sides of the alley at the same time. Near Liaqat's front door is an electricity pylon on which I've seen a barefoot boy of about five climbing and playing. Children of very young ages are everywhere, usually playing unattended. I am often passed by bicycles and motorcycles on this street when I visit. Men and women are often talking in the street, frequently congregating around doorways, which seem to be open more often than not. Liaqat's home in 44 Quarter is a three-story brick and cement building that has not seen any new paint in some time. Liaqat and his wife and children live on the ground floor of their house, and other members of his extended family live on the upper two stories. The two rooms on the ground floor are a living room and a bedroom. The floor is bare cement. The ceiling is perhaps seven feet high and gives me a distinctly claustrophobic feeling when I stand. There is a small fridge in the bedroom—that is the only visible appliance. Located in the middle of an affluent residential area, 44 Quarter is well situated for access to employment and municipal services. The same electricity lines that serve the well-off neighborhoods run through 44 Quarter. For most of its history, 44 Quarter was served by undocumented connections, known in Urdu as *kunda*.[16]

According to Liaqat, the type of theft occurring in Islamabad's *katchi abadis* occurs with the participation of the distribution company employees. Liaqat tells me that "The same money, instead of going to IESCO's treasury, went to police and IESCO staff."[17] Liaqat says that the distribution company employees were paid off to leave illegal connections alone, as were the police. Although I found no distribution company employees admitting to their participation in this specific case, many of them accepted such arrangements as being relatively common.

Some 11 years prior to the time of my study—probably in 1998—44 Quarter's illegal connections were forcibly taken down in an army-backed intervention. The army's role in power sector management came about at the invitation of the elected Prime Minister Nawaz Sharif. In an admission of his government's incompetence at public administration, which foreshadowed his own government's removal in a coup the following year, Nawaz Sharif asked the Pakistani army to take over the management of electricity distribution companies in order to reduce theft. IESCO and the other distribution companies had serving army personnel assigned to them, including at senior management levels. The chief executives of the distribution companies were replaced by brigadiers on deputation from their usual military assignments.

The residents of 44 Quarter responded to the disconnection of their electricity supply by forming a committee to approach the brigadier in charge of IESCO. The gist of the argument they put to the brigadier was that if they were not allowed *kunda* connections, they should be allowed legal connections. My informants at 44 Quarter feel no qualms about the *kunda* connections. Liaqat tells me that 'It's our right [to electricity]. If you won't give it to us, then we'll take it like this' ("Hamara right banta hai. Aap nahiN daiN gey tau hum iss tarah laiN gey").[18] Another informant states that it is 'inevitable, in this heat,'[19] that people will get electricity connections however they can. The 44 Quarter residents see electricity as something fundamental for decent living to which they, too, should have access, and their appeal to the brigadier was on largely humane rather than legalistic grounds.

The meeting of the 44 Quarter residents' committee with the IESCO brigadier went well. The compromise reached by the parties was that 44 Quarter would be served by a few documented meters, but that all the wiring and management of the system beyond the meters would be the responsibility of the residents.[20] This decision served IESCO by ensuring that 44 Quarter residents would pay for their electricity consumption and met the needs of 44 Quarter residents by ensuring their electricity supply.

These arrangements, however, are distinctly an exception to the rules, which define a consumer as "a person or his successor-in-interest who purchases or receives electrical power for consumption and not for delivery or re-sale to others, including a person who owns or occupies a premise where electrical power is supplied" (Islamabad Electric Supply Company, 2010, p. 4). The provision of electricity for delivery and resale to others is the job of a distribution company. The brigadier's decision contravenes these rules, but IESCO's consumer services manual limits service provision to applicants who can provide "ownership proof of the premises" (Islamabad Electric Supply Company, 2010, p. 8), and it thus cannot be provided to individual *katchi abadi* residents so long as the regularization process is incomplete. In the absence of NOCs and legal individual connections, the committee representing residents of 44 Quarter accepted the compromise of communal metering. The residents of 44 Quarter would be allowed a single communal connection at commercial rates (higher than domestic rates).

The committee managed the process and the money for connecting the several hundred households of 44 Quarter to the communal meter. Shoaib was a member of that committee (he mentions that the brigadier was a 'very nice person')[21] and tells me that his inclusion was on the grounds that he is considered educated ("*paRhay-likhay*"). Shoaib lives in 44 Quarter and is employed by the residents' committee to manage the billing and maintenance of the electrical system. He says,

> The committee met for 2–3 days [prior to the negotiation with IESCO]. They formed a constitution for the committee (I asked to see this later in our conversation, he smiled and said that they made it once upon a time and that no one knew anything about it now).[22]

The committee members are the respected elders ("*bazurg*") of the community. Shoaib has in fact taken on many of the functions of the distribution company. He manages billing, collects the money, gives receipts, keeps records, and also handles the maintenance of 44 Quarter's electricity system. Shoaib does many of the same tasks a subivision officer would. He also handles situations where there is difficulty in paying bills. 44 Quarter prints its own bills with instructions on the back for making payments. Paying in installments is not unusual, and sometimes the committee can reduce the bill somewhat. Strictly commercial arrangements are also not observed for churches and those individuals whom the committee deems needy and worthy of help. Instead, the moral underpinnings of the collective organization for service delivery are reflected in the departure from commercial logics. Each household is charged a fixed amount based on an assessment of the household's consumption:

> I ask how they determine the charges for each household. Shoaib says he knows every house on every street. They are 'like a family.' He knows everyone's name, and his paternal grandfather's (dada) name. We have no formality in going to each other's houses. Paying for extra facilities (fridge, a motor for pumping up water) costs up to extra 300 per month.[23]

Shoaib is confident that he knows the ins and outs of every household. His deep local knowledge is essential to keeping the communal system going.

The residents of 44 Quarter have mobilized on the basis of collective solidarity and make their claim for service delivery on a moral basis. They do not exercise purely commercial reasoning in determining how much each household must pay. Instead, assessments are based on Shoaib's intimate knowledge of each household. Shoaib attributes his position to his good character and reputation.

Imagining Rights

Sharing of a common meter is also present in 75 Quarter and 50 Quarter (two other *katchi abadis* in Islamabad where I interviewed residents), but their committees have been less scrupulous than Shoaib. Collection for the municipal electricity bill is handled by a leadership committee comprised of *katchi abadi* residents. Neither in 75 Quarter nor in 50 Quarter was anyone able to explain how the current leaders obtained their position or describe what was entailed in being a "leader." Their inability to explain the nature of a leadership position suggests a lack of a formalized process for selecting and changing leaders. Rates in 75 Quarter are higher than in 50 Quarter, but 50 Quarter has accumulated arrears worth approximately two months of billing.[24] One resident of 75 Quarter suggested that members of the *katchi abadi* leadership committee were embezzling some of the money. Another informant chided me for being so naive as to think that the 44 Quarter leaders were not also embezzling the committee funds.

Even in 44 Quarter, the communal system has not always worked out well. The communal meter must be put in someone's name, which creates the opportunity for that person to take advantage of their position. Liaqat told me the following story based on 44 Quarter's earlier experience with communal metering, which predated the current solution:

> A committee of about 20 people got together to choose the person whose name the meter would be put in. 'That man had not even a cycle to his name. He was a government employee (*mullazim*), went to work wearing slippers. Now he has cars. He's become a big-shot (*Chaudhry bun gaya hai*).'
>
> 'This is Pakistan. (*Yeh Pakistan hai*). Who has money is king (*badshah*).' 44 Quarter residents brought legal suits against him, but 'we'd talk and he'd use his money to get away free.'[25]

Liaqat sees how the communal system that now serves them well was once an opportunity for a member of their own community to exploit the residents of 44 Quarter. In his eyes, the legal system offered them no recourse to justice against someone with substantial resources.

In their quest to formalize their land tenure rights and secure service delivery, the residents of 44 Quarter have engaged with various political actors in a very pragmatic manner. Liaqat tells me that 'We're not with any political party. We work with whoever is in power.' Through their different contacts—activists, academics, politicians, and also foreign embassies—the *katchi abadi* dwellers bring to bear whatever pressure they can on the CDA to complete the regularization to which they are already committed. Liaqat proudly tells me of how the 44 Quarter residents secured a majority of votes for the candidate they backed at their local polling station. The delivery of votes is an exchange for political representation in a purely transactional sense, as Chatterjee describes for political society, with no regard to party platforms.

The residents of the *katchi abadis* used the language of rights more than anyone else I spoke with in Pakistan. In the blunt terms of Liaqat, 'With a meter you get rights':

> We've spent hundreds of thousands of rupees (*lakhs*) on our houses, but there's no benefit. When you have rights, you benefit if you invest in your house. With a proper road you could get a car in. That would be very valuable.
>
> After plotting only 300 houses would be possible. Some people would be moved away. The Capital Development Authority initially offered

> [the outskirts of Islamabad], but that is too far away. Each household has 3–4 earners to sustain it. Their jobs are in Islamabad, the commutes would cost too much. The Capital Development Authority board has the plan for approval. It's almost done. ("*Taqreeban tai ho gaya hai.*")
>
> [Liaqat thinks it will go through in a week.]
>
> After plotting [regularization], everyone will get No-ObjectionCertificates. Each plot will have value. No problems with authorities in getting gas and electricity connections on our own.[26]

Liaqat is acutely conscious of the material benefits that can accrue from formal land titles. He hopes that the shady dealings with state officials will cease. His approach is entirely consistent with neoliberal arguments for the importance of property rights, which draw on Hernando de Soto (2000). Far from challenging the status quo structures of power and domination, it is a middle-class aspiration. In some instances, *katchi abadi*'s leaders exploit institutional failures to extract rents of their own, adding one more obstacle to service delivery for the squatters. Perhaps unsurprisingly, the world of formal rights exemplified by a personal electricity connection takes on the appearance of an escape from these webs of exploitation and patronage. However, a more careful look at the experiences of those with established formal claims on electricity services exposes just how unreal the social imaginary of citizenship with recognized rights is.

"This Is Pakistan"

Focusing on the *katchi abadi* residents alone gives an incomplete picture of claim making on the electricity infrastructure of Islamabad. Examples taken from those who have more substantiated formal claims for service as well as more wealth, connections, and education reveal the tenuousness of formal claims and the pervasiveness of informality.

Industrial consumers are some of the most prized consumers for a distribution company as they are very easy to monitor and service. Zeeshan's family owns an industrial facility in one of Islamabad's industrial sectors, which he and his brother run. Zeeshan has a leadership position in a local business association, has a master's in business administration from the United States, and drives a very expensive SUV. His industrial facility is served by a legal connection, but even in this situation his experience is that the formality of the relationship is not relevant:

> To have a relationship ("*ta'aluqaat*") with a government officer here means that you are giving them money. Nothing else ("*bus*").

> At every level they take money. To get a new connection you have to give money. Else you'll wait 10 years. Since Pakistan was made, you have to pay to get work done. Everything's foundation ("*bunyaad*") is money. They won't do for you an unpermitted ("*naajaiz*") thing, but you have to pay for your rights.[27]

Zeeshan's view is that one's rights may or may not exist on paper, but it is money that determines whether you can enjoy those rights. As an industrialist, Zeeshan's main concern (along with cost) is the predictability of the electricity supply so that he can schedule his shifts, and it is on this topic that he meets regularly with the IESCO staff. He needs their cooperation for the success of his business, and in those relationships with IESCO officers he has to pay for the predictability of his supply.

My personal experience as an Islamabad resident also speaks to the nature of paralegality and the urban bourgeoisie. When the house I lived in developed some electrical problems, I called the local subdivision office to register my complaint. I lived in a suburban neighborhood where I rented the top half of a two-story house. Many of the residents of this neighborhood were college graduates, professionals with good salaries, and relatively well-off. After six attempts over three days, I succeeded in having an IESCO lineman come to my house to look at the electrical problems. He found a loose connection in my distribution box[28] and tightened it, but the problem reoccurred two days later. I then had the problem fixed by Bilal, an independent electrician whom I had hired a few times in the past. Bilal and I had the following exchange:

Bilal: Everything after the meter is done by the electrician, everything before is IESCO's responsibility. We aren't allowed to touch it. If I had dropped my pliers and it had touched two wires then the transformer back there could have blown up.

IN: I asked if he could do it and he said that it was my responsibility to arrange for it, but that he could do the work for me if I wanted.

Bilal: He wanted to get some money from you. This is Pakistan. This is how things work here. Don't give him any money for this, or else he'll loosen it every time he goes by so that you'll call him and he can get a little more money for it.[29]

The source of the fault is located in the distribution box. As Bilal stated, that can only be attended to by the IESCO staff because any errors on Bilal's part could have damaged equipment that served my neighbors as well as me. The lineman misinformed me in an effort to get some money from me. Bilal feared (rightly) that my naivete would cost me money. Even though my relationship with IESCO is based on the formal rights of a contract for electricity supply, in practice those formal rules form the basis for transactions of favors, money, and power relations. To secure the electricity supply I needed, I had to employ a private contractor to do the work of the electricity company. The work entailed some risks and was completely against IESCO rules, but the alternative was to pay the IESCO lineman to do the same task in his personal capacity even though it was actually in his official job description.

Although the *katchi abadi* residents are pushing for regularization so that they can obtain legal metered connections on an individual basis, having a meter is by no means a complete solution to electricity woes, as it opens up a new relationship with the distribution company based on the legal obligation to pay. The primary school next to the *katchi abadi* upgraded its electrical system and had a new meter installed, but the first bill was for an exorbitant amount because the new meter didn't have a zero reading. The headmistress refused to bow to pressure from IESCO officers, who eventually dropped the matter without explanation. Separately, IESCO officers describe government facilities such as schools, streetlights, and water pumps as 'parking lots' for spurious charges through which they seek to offset losses incurred elsewhere—including theft in which they may be complicit.

The school was able to see off the attempt at extortion from the distribution company employees, but without a resolution to the case there is every chance that a future headmistress will have to respond to the same outstanding bill. Even for a government school—well established in the formal system—formal rights and an individual electricity meter are opportunities for predation rather than a solution.

The situation with the school and the industrial facility, and my own encounters with the electricity utility, all show the pervasiveness of informality even in the public sector, for wealthy businesspeople, and for a relatively well-off resident of a good neighborhood.

The Challenging Transition to Formality

Unfortunately, many of the 44 Quarter residents who have succeeded in getting a toehold in the world of formal rights via an electricity meter in their name have come to regret it. Although IESCO's compromise with the residents' committee to provide electricity to 44 Quarter through communal metering is a functional solution (every household in 44 Quarter has electricity), it is viewed as second best by the 44 Quarter residents. The communal arrangements notwithstanding, the 44 Quarter residents have continuously pushed to try to regularize their *katchi abadi* and secure the right to have individual meters for electricity supply. A local NGO has been at the forefront of these efforts, chiefly in engaging with politicians and activists in putting pressure on the CDA to complete the process in a timely manner. 44 Quarter has been surveyed twice by the CDA. Households identified in the survey are noted by the CDA as residences with rights to municipal services. Liaqat tells me that for meters approved after the second survey, the demand notices (the distribution company's equipment orders for the connection of new premises) were issued five years later, and that it was 18 more months until the meters were finally installed. The money for these demand notices was given by a member of the National Assembly out of their official budget for development projects. Liaqat's explanation for the delay is that the distribution company employees resisted because it would reduce their monthly earnings from the communal meters. Nonetheless, Liaqat and the 44 Quarter residents' fight for individual meters had partly been won by the time of our meetings.

When some individual meters were installed in 2009, 44 Quarter residents were told by an IESCO officer that they would regret it and that they would want the old shared meters back. That prediction was borne out in 44 Quarter in many cases. An individual meter can be a mixed blessing, as it requires a greater degree of direct dealing with the distribution company. The buffer from a communal meter is gone, and so are the protections that come with it.

The experience of having an individual meter for a house is described to me by Adam, a young man of about 21 who is working in a community-based organization in 44 Quarter. Adam's family had received an unreasonably large bill exceeding 10,000 rupees:

IN: What happened in the [IESCO] office?

Adam: The first man I went to see sent me to another one. The next one sent me to another one. He told me that there was no meter assigned to our house. I said then how are we getting a bill? He told us that they'll check it out. That they'll come and see if the meter is working properly. They said there's a leak in our house, that the electricity is being wasted.

Liaqat: How can you have a leak with electricity? This isn't a gas pipe.

Adam: They are taking the money from us in installments. And the next bill came to 7000. So we switched back to the shared meter, which is 1200 per month. And now our bill from the meter—which we aren't using—is 75 rupees.

Adam: We aren't the only ones. Our neighbors have complained about high bills too.

IN: There must be a form you have to fill in to complain about your meter.

Adam: I don't know what form it is. They didn't give me any form.

'We aren't educated enough' ("*hum itnay paRhay-likhay nahiN haiN*") that we can deal with IESCO.[30]

Adam and his family were poorly equipped to handle the challenge of dealing with the state on its terms. Although Adam describes himself as insufficiently educated to deal with IESCO, he tells me that he passed his Matriculation (10th grade) and, in conversation with me, is reasonably confident and able to express himself. Nonetheless, the opacity of the process at the distribution company office and the behavior of the distribution company staff are enough to deter him. Adam tells me that his family is resigned to paying this bill that they cannot afford and did not incur. Their retreat to the communal system is a retreat to a system where they will be protected from state officials' efforts at predation by Shoaib and the other committee members.

A related experience to the abandonment of an individual electricity meter comes from some households from Islamabad *katchi abadis* who were relocated as a result of the regularization process. These families were given small plots of land in the residential sectors of Islamabad, including the relatively well-off area of F-10. These families took possession of the land, but most of them sold their properties and returned to *katchi abadis* in Islamabad (Rasool, 2010, p. 20).

The choice to sell the land to which they had formal title in order to return to *katchi abadis* throws a different perspective on the value of formal rights and also the state's responsibility to continue to provide such regularization programs to *katchi abadi* residents. Matthew Hull (2012) reports a related set of circumstances, with villagers on the outskirts of Islamabad being compensated when they are relocated as a result of the city expanding, only for them to anticipate city planners by moving to the next area where expansion will take place in order to seek out further compensation. The decision of the relocated *katchi abadi* residents to return to informality suggests that the program for their relocation was poorly conceived. On the other hand, these families were best placed to judge how to manage their resources, and their actions suggest that living with a cash windfall and returning to informality can be preferable to having formal rights. Nonetheless, in all the fieldwork and other interactions I had concerning electricity in Pakistan, the *katchi abadi* residents were the only people to invoke regularly a language of rights.

What are rights worth in this context? Formal rights seem to be worth very little. Claim making on the state through formal channels is an exercise in frustration. Power relations (sometimes reduced to wealth) dominate proceedings, making it difficult to claim an entitlement regardless of the black letter law underlying the claim. The natural right to basic necessities is more compelling in achieving a compromise solution to the impasse between the electrical utility and the squatters who are prevented from formal access to a service they are ready and willing to pay for.

Discussion and Conclusion

The phrase 'this is Pakistan' is inevitably followed by a view of the conditions of life in Pakistan, both in the *katchi abadi* and elsewhere, of a Hobbesian state of nature where law offers little respite from a dog-eat-dog world. The social imaginary invoked is one in which dangers abound and must be navigated carefully. Formal rights are relevant in this collectively imagined Pakistan, but formal rights do not protect people, nor are they on their own sufficient to secure access to crucial state services. Paul Brass' account of villages in Uttar Pradesh somewhat shockingly (given that Islamabad is Pakistan's capital city, compared with relatively less developed rural villages) holds true in Islamabad: formal law is weak in the face of power relations, and there exists "a set of formal rules and practices obeyed by a few, a set of informal rules and practices followed by most, and a lack of legitimacy attached to both" (Brass, 1997, pp. 273–279). The fact that claim making based on formal rights is so ineffective in Islamabad implies that the challenges faced by 44 Quarter residents will only be worse in squatter colonies elsewhere, and it suggests that the writ of the state is still remarkably weak even where it is strongest.

Liaqat, who talked about securing rights through a meter, also says, 'This is Pakistan (*Yeh Pakistan hai*). Who has money is king (*badshah*),' in the context of legal suits brought by 44 Quarter residents against an individual accused of embezzling the fees for a shared electricity meter. Liaqat described the lawsuits by saying, 'we'd talk and he'd use his money to get away free.' In the collective imaginary of Pakistani citizenship articulated around access to electricity, outcomes in the formal justice sector can be bought and sold.

At the other end of the social ladder from the *katchi abadi* residents, Zeeshan—the industrialist—states that you have to 'pay for your rights,' and that it has ever been thus since Pakistan's founding. Zeeshan has all the advantages of wealth and power that one can imagine, and he uses them to secure his rights in terms of the access to electricity he needs to run his business. At my rented accommodation somewhere between these two points, the electrician repairing the electricity supply to my house invokes the phrase 'this is Pakistan' as a cautionary injunction against trusting the honesty of street-level bureaucrats. The shared imaginary invoked by the phrase 'this is Pakistan' is a harsh and hostile setting in which the state is just one more battleground. The people who invoke this phrase span all social settings and speak from personal experience. The idea of formal rights as having much purchase is unsentimentally dismissed. Street-level bureaucrats will take advantage of naivete, rights must be secured through payments, and the courts serve those who can buy justice. The shared web of meaning around the phrase 'this is Pakistan' constitutes an unsentimental and cruel imaginary.

In many respects, Chatterjee's (2004) description of political society closely corresponds to the experience of 44 Quarter residents. The 44 Quarter residents obtain a communal meter after meeting with the electrical utility and arguing that they are neither being allowed to steal electricity nor to pay for it. They describe access to electricity as a right, but the use of the word "right" (in English) is semantically vague and more moral than legal. The establishment of the squatter settlement as a moral community is reflected in how Liaqat describes his knowledge of the residents and his description of them being 'like a family.' The sentiment that underlies this claim is that the 44 Quarter residents are human, too, and to deny them electricity is unjust. The 44 Quarter leadership is aware of their legal rights and actively pursues the regularization of their land tenure. They use their vote instrumentally and align themselves with such politicians as will support them. More recently, the Awami Worker's Party won three seats in the 2015 local government elections in Islamabad by fielding candidates from *katchi abadis*. While this young movement is still a work in progress, it could be on its way toward generating a "counter-politics that destabilizes the dominant regime of citizenship, renders it vulnerable, and defamiliarizes the coherence with which it usually presents itself to us" (James Holston, 2008, p. 15).

The 44 Quarter residents who secure a personal meter merit further consideration because they have moved from the moral claim of the community in political society toward the individualized claims of civil society. Chatterjee does not discuss individual or communal movement from one terrain to another, but in 44 Quarter the transition to civil society is not straightforward for some. Engaging with the state with a contract on the basis of individual rights is also a contested and negotiated terrain, and very much subject to predation. That the electricity bill is the vehicle for this particular form of predation underscores how it is targeted at formal rights holders. To contest this predation requires a facility with bureaucracy (or power and resources) that Adam and his family can't muster. Their response, to retreat to the communal metering engagement, is driven by the assessment that they are better equipped to deal with the vagaries of a familiar informal system than with the unfamiliar realm of formal rights.

As shown in the example of the school and Adam's family, formal rights and an individual electricity meter bring with them new opportunities for predation. This category of claim making exposes distinct vulnerabilities because it is individually exercised. The poor are unlikely to manage these vulnerabilities successfully because they may be socially disadvantaged due to their minority status, lower levels of schooling, or lower incomes. The implication is that effective claim making for the poor is more likely to be informal—such as the moral claims of political society or even through quiet encroachment. Even wealthier individuals, state actors, and businesses have reason to be wary of the predations of the state and put little stock in the protections of law. Local governance regimes are themselves highly resistant to rule-based governance imposed on them from above and also resist when it is imposed on them from below.

Both among the residents of 44 Quarter and the international development agenda following de Soto, formal rights are assumed to be preferable to informal claim making. The bourgeois urban residents have a greater degree of formal rights, and there is a palpable inequality in life chances that corresponds to the apparent availability of formal rather than informal modes of claim making. But, as Zeeshan explains, when he does use his wealth to influence the electricity bureaucracy, it is to ensure delivery on his formal claims rather than to have the street-level bureaucrats exceed their job scope. Nonetheless, it is certainly the target of squatters to achieve formal status. State agencies, aided by development actors, both deny services to squatters on the basis that they do not own property and have formal documentation, and undertake reforms—at least on paper (Lant Pritchett et al., 2013)—to eliminate informality in their own ranks and in their engagement with the society around them. Yet as the examples in this chapter show, formal rights come with their own challenges that must be contested and negotiated. As Rao (Rao, 2010, p. 413) observes, "Buying, selling, possessing or defending a plot is a condition of negotiation." The predation is of different varieties, but individuals and organizations in civil society are very much subject to it. After all, 'this is Pakistan,' where predation is a universal condition. In political society, much of the work of resisting predation is managed through collective mobilization. Among the wealthy and middle classes, the work of managing predation is a more individual function. In both cases, these are contested and negotiated processes. Wealth, personal networks, and education are key factors for dealing with the state for everyone—regardless of the type of claim that they make. The transition to formal claim making may create new vulnerabilities for the poor and take away their most successful strategy for dealing with the state.

The residents of the *katchi abadis* can be savvy navigators of the tension between formal rules and their capacity to claim service delivery effectively. In the examples above taken from Hull (2012) and Rasool (2010), formality has an instrumental utility unrelated to the actual occupation of the land in question. Securing individual rights isn't necessarily the most advantageous position because it involves a transition from negotiating with bureaucratic agents as a group to negotiating as individuals. Trying to take advantage of those individual rights can be a losing proposition, as squatters aren't always well placed to follow de Soto's path to prosperity through leveraging property values (de Soto, 2000; for a counterargument to de Soto, see Gravois, 2005). The land title itself is just one component of the struggle for voice and recognition by the landless poor (Hetherington, 2011).

The transition from being a squatter to holding and enjoying the benefits of formal rights is poorly understood and is a worthy topic for further research on service delivery to the urban poor in the Global South. We need to understand the conditions under which the poor struggle to benefit from formal rights, and whether these challenges can be mitigated by some systematized form of collective bargaining as is prevalent in the more informal arrangements common to squatter settlements. Engagement with the everyday state has some similarity for rich and poor alike in terms of process, though the impact of predation on the poor is, of course, much greater, and it is much harder for them to negotiate those same processes. The desire for formal rights animates much of the engagement with the state in *katchi abadis* but can be unrewarding for them when it is achieved. Formal rights do not end the practices of rent-seeking and personalistic relations, which make up the encounter with the state. Where subordinate groups in *katchi abadis* have succeeded in achieving some level of service delivery, they have done so by internalizing many of the functions of the distribution company and organizing to deal collectively with public officials and elected representatives.

There is little evidence here in support of an insurgent citizenship.[31] Instead, the neoliberal logics of property rights have been internalized by *katchi abadi* residents in their focus on formal rights. Misrule was more likely to be perpetuated than repurposed. Much as described by Chris Fuller and John Harriss in their introduction to the influential edited volume on the everyday state in India, ordinary people are "using the 'system' the best they can" rather than resisting it (Fuller & Harriss, 2000, p. 25). The ideal-typical form of political society and its central dynamics were largely borne out in the examples of the urban poor of the Global South explored in this chapter. However, civil society remains elusive in this study, and the holders of formal rights also described contestation and negotiation in securing the benefits of those rights while avoiding the predations of the state and others. The experience of those holding formal rights and the challenges faced by the squatters who have attempted to transition to individual meters suggests a poorly understood condition in which formal rights must be continuously secured through struggle. In this vision of the Global South, a regime of formal rights is more illusionary than imagined. Even for those who have formal rights, there is no shared imaginary of how these might effectively translate to service delivery.

PART III

THE INDIVIDUAL LEVEL OF ANALYSIS

The city level of analysis exposes the ways in which formality is neither the determining element of governance processes nor a panacea for addressing the needs of the socially excluded. The individual level of analysis, explored in Chapters 6 and 7, takes these same themes further and relates them to ethnographic observations from the individual citizen's encounter with street-level bureaucrats in the offices of the electrical utility. In considering the encounter between formality and informality as a contest, formal rules are just one strand of the larger picture, and the capacity to enact the latent potential of these formal institutions is wrapped in informality.

For most citizens of Pakistan, the encounter with the state is a personal one, often taking the form of a visit to the local utility office in order to address the everyday business of securing access to electrical power. Although the parameters that shape one's capacity to move the state are most visible in the breach (Wedeen, 2003)—that is, at times of overt violence or corruption—it is far more common for these considerations not to be voiced as the relevant accommodations to power and position are made. While the visible incidents are instructive, one must also note the delicate diplomacy of the dance around what usually remains unsaid. Indeed, the processes of managing governance transactions are more art than science, and a constant compromise through which the shape of governance emerges.

As Chapter 6 argues, governance can be understood as an emergent compromise. It is emergent in the sense that it is a property of the system rather than of individual actors, and that it is co-produced through path-dependent processes in which actors coevolve with their environment. Governance is a compromise in the sense that it is a negotiated outcome, determined neither by any one party—witness the ability of the disadvantaged to maneuver in the margins of the state and the unevenness of state capacity across the city—nor by the mere existence of a formal rule set. Street-level bureaucrats who hold the key to one dimension of the city are obliged to adapt to social and political reality. In this manner they reproduce existing power asymmetries, and the inequality by design that results from these many small compromises reflects the larger patterns of power and inequality in the society. As with the case of the Islamabad squatter settlement, however, the bureaucratic exercise of discretion in navigating the sometimes-conflicting demands of formality and informality produces workable outcomes catering to human needs even as they do not challenge larger power structures or threaten the status quo.

Chapter 7 brings the book's exploration of governance in Pakistan through the lens of the infrastructural state down to the personal encounter with street-level bureaucrats of the public utilities. In this field, governance outcomes are shaped by money, personal connections, and also the threat of violence. It is through all these informal modalities that the wealthy and the powerful access their formal rights.

6

Governance as an Emergent Compromise

Introduction

Governance is always an emergent compromise produced by "the complex web of unfolding transactions and processes" in which bureaucrats must operate (Silbey, 2011, p. 3). Compromises between the formalizing imperatives of modernization and the flexibility of bureaucratic agents to adapt to social and organizational constraints are essential to shaping the patterns of coordination and regulation that make up governance in the Pakistani electrical power sector. Discretion, and the opportunity for idiosyncratic outcomes it entails, is unavoidable and can be exercised with a sense of social responsibility or for narrowly construed personal gain. This chapter argues that the capacity of individual bureaucratic agents to choose among multiple courses of action—and go beyond their formal bounds—can serve the organizational mandate of public good provision better than the pursuit of modernization in terms of increasing formality. However, the task of preventing this autonomy and discretion from leading to the abuse of public office for private gain depends on the effectiveness of social and organizational constraints on bureaucratic agents, which may fall short of the task.

The primary shape of governance reform in the Pakistani electrical power sector is a formalization that was intended to promote market mechanisms. As in other countries, international financial institutions pushed a standardized template of reforms toward increasing competition and private sector participation, with poor results (see Chapter 3). Electricity in Pakistan is primarily supplied through state-run regional electrical utilities known as distribution companies (or DISCOs). In principle, electricity connections, ongoing maintenance, and payment for the consumption of electricity are all managed according to the bureaucratic rules of business. However, at the individual, group, and national

Access to Power. Ijlal Naqvi, Oxford University Press. © Oxford University Press 2022.
DOI: 10.1093/oso/9780197540954.003.0006

levels, engagement with bureaucratic rules is an imprecise process in which the codified rules are one reference among many, such as culture, language, rents, and politics.

The challenge of producing good outcomes through interventions such as formal rules is at the heart of the literature on regulation and governance. The principle that formal rules do not pass unscathed through the organization that must implement them is well established (Wilson, 1989). Moreover, going by the book and not showing flexibility in the application of rules gives rise to the problem of "regulatory unreasonableness" (Bardach & Kagan, 1982). Nonetheless, many organizations offer routinized solutions, particularly as under-resourced street-level bureaucrats must manage an unworkable caseload (Lipsky, 2010[1980]). In these circumstances, discretion, wherein the public officer must choose among possible actions (Davis, 1969), is unavoidable.

A new direction in studies of regulation and governance places discretion at the heart of the possibility of "rewarding regulation" when exercised judiciously by a "sociological citizen" (Schrank, 2013; Silbey, 2011). Regulators who can exercise their discretion produce insightful and tailored interventions that serve their organizational mandate under challenging circumstances, but uncontrolled discretion can also lead to idiosyncratic decisions and the abuse of public position for private gain. These authors identify limits to discretion that are social and organizational in origin, and thus probabilistic and pragmatic rather than absolute (Feldman, 1992). As the "identity and self-conception" of the bureaucratic agents implementing policy at the street level becomes "entwined with their organizational roles," the pathway to improved organizational performance lies in managing organizational culture rather than directly managing the agents (Piore, 2011).

In the sections that follow, I first lay out the paradigm of reform based on formal institutions. I then examine the reality of governance—first at the offices of the utility company conducting its routine operations, and then at the national level where internationally led initiatives to reform the power sector have been introduced.

The vignettes that follow illustrate formal rules in action in the Pakistani electrical power sector. They show the interdependence of the formal and the informal, and how the patterning of governance is produced through their interaction. Additionally, they show how increasing levels of formality can sometimes produce undesirable outcomes. In each of these cases, discretion on the part of the bureaucratic agent is a key part of shaping the patterns of governance, and the degree to which this discretion can be tamed to serve the organizational mandate is linked to the influence of social and organizational limits on discretion.

At the Offices of the Islamabad Electric Supply Company

This first vignette of interactions at the offices of the Islamabad electrical utility shows the unavoidable role of individual bureaucratic agents in the passage of formal rules into concrete actions. Personal contact is a necessary step in dealing with the Islamabad Electric Supply Company (IESCO), and consequently, dealing with personal requests is a major component of what IESCO employees do in a day. These demands do not relent even when employees are otherwise engaged, as illustrated during one field visit with Omar sahib, an executive engineer (XEN) with operational oversight for an entire division:[1]

> Throughout this time there has been a steady stream of IESCO employees and consumers bringing in papers to sign, particularly bills which need to be adjusted or addressed in some way. One example. A youngish fellow in jeans, collared t-shirt, with shiny black shoes (cheap and flashy) asks to pay in installments. He brings in the bill, Omar sahib signs it, and he says "most kind" (in English). At least 20 such people come in during the 2 ½ hours I'm there, at least 30 phone calls too. Omar sahib has two mobile phones.[2]

Complaints regarding the size of a bill are frequently put to IESCO employees. In his capacity as XEN Omar sahib can permit a bill to be paid in installments, though this request must be made in person as the XEN's signature is required on the actual bill. Almost every such request is granted, so long as the customer has a reasonable record of making timely payments. Omar sahib tells me that it serves IESCO to allow payment in installments because at least some payment will be made on time and there is more chance of the entire bill being paid over time. Allowing a bill to be paid in installments also pleases the consumer and is far less effort than denying the request, as a consumer will typically protest and argue with the IESCO employee if rebuffed.

Omar sahib's role in allowing consumers to pay in installments personalizes bureaucratic operations. Requests are made in person, verbally, at his desk. IESCO consumers can't avoid encountering him and making a polite request if they wish to pay in installments. Similarly, getting a new connection involves dealing with Babur—the line superintendent in charge of new connections—in person. Aside from the need to follow up with an application to ensure that it is being processed, people have to deal personally with Babur because they don't know the requirements of the new connections process. While documentation is available and given out on request—such as the "Abriged [sic] Terms and

Conditions" for a new connection—the information deters and confuses, rather than informs, the average applicant:

> Babur gives me a copy of the "Abriged" [sic] Terms and Conditions. They're 4 pages of single spaced, dense prose [in English]. I ask if he's read them. Babur shakes his head, laughs, and says no. Babur: "Zubair Sahib [a clerk in the same office], have you read them?" Zubair shakes his head. He doesn't even look up from his files. Babur laughs again: "How many years' service and even he hasn't read them . . . when you read them, let us know what they say!"[3]

The formal rules governing new applications are literally in a foreign language to Pakistanis. While many Pakistanis do read English, their facility with it is far less than with Urdu. Nonetheless, the written language of the Pakistani government is usually English.

Formal procedures are obscured and only accessible through in-person requests to the IESCO officers. Simple requests, politely stated, are a way to get things done, but they require the applicant to appear at the office in person (sometimes repeatedly) and to be grateful to the IESCO employee who helps them. The performative component to the encounter at the office is essential because people need the assistance of an IESCO employee; they are usually the only ones who know what has to be done. Further, contact must be personal—usually face to face—or else the IESCO employee will turn their attention to whichever task someone is pursuing in person.

The necessity of personal contact is the first plank toward the mutually constitutive role of codified rules and informal norms in establishing the institutional field of governance. IESCO procedures are tedious—assuming one even knows them. For example, the process for getting a meter reconnected after it has been disconnected for nonpayment requires the customer to: (1) pay the bill at the bank; (2) take the paid bill to the subdivision office to receive a reconnection order; (3) take the reconnection order to the revenue office in order to receive a notice demanding a reconnection fee; (4) pay the reconnection fee, which must be paid at a bank; (5) take the receipt of the reconnection fee back to the revenue office, where the customer will obtain a reconnection order; (6) take the reconnection order back to the subdivision office, whose staff will reconnect the disconnected meter. Each stage requires paperwork to be completed by hand and the receipt to be carried by the customer to the next step in the process. The subdivision office, revenue office, and bank are not at the same location, nor will the relevant personnel necessarily be available. Unsurprisingly, IESCO employees will help customers out for a small fee (sometimes called "speed money" or described as money for petrol or bus fare). Qasim is an IESCO employee in the disconnection and reconnection department of a subdivisional office that serves several unfashionable neighborhoods of Islamabad:

> While I am in his office, Qasim receives a phone call. He tells the caller that he's in his office, to come upstairs. A young man comes in, they chat briefly, and he gives Qasim a bill along with about Rs 2000. After he leaves, Qasim turns to me to explain that guy is a 'someone he knows' ("*jan-nay wallah*") and their meter has been disconnected for a while. He's going to get their RCO [reconnection order] for them. He goes on to explain that "to get an RCO is complicated." For older people and ladies—or the people one knows—he or other IESCO staff will help them out. And they'll get a small Rs 100–200 payment for this. He says, 'There's nothing illegal in this' ("*iss meiN kuchh illegal nahiN hai*"). Qasim looks at me as he says this, but his eyes meet mine only briefly and then flick downwards. Qasim starts explaining the RCO procedure and I make him repeat it so that I can write all the steps down.[4]

The procedure to reconnect a disconnected meter is a good example of a codified rule controlling service delivery, but this example also demonstrates how such codified rules are filtered through social norms and expectations in truly becoming the rules of the game. Qasim is in effect a gatekeeper because those codified rules are generally unknown. I never saw anyone ask for them at the subdivision office during my fieldwork. The terms of a reconnection are included in the 2010 Customer Service Manual available on the IESCO website,[5] but this laudable step toward transparency wasn't in place at the time of my fieldwork and will not (on its own) serve the 88% of Pakistanis without Internet access or those unaware that a handbook exists. At a minimum, a consumer seeking a reconnection will have to approach Qasim in person at least once in order to simply learn the procedure. The tediousness of the procedure—trips to different locations to secure receipts and approvals—also represents a significant transaction cost. Weighing up a tedious and unknown procedure, it is little wonder that many consumers will gladly pay a small amount to Qasim to process their paperwork. The written procedure will be followed in the end, but only when mediated by an officer who gains a rent due to their exclusive knowledge. The rules of the game are social because they must be accessed through a gatekeeper and oriented toward rents, both because of the gatekeeper's role and the tedious nature of the tasks.

The everyday experience of securing service delivery reveals how the cultural norms and expectations of behavior in state service delivery leave little room for the operation of formal rules—rules that are neither possible nor desirable to observe. As my interviews and fieldwork show, the rules of game in service delivery are shaped by language, power, rents, and violence as much as they are by codified rules. They are not defined either by the rulebook or social reality on their own but are instead mutually constituted by the interaction of the two.

A focus on changing written rules is well suited to a technocratic mindset and a top-down administration. Yet in Pakistan, as in many developing countries, an important cause of poor service delivery is the ineffectiveness of internal administrative mechanisms. Bureaucratic commands are simply not fulfilled, though the paperwork may suggest compliance. Because behavior in public service is not effectively governed by formal rules, changes in those rules are unlikely to bring about the desired changes in behavior.

The limited ambit of the codified rules of the state form only a small part of the rules of the game, as the discussion in this section has argued. This should not, however, be viewed in a purely negative light. On many, many occasions I've seen or heard about IESCO employees working to make their underfunded distribution network continue to function despite their lack of resources and the resultant danger to their lives due to the lack of appropriate equipment.

One example of this can be seen in transport, a constant problem faced by IESCO employees. There are too few official vehicles to get them around the area that they work in, and there is not enough money to pay for the fuel consumed by these official vehicles. In the case of meter readers, they arrange for their own transport, from the subdivision office where they will start the day to the location where they will do their allotted meter readings for the day. This transport can take a variety of forms. I shared a cab with four meter readers one sunny summer morning, which meant that six adult men were crammed inside a miniature 800cc Suzuki. We had to open the windows both for ventilation and to give us space for our bodies. With another meter reader we took a wagon (a privately operated bus route) in which we were shortly joined by someone taking a chicken home from market. The chicken was apparently a fine specimen and received compliments from all sides. With another meter reader I rode pillion on his motorbike. Transport costs for a meter reader will easily add up to Rs. 1000 per month out of a salary that may only be Rs. 6000 a month. In the case of the line superintendent for maintenance, his job required him to supervise fault repairs all over the service area of his subdivision. When I joined him to observe his duties, he drove me to these locations in his 20(or more)-year-old car at terrifying speeds. But without these IESCO employees arranging their own transport, there is no way the system could function.[6]

Basic equipment is rarely available at IESCO in sufficient quantity or quality. Two line superintendents in charge of maintenance described buying tools such as axes for their workers themselves. Helmets and boots are nonexistent and ladders a rarity. The only time I've seen such equipment on IESCO workers is in the promotional materials or safety brochures. I've seen men climbing up a pylon wearing plastic flip-flops without any ropes or ladders or protective equipment. From July 2009 to June 2010, IESCO had 12 fatal accidents among its linemen (MWP-USAID Power Distribution Improvement Program, 2011, p. 30). Like many Pakistanis, IESCO staff are forced to take risks that could be avoided with more money and better equipment.

This role of IESCO staff in trying to do their job despite the missing equipment and dangerous conditions is recognized by consumers at times. A professor at a public university told me about the following events he had witnessed near his home in one of the nicer Islamabad neighborhoods:

Professor Nadeem says that some time ago there was a loud bang on his street and the door of the transformer housing was blown away never to be seen again. The transformer on his street had burned up. The maintenance people came after a while and he spent some time observing them. Professor Nadeem said: "They couldn't afford a new one so they had to repair this one. The lineman got some old newspaper from the neighboring houses and they made a small fire which they used to heat the cables they were joining together. I looked at the leaflet of maintenance instructions that they had and it described how everything was to be done, but they didn't have a blowtorch or any of the tools that were described in the leaflet."

IN: One thing I'll say in their defence is that they don't have money for spares or the equipment they need, but somehow they do what they need to do. They don't follow the proper procedures, but they'll get a result which is close enough.

Professor Nadeem: I agree. They adapt themselves to working with these limitations and we adapt ourselves to living with the constraints of the electricity supply.[7]

Focusing only on the negative aspects of informality doesn't do justice to the risks taken and efforts made by IESCO staff. Formal procedures and regulations are not the major determination of what work gets done or how it gets done. The positive aspect of this approach is that when the IESCO staff are on the job, they routinely look to overcome the lack of resources and equipment to which they are entitled.

The patterning of regulation and coordination for the mundane tasks described in this vignette is heavily shaped by personal interactions. Thus, there are substantial social and organizational constraints on the discretion of bureaucratic agents. While the bureaucratic agents are the key actors in moving from formal rules to concrete action, and they take action in a manner guided by their organizational mandate, there is ample opportunity to apply power and leverage for decision-making that can either produce a steady stream of payments or conform to the needs of influential clients (or both).

Policymaking and Structural Change at the National Level

The previous examples illustrate the emergence of compromises between the formal and informal that still serve the public in some oblique, imperfect way; individuals' cash flow problems are accommodated, and IESCO employees find their own transport around the city. The compromises are shaped by social interactions among street-level bureaucrats and the people they serve. This last vignette is at the national level rather than the street level and illustrates how the idiosyncratic filtering of the formal through the social realities of how state power is exercised can be abused for personal interest. This case is not intended to produce surprise that public office is sometimes abused; other examples could, instead, have shown more constructive compromises (e.g., among provincial representatives at the Council of Common Interests) in line with the previous two examples. What this case illustrates is how hard it can be to prevent this abuse of power even when the perpetrators are caught in the act by the media and elected representatives.

Over the years, power sector reform initiatives have introduced several major structural changes in an attempt to change the processes and outcomes of the power sector. These initiatives have typically been backed by international donors and multilateral lenders, with—at best—mixed success. In this section I will examine the National Electric Power Regulatory Authority (NEPRA), which was established in 1997.

NEPRA, like any regulatory authority, can only fulfill its role with the right staff with relevant expertise. The NEPRA Act of 1997[8] states that the chairman "shall be an eminent professional of known integrity and competence with at least twenty years of related experience in law, business, engineering, finance, accounting, economics, or the electric utility business." To recruit such a person when the post was vacated in September 2007, NEPRA placed an advertisement in Pakistani newspapers, for which it received 72 applications to the post of chairman by October 20, 2007.[9] A shortlist of 17 applicants was interviewed by a committee headed by the secretary of the cabinet division, and the committee sent its recommendations to caretaker Prime Minister Soomro[10] for approval on January 18, 2008. The committee's recommendations were returned without decision on February 14. The next day—three days before parliamentary elections, which would lead to a new prime minister being installed—the caretaker prime minister appointed his Principal Secretary Khalid Saeed to the post of NEPRA chairman but also had him retain his then post of principal secretary to the prime minister. Saeed had not applied for the position of NEPRA chairman and did not have the required 20 years of related experience. On February 26, 2008, the Pakistan Senate passed a near-unanimous resolution against Saeed's appointment, noting his lack of qualifications, noting his occupation of two government posts simultaneously (which is unconstitutional), and describing the process as "against accepted norms."[11] Saeed resigned from his post as principal secretary to the prime minister as the senate resolution against him was moved but retained his new post as NEPRA chairman.[12] Despite the senate resolution, a petition before the Lahore High Court challenging his appointment,[13] and the fact that he was near retirement age, Khalid Saeed stayed in his post as chairman of NEPRA. Moreover, an amendment to the NEPRA act on August 12, 2011, added "and public administration" to the list of fields in which NEPRA chairmen can use as their requisite 20 years of experience.

As this example shows, not only was the appointment process circumvented to appoint an unqualified candidate in 2008, but now administrators with no relevant experience can legally head NEPRA. The post of NEPRA chairman is now primed as a ripe cherry for retiring bureaucrats wanting to stay on the government payroll after retirement. The lesson is not just that the newly formed regulatory agency was subverted by existing power structures, but also that media attention,[14] a senate resolution, and continued involvement by international donors in electricity reform could not prevent it from happening.

A Fractious Federation

Pakistan is a fractious federation. Power sector policy can either reinforce the stresses between the provinces or diffuse them. Each province has its own profile of generation and distribution, and there is a rough symmetry in that the fuel-producing provinces have poorer performance at the distribution level. Disaggregated pricing for distribution and generation will damage the sector as a whole and be politically toxic. One way in which the balance between the different provincial profiles for generation and distribution is recognized is through the uniform national tariff, that is, the principle that all Pakistani electricity consumers are charged the same rate anywhere in the country. This idea is an anathema to neoliberal reformers who insist on local cost recovery and the operation of each distribution company as a commercially viable entity in anticipation of privatization, but the uniform national tariff serves an important function in maintaining the harmony of the Pakistani federation. While the best performers among distribution companies are in Punjab, the cheapest generation options come from sources in Khyber Pukhtunkhwa, Sindh, and Balochistan. Investment in hydroelectric power is largely done by the federal government, and each province (mostly Khyber Pukhtunkhwa) gets profit shares for their hydroelectric generation. However, Khyber Pukhtunkhwa has not been paid royalties in a timely fashion in the past, and they may still feel ownership over the hydro projects located in Khyber Pukhtunkhwa. Just as the benefits of preferred fuels are shared through the common generation pool, the uniform national tariff shares the strengths and challenges of the different distribution company's territories across the federation.

Arguments for approaching electricity as a provincial issue have some merit but come with substantial risks. The benefit is that ownership of the major distribution problem—preventing theft and collecting payments—would be in the hands of provincial politicians with the deep local connections to address these issues. However, there is no guarantee that these politicians would seek to do so rather than continue with some variation of the status quo, in which they seek jobs for their constituents and rents for themselves over reforms that give a long-term benefit to the whole province. Moreover, a complicated new electricity market would have to be designed to adjust for the allocation of different sources of power generation. Breaking up the common generation pool would mean that provinces would compete to have the cheapest energy allocated to them. Regardless of the qualities of the market design (no doubt drawing on best international practices), tremendous pressures would be put on the people deciding on these allocations of power to favor one province or distribution company. The private sector cannot remove institutional weaknesses by magic, and in many instances of infrastructure governance "the process of involving the private sector has itself been a significant source of rents" (Kenny, 2007, p. 10). Every previous experience of such structural reforms in the Pakistani power sector suggests that the capacity of existing power structures to subvert new structural arrangements exceeds the capacity of pro-reform constituents to prevent such abuses.

Social and organizational constraints did operate in the case of the NEPRA chairmanship. It is difficult to imagine what more could be done in such a case than to have the senate take notice and for the media to cover it. However, social and organizational constraints are probabilistic rather than absolute. This case may just lend support to the view that Pakistani elite bureaucrats indulge in self-serving practices against their organizational mandate (Niaz, 2010). It also differs from the earlier vignettes where the social and organizational constraints on behavior were more immediate and personal than at the rarified level of national government. Although the evidence presented here is insufficient to conclude the argument, these vignettes suggest that the capacity of social and organizational constraints to limit discretion in accordance with the organizational mandate is dependent on the immediacy and persistence of those constraints, particularly when manifested as a communal or moral right such as in the case of the *katchi abadi* in Chapter 5.

Discussion and Conclusions

The dichotomization of formality and informality is an incomplete representation of the rules of the game for governance in the Pakistani power sector. Rules are encountered through the state, in person, with documents in hand, as has been richly examined by anthropologists of the state. By exploring the paradoxes of the lived encounter with the state in Himalayan India, Nayanika Mathur invites us to "radically reimagine bureaucracy as . . . a space in which life unfolds within and at the intersection of varying orientations, disciplines, and affects of social time and material practices" (Mathur, 2017, p. 163). The materiality of documents is central to Matthew Hull's (2012) account of citizens seeking compensation for displacement from—and seeking opportunities to be displaced by—the Capital Development Authority of Islamabad. Kregg Hetherington (2011) describes the tactics of guerrilla auditors in Paraguay who track down illegible official paper records documenting hopelessly tangled land ownership claims and then wield these papers as if they were entry passes to fiercely contested meetings with state bureaucrats. At IESCO offices, individuals paying a bill in installments or seeking to avoid a disconnection have to work through the street-level bureaucrats through whom the official procedures are managed. The rules of the game are neither formal nor informal; instead, they are mutually constituted by the interaction of the formal and informal through social processes. And, as social processes, the construction of the rules of the game reflects the power and relative position of the actors involved.

In the framework of the infrastructural state, the characterization of electricity governance as a field brings the focus to a dynamic and emergent reconsideration of how formal rules shape patterns of governance. Modernization, and the responses to it, can take different guises and produce different responses at different levels of analysis. The governance compromises at the national versus the local level have different dynamics and outcomes, but in each field the modernizing impulse is shaped and reformed through its interaction with power and politics. At neither the individual, the city, nor the national level do increasing levels of formality produce uniformly desirable outcomes: the squatters who secure individual meters find themselves vulnerable to new forms of predation, collective negotiations can provide more security than an individual contract, and seasoned bureaucrats can outmaneuver local media and irate politicians. Retreats from formality take place at both local and individual levels as exposure to predation and relative advantage are influenced by modernizing impulses. Whether these discretionary moves are constructive in serving the organizational mandate toward the public good of electricity service provision, however, is hugely shaped by the extent to which social and organizational constraints weigh on the bureaucratic agents who are key actors in these processes and transactions.

The cracks that are revealed in the modernization process can vary from constructive accommodations to local power realities, necessary political compromises, or opportunities for predation by local notables. These adaptions to the modernizing impulse are not always negative: they can also be practical adjustments to an unwieldy process or accommodations of a pressing social need. However, the patterns of coordination and regulation that emerge in the local and national fields of electricity sector governance are always the products of a compromise produced by the interplay of actors navigating formal rules, culture, and power.

7

Money, Violence, and Connections

The Culture of Power

At the heart of the relationship between citizen and state over access to electrical power lies a personal encounter between consumer and street-level bureaucrat. The parameters of this encounter are shaped by power in the form of money and personal connections, with an underlying threat of violence that usually remains hidden. This is the lowest of the three nested fields that form the scaffolding of this book, and in many senses it forms the basis for the phenomena discussed at higher levels. Earlier chapters examined sub-national unevenness in electricity governance between the provinces and showed how this unevenness was produced by the state as a strategy of rule. The analysis of unevenness of electricity governance within the city of Lahore showed how demographic characteristics were the strongest influence on the state's ability to extract payment for services, implying a differentiated urban citizenship in which the state has limited capacity to extract compliance from poorer residential or agricultural consumers. The immediately preceding chapter discussed institutions and the inability to disentangle formality and informality. Codified rules exist, and certainly matter, but access to them is wrapped in layers of social negotiations and contestations. In this chapter the arc of the book descends to the most basic and direct form of contest over the terms of engagement with the state, which is mostly conducted face to face.

The form of power examined in this chapter relates most closely to Lukes' (Lukes, 1974) first face of power. In his seminal treatment of how power works, Lukes described a first face of power that consists of direct and confrontational challenges over who determines the outcome of a contest, a second face that involves agenda setting, and a third that is about shaping preferences. The situations examined in this chapter unfold in a setting where the agenda is largely predetermined by the existing institutional structures, and societal preferences are determined outside of these encounters, hence the focus on the first face of

Access to Power. Ijlal Naqvi, Oxford University Press. © Oxford University Press 2022.
DOI: 10.1093/oso/9780197540954.003.0007

power. An emphasis on power is central to the argument of this book because the conceptualization of a field requires that we consider the relative power and position of actors as well as the rules of the game. The illustrations of how power is exercised in this direct and personal level of analysis touch on the central importance of money, of personal connections, and of violence.

Money influences the individual encounter with the state in multiple ways. The situation of the street-level bureaucrat is structured by their low wages contrasted with the influence they have over much larger public sector expenditures and private cash flows. The group setting of the organizational work environment also imposes requirements and expectations. The inadequate budgets of the distribution company also impose its own pressures. Against these limitations, the street-level bureaucrat must work to maintain their own dignity while handling the consumer's requests.

The consumer's personal connections and standing often establish a power differential relative to the individual street-level bureaucrat, particularly in Islamabad, where high-level government officials (and their close relatives and acquaintances, etc.) are plentiful. In other words, both parties rapidly size up their own position within this field of interpersonal power. Anand Ghiridharadas captures this process beautifully when he describes the occasion of returning to a friend's flat in Mumbai that he had visited earlier for coffee, but now to return a mattress that he is carrying himself while casually dressed. The servant, previously meek and submissive, receives him roughly until he recognizes Ghiridharadas, which prompts the following reflection:

> I had a privilege that morning that I never knew before or afterward. I saw the truth of what it means to be Indian, an ordinary indian, not a foreigner like me, not an educated elite. I had felt impotence and then omnipotence in the same minute; I had gazed up from, and then down into, the Indian abyss. For the Indians around me, it was the calculus that governed life: Am I his sahib or is he mine? Who should shout at whom? Whose body must apologize for its presence and whose must swagger? Whose eyes must stay down? Who can use "*tum*" and who "*aap*"?[1] Who must hide his hands behind his back and who can gesticulate with them? (Giridharadas, 2011, pp. 39–40)

Ghiridharas goes on to say that there is "no more urgent knowledge in India than the knowledge of one's place, and to commit such an error with any frequency was to risk one's survival" (pp. 39–40). As befits the shared history of India and Pakistan, Ghiridharas' observations apply to my fieldwork as well—including the rarity and danger of mistakes on this front. The relative standing of the street-level bureaucrat is an odd one because, although individually neither wealthy nor influential, they sit—for a time, at least—with influence on an important lever that can affect the lives of many. For the most part, there are workable accommodations to be found by which consumer needs can be satisfied.

Rarely does a contest over the delivery of services descend into actual violence, but, when it does, this tear in the thin skein of civility reveals how close these negotiated power relations bring us to brute violence at any given time. Violence is the ultimate degeneration of Lukes' first face of power, from which we cannot go lower. The final vignette in this chapter brings together these alternative routes to direct influence and power.

The qualitative data presented in this chapter was collected from 2008 to 2010. In a concentrated set of visits over four months, and then regular visits over the following 18 months, I spent time with each of the departments in multiple urban subdivisions of Islamabad. In this time I interviewed Islamabad Electric Supply Company (IESCO) employees, observed them dealing with customers, and talked more generally with them about their work and their lives. I was not an employee of IESCO and did not contribute toward their work in any way.[2]

I introduced myself to people at the IESCO offices where I conducted my field research as a Ph.D. student studying service delivery in the electrical power sector. Despite being a graduate student on a limited stipend, there was no escaping the "urgent knowledge of one's place" described by Ghiridharas (which ethnographers would call my "positionality"). In background, appearance, speech, and so on, I signal a privileged Pakistani background. However, thanks to my Austrian mother, I look very little like your average Pakistani, and this combination of visible insider and outsider statuses, along with my unusual behavior, marked me as an oddity. In general, Pakistanis who can avoid it just don't spend much time talking to low-level public service employees, let alone spend long stretches of time in their offices trying to learn about government work. In my opinion, this oddness of my appearance and behavior made me interesting to my research subjects, who were no doubt trying to make sense of me as much as I was trying to make sense of their world.[3] My suspicion is that their difficulty in placing me easily gave me more opportunities to talk to them while they tried to learn a little about me during our conversations.

Gaining access to the environment of the subdivision office was a challenge that I addressed in much the same way that most everyone else navigates the bureaucracy—through connections and introductions. My goal was to get introduced to the subdivision level, but my only starting point was at the top. Through previous experience working at the Pakistani government, I knew a senior bureaucrat with ministerial-level experience in the power sector. With his reference, I introduced myself to someone who introduced me at IESCO headquarters, and so on down the chain until I made it to the subdivision level. I was strongly and repeatedly advised not to have an official affiliation on the basis that any sense that I was working for their superiors would limit the lower-level staff's willingness to talk to me. While I was introduced from the top of the organization downward, this was an introduction rather than a command, and my presence was always unofficial. Throughout my fieldwork my only public role was as a student researcher studying the power sector, and this is exactly what I was.

My presence at the subdivision and other offices was always quite visible. These are spaces through which there is a relatively constant flow of human traffic as people come to transact their business with IESCO. Further, it is entirely common for people to be sitting around with no particular purpose—as I no doubt appeared to be doing as well. In any given Pakistani government office, there are always people waiting for their case to be attended to, or to serve at their superior officer's pleasure, as the situation may be.[4] This gave me ample opportunity to be present in public offices as cases were attended to, and in the times in between when I would talk to the street-level bureaucrats about those cases and their work.

A major shortcoming of my fieldwork is the lack of attention paid to the role of gender. As a cisgender male, my presence in the entirely male spaces of the IESCO subdivision offices was unremarkable in and of itself. I encountered no women in operational positions at IESCO other than at a central call center. I hardly ever saw a woman at an IESCO office, and social conventions made it extremely difficult to speak to women I had not previously met. And, rather than speak directly to women, I would instead be expected to speak to the male family member who invariably accompanied them. I was unable to solve this problem during my fieldwork and had no funding for a female research assistant.[5]

The office of the IESCO subdivisional officer (SDO) where I did much of this fieldwork is a drab building between a small market and a street of bungalows. An educational institution and an office also operate out of the residences on this street. The paint on the exterior of the building has faded, peeled, and weathered to a mottled gray. Spare electrical equipment, a pickup truck, and the personal motorcycles and cars of the employees are usually parked outside. A small blue board outside identifies the office as the "Office of SDO (Engineering)."[6]

The SDO is responsible for operations in his subdivision of some 25,000 households, and this office is the primary point of contact for customers with any questions such as those about the duration of outages, inquiries about new connections, or billing complaints. This subdivision is organized on functional lines into four departments: new connections, meter reading, disconnection and reconnection, and maintenance. Each department is headed by a line superintendent (the rung below the SDO in IESCO's hierarchy), who can have up to 25 years of experience. Within each department there may be a second (subordinate) line superintendent as well as linemen and assistant linemen, who report to the line superintendent heading the department.

In the sections that follow, I explore how the practices of governance on an everyday level are shaped by money, personal connections, and the possibility of violence.

Money

Money pervades all three nested fields of electricity governance in Pakistan. At the national level, accumulating debts resulting from inadequate electricity sector cash flows figure heavily in the growing national debt and the ability to generate sufficient electrical power on a daily basis. Across the city, seeing who pays and who doesn't is an indication of the integration of different populations into the fullest ranks of urban citizenship. For the individuals involved, particularly on the part of the distribution company employees at the lowest levels of the official pay scale, the challenge of living decently on a very limited paycheck—all the while influencing a vital facet of urban infrastructure—is an immediate point of pressure in their relationship with the citizens who demand electricity.

Salman is a line superintendent for Disconnections and Reconnections. This is the same position as Qasim from the previous chapter, but in a subdivision serving generally wealthier areas. Salman, too, is familiar with speed money:

> Salman differentiates between taking money for acts which don't harm the "*mehkama*" (institution, meaning IESCO) and acts which do. Expediting paperwork, possibly 'cutting the process' (*process ko kaatna*), on additional payment by the customer doesn't harm WAPDA.[7] Salman clarifies that the parent organization hasn't lost anything in this exchange—it gets its full payment. Expediting a connection can mean a lot of revenue to a business. 'There's no harm (*nuksaan*) to WAPDA in this.'[8]

For Salman and others, the distinction between that which harms and does not harm IESCO is carefully maintained when describing instances where IESCO employees take money. To speed up an otherwise legitimate procedure is acceptable, as is taking charge of the processing of someone's paperwork. In a later exchange on the same topic,

> Salman says that he only knows one or two people in this office who would take a payoff to enable the theft of electricity.
>
> Salman carefully distinguishes this from taking a fee to help someone navigate IESCO paperwork. He admits that that practice too has "*rishwat ki shakal*" ('the appearance of corruption'), but that there is "no loss to the authority."

Salman's colleague Haroon Sahib, an older Line Superintendent with a wry sense of humor, says that I might call this a "service fee."
I suggest that he might for example take Rs 100–200 to help someone get a meter reconnected as a "facilitation fee"—Haroon Sahib smiles at that term.
Salman: "*Jiss level ka kam, uss level ka . . .* " ('the level of work, that level of . . . ') Salman raises his hands upward, fingers extended. He doesn't name the act of receiving a payment.[9]

Salman and Haroon sahib are entirely comfortable admitting to taking money to help people navigate the formal procedures of IESCO. Taking money when IESCO is harmed, however, is presented as immoral and not the work of a good employee.

Rent-seeking on any scale is typically a collaborative exercise that requires the active participation of many staff members.

> Salman describes an episode where he was offered 1 lakh.[10] The man was setting up 4 cell phone towers and needed electricity connections. When getting a connection you can get it done on a cost-sharing basis [cost of infrastructure shared by IESCO], which is cheaper for the customer. His cost was going to be 6 lakhs because Salman wanted him to install his own transformer, which was the technically superior solution. He wanted cost-sharing so that his cost would only be 90,000. He offered Salman 1 lakh to do it that way.

IN: he showed you the notes?
S: 'Cash on the table.'
IN: Won't everyone else in your office know if you are taking money like that?
Salman: 'only 30,000 would have ended up in my pocket.' Not only does everyone else know but they have to take part. 'It can't happen unless the whole team takes part.' Salman would have 'to give 2000 here, 3000 there to get the paperwork done.'[11]

It can't be kept secret because of the paperwork requirements for any substantial initiative, or the variety of resources that must be mobilized, all of which will necessarily involve many different employees. For rent-seeking of this kind to exist, it has to be widespread in practice and generally tolerated, including by administrative superiors.

The IESCO employees are conscious of their own moral responsibility for their behavior despite being tied into a corrupt system. A common refrain that I heard from IESCO employees was that 'Both the giver and taker of bribes (*rishwat*) are going to hell (*jahanami*).' The speaker gave what I understood to be an Arabic equivalent to the above phrase, but then quickly added a movie reference and then—after glancing around at his colleagues in a manner that implied he was referring to them—'sometimes the taker is compelled (*majboor*).' All of us laughed, but the use of the word *rishwat* (a more formal invocation of corruption), the Arabic phrase that I understood to be a quote from the Qu'ran, and the reference to hell mark his acknowledgment that some of what they do is wrong, even if their hand is forced.

For these and other discussions of corrupt behavior, I was in no position to query or verify anything beyond the frequency with which they were stated, the number of different people independently making related claims, and the responses of other colleagues. However, for all the openness with which IESCO employees discussed how they themselves and others took money from consumers, I never witnessed such an exchange firsthand. I almost never broached the topic of corruption myself. All of these attributions of taking and receiving money (including self-incrimination) were volunteered in the course while discussing the ordinary business of IESCO.

The necessity of corruption within IESCO is underscored by the practice of purchasing appointments. I asked Babur, a twenty-something line superintendent in charge of new connections, how an IESCO employee could join the audit department.

IN: "How do you get appointed to be in the audit department?"
Babur explains that you do a B. Com or an MBA, then apply in response to the ad in the newspaper announcing the hiring. [The same process as for other positions.]
IN: "But how do you actually get appointed?"
Babur doesn't immediately respond and continues to look at me.
IN: "Are these positions filled according to merit?"
Babur: "It would take *lakhs* to get an appointment."[12]

The phenomenon of paying for an appointment is not unique to the audit department but is in fact common in IESCO. When I asked Salman what was different in the time when the army was running IESCO,[13] the first thing he tells me is that people didn't have to pay for their appointments. Salman tells me that it now takes 2.5 *lakhs* to be appointed as a line superintendent and 5–6 *lakhs* for an SDO. This was not the case when Salman joined under Brigadier Waseem Zafar. Salman did not have to pay for his appointment. Salman pointedly asked me, "The person who paid this, won't he make it back though corruption?"[14]

Having paid for a position—whether an internal transfer to a post or the initial hiring—there is a financial imperative to make that money back. A clerk in the drafting section had his promotion to a higher pay grade held up because he wouldn't pay the 25,000 that was being demanded of him to process his promotion. When I suggested that at least he didn't have to seek out bribes to pay back the bribe he would have paid, he pointed out that the salary increment over the past year would have covered the initial cost of the promotion. The clerk regretted that he had waited so long to pay the bribe and was reconsidering his stance. The purchase of more lucrative postings than a clerkship in a drafting section, however, necessarily leads to rent-seeking because the sums involved are far greater than the compensation provided through salary increases. Those disinclined toward rent-seeking may well be channeled to lesser posts, or—if they pay for the appointment—then become part of the system they despise. To fight continuously against corruption would pit an individual against both their subordinates and superiors who are part of that system.

Pakistanis working in the state-owned power sector are aware of the distinction between the formal and the informal and carefully shade the moral valence of their actions. They can peer outside the limitations of their social environs but find it very hard to act outside of them. Robert Wade's study of canal networks in South India describes a similar environment where the giving and taking of money related to the performance of official duties by employees of the Irrigation Department is pervasive:

> the line between "taking gifts" and "corruption" is blurred—especially because part of the maintenance budget rake-off is well institutionalised and an engineer would have to go out of his way to avoid receiving the money. Hence one can understand why, from the point of view of farmers and contractors, an "honest" engineer is not one who does not take money, but one who takes no more than the normal rate, who does not haggle, and who having taken your money at least tries to help you in return. (Wade, 1982, p. 308)

Although Wade's fieldwork dates 30 years before mine and is located in an entirely different part of South Asia, there are many similarities. In particular, the attribution of "honesty" to a state official who only takes a normal amount of money and then is true to their commitment indicates a morality that reflects the context and its constraints.

Paying to get what one needs from IESCO is a pervasive practice both within the organization as well as in dealings with consumers. For consumers, the payments described in this section enable the workings of the codified rules by greasing the cogs and wheels of the bureaucratic machine. The existence and validity of the codified rules is never questioned, but the parties involved understand that—unless they have other pressure to apply—paying for what one wants is the way to benefit from the application of the rules. For IESCO employees, they pay for appointments, pay so that their promotions are processed, and pay their superiors a share of their own takings. The type of institution described by these pervasive practices of paying for one's due is one in which the formal rules are reduced to a preamble. The outcomes of this game are dictated by power, relationships, and money rather than rules.

An important companion to theft is overbilling, a process through which one meter's electricity consumption will be underreported and instead added to the bills of various neighboring houses. This isn't an attempt to prevent losses in any way, only to compensate for them. The role of the meter reader is central to overbilling because they manually note down meter readings. Hajji sahib—so-named for his performance of the hajj, the pilgrimage to Mecca—is an older meter reader nearing retirement age whom I joined on his meter reading rounds:

> Hajji sahib tells me about an *angraiz* (English) consultant who came to IESCO years ago. Hajji Sahib says that his first question was "how much is the salary of the meter readers?" On being told how low it was, he simply said "goodbye." Hajji Sahib describes the argument that you can't expect a company to function well and avoid corruption when you aren't paying people decently.

IN: "How much would be enough?"
Hajji sahib: "Look at the Motorway police. They are paid Rs 25000 per month and have an easy life"
"kiss naiN apna qabar ganda karna" ('who wants to dirty their grave,' to dishonor themselves and soil their legacy).[15]

Hajji sahib justifies his own—unspecified—misdeeds as a meter reader with reference to his poor paycheck. The moral dimension of his behavior is clear to him:

> Hajji sahib describes his return from the Haj, which was an awesome experience for him.[16] He 'swore to stay straight, made a careful budget, no swearing and no *sharartaiN*' (literally, naughtiness, but he's referring to corruption in his work), and he stuck to this for a month. The prices rose on basic goods and he went back to being "*shararti*."[17]

Hajji sahib is not the only one aware of the moral consequences of participating in the theft of electricity. In the Ministry of Water and Power offices I spoke with a retired military officer who was now working at the ministry. When we agreed on electricity theft being the domain of the rich and powerful, he said, "Look at me. I'm an educated man. I'm wearing a suit and tie. I steal electricity." The retired officer acknowledged that a man of his education and position should do better, but that he stole electricity because he could.

Get Yourself Connected

Personal connections are the ubiquitous *desi* (South Asian) currency of getting things done. Suketu Mehta, who grew up in the United States, discovered the importance of personal connections when he returned to Mumbai as an adult:

> We learn the uses of "influence." The WIAA club, when I phone to ask for a reservation for an out-of-town visitor, say is there are no rooms available. Then my uncle called a friend, who uses his influence, and a room miraculously materializes, like the universe manifesting itself from nothing. I had forgotten the crucial difference. There's very little you can do anonymously, as a member of the vast masses. You have to go through someone. The reservations clerk needs that personal touch of a human being he recognizes. It is the same with railway reservations, theater tickets, apartments, and marriages. It has to be one person linking with another who knows another and so on till you reach your destination; the path your request takes has to go through this network. You cannot jump the chain by going directly to someone who doesn't know you, connected only by the phoneline. A friend went from Bombay to London and told me she was horrified that she could spend an entire day—buy tickets on the tube, go to a play, eat—without ever needing to make a personal connection. When you want to book a hotel in Matheran or a movie ticket at Metro, you ask around: "Who has influence?" This is why people stay on in Bombay, in spite of everything. They have built a network here; they have influence. (Mehta, 2004, p. 256)

Who you are and what you can do is shaped by who you know. Things work through people, rather than in the abstract. This is as true for Mehta's Mumbai as it is for other parts of the Indian subcontinent, including electricity access in Islamabad.

Powerful consumers behave and are treated differently from the ordinary and even middle-class consumers. In following Babur at the subdivision in a wealthy area of Islamabad, I saw several encounters with powerful customers and the different approaches they employed. The first instance pertained to a new connection for a security barrier that was being installed at the entrance to a parking lot serving several government offices. One of the offices was expecting a visit from the interior minister the next day and needed this barrier in place before the visit. Babur received a phone call from the office in question, promised to take care of things within 20 minutes, and then had the paperwork ready for a driver who was sent over with some supporting documentation some 15 minutes later. Normally, customers must pursue such matters in person, and it can take days or weeks to get this sort of thing done. The idea of an IESCO officer completing his end of the formalities for you in 20 minutes after a request on the phone is unheard of for an ordinary consumer.

In a second incident Babur was visited by Rehman sahib, who wanted to get an electricity connection for a girls' school in a middle-class area of Islamabad. Babur wasted no time in making enquiries about the cost of the connection by phoning his colleagues who deal with construction. Further, he and a lineman who had joined the conversation told Rehman sahib how to file a report on a burned-out transformer that had served a mosque neighboring the girls' school. Rehman sahib claims that he'll have the transformer replaced "before you've even sent on the report" by speaking to Raja Pervez Ashraf, the Minister of Water and Power. Rehman sahib names his contacts to underline his own importance. While he accomplishes what he needs to, his manner does not impress all of the IESCO employees:

> I speak with [an experienced lineman] in the entry way to the office regarding Rehman Sahib and the school. 'Our officers listen to him out of fear' ("*officers hamaray dar sey baat maantay haiN*"). 'He takes the names of [President] Zardari and the Minister, but he's really nothing.'[18]

Powerful people intimidate IESCO employees, and claiming to know one or to be acting on behalf of one is a good way to get things done. IESCO employees usually won't directly oppose someone making those claims, even when they don't entirely believe what they are told about the citizen's powerful connections, because it isn't worth the risk to challenge such a claim.

A lack of timely and complete bill payments is a long-standing problem for Pakistan's electricity distribution companies. The problem is even more prevalent with public sector customers than it is with private. For IESCO this is a particular concern given the density of public sector organizations located in and around Islamabad. A summary of arrears displayed on the office wall of an IESCO executive engineer indicates that public organizations owe 80% of all arrears in his division despite consuming only 20% of the electricity supply.[19] Media reports ensure that the public is aware of this component of the national electricity crisis:

> An IESCO notification said the President's Secretariat owed it Rs 21.6 million, the Azad Kashmir government Rs 1.3 million and the Immigration and Passport Secretariat Rs 1.5 million.
>
> Also, the chief commissioner's office owed Rs 16 million and the Senate office Rs 10.5 million to IESCO.
>
> It said the Federal Government Hospital, Education Ministry and Punjab police were also among the defaulters.[20]

IESCO undertakes periodic drives to recover its outstanding dues. At one of these times I spoke with Haroon, an older line superintendent in the disconnection and reconnection section of an Islamabad subdivision, about his experience in getting public sector organizations to pay their bills:

> I ask Haroon if he was involved with the collection of bills and he says yes, but that it is the XEN and SE [a Superintendent Engineer, two levels in the hierarchy above an SDO] who have to deal with the large government customers.

IN: Do you go to them?
Haroon: Yes, but they tell me they don't have the funds and I come back
IN: Who can you get money from?
Haroon: Those orphan departments (*yateem*),[21] we can get them to pay. We aren't allowed to cut off the Police, the CDA streetlights, the CDA main office, or the Army.
IN: Is that a rule?
Haroon: Yes definitely that's an order. We can't just do it according to our choice (*marzi*). There's an order from above.
The army will make partial payments, perhaps 60,000 on a bill of 100,000. They always clear everything in June. [June = end of fiscal year]. In June they take whatever money they have left and pay off the WAPDA bills. They know they have to pay WAPDA ("*daina he daina hai*"). Plus it is not from their pocket—the government is paying to the government. So they clear the bills.[22]

Haroon presents IESCO's dealings with the army—which in this case will be any one of many military organizations with offices in Islamabad—in terms of the power dynamics of the Pakistani state and the unassailable primacy of the army. The army cannot be browbeaten or threatened into paying its bills on time—that is only for "orphan" departments lower down in the status ranking of Pakistani state organizations. Yet IESCO does have enough clout that it must eventually be paid, although occasions when IESCO has disconnected the electricity supply to the Capital Development Authority (CDA), police, or some military offices are rare. As Haroon rationalizes, it's not as if they're paying out of their own pocket. Haroon understands payments between state organizations as being conceptually different from private consumer payments. When I ask him if there will be late charges on the arrears, he flatly says, "No," because "the government doesn't charge late fees to the government."

On another day I hear Farid sahib, the SDO in the subdivision where Haroon works, on the phone regarding the disconnection of the electricity meter of a director of finance for an unspecified public sector organization:

> I can't just disconnect the meter of the director finance like that.
>
> . . .
>
> I've been authorized to cut off your meter.
>
> So send me that voucher.
>
> Sir, just send me something [voice rises in pitch] so that I don't have to cut off your meter.[23]

Farid sahib is going out of his way to avoid the ugliness that would doubtless occur if he had to confront a senior bureaucrat and try to enforce their compliance.

Abbas, a senior officer at LESCO, explains the functioning of the Water and Power Development Authority's (WAPDA's) successor organizations in terms of the society they are in:

Abbas: The development of a society, in all sectors, goes side by side. Can't have one institution on U.S. or European standards and the others are on subcontinental standards. They either all go up together or not at all. WAPDA is an integrated department of the government of Pakistan. If you think WAPDA can elevate itself from the *gund* (dirt) and become a super institution, it can't happen. We all live in the same country. It isn't possible.

IN: But what about the motorway police?[24] They are the same people as in the normal police, but they function well.

Abbas: You might think you know the motorway police but you don't know them like I know them. I was posted to [location] as a punishment while I was an SDO. It's on the motorway, far from Lahore. I was afraid that I would have to leave my job because I couldn't afford to go there every day, but a colleague told me that it would be no problem. Here's what I did. Every day I got on a motorway bus for free. I got off on the motorway, walked across the motorway to the motorway police's facility. They received me there and gave me tea. My car was parked there—illegally—and I drove it out of a back gate—which they are not allowed to have—and went to my job. When I came back I would park my car inside the compound again. They would give me tea and we would talk. They would flag down a bus, have them seat me for free, and I would return to Lahore. Every day. Except Daewoo. I never went on the Daewoo buses.

What they do for their own relatives I can't speak about.

Sometimes I would drive my car from there to my house.

IN: but you need a motorway ticket at the other end. [exiting the motorway involves presenting your entry ticket at a toll plaza]

Abbas: They would give me a fake ticket from the nearby entry point. The motorway police won't stop a bus, but they are better than the normal police. They'll stop a general to show it [their enforcement of the law]. The motorway is a very small area. You can watch it closely. You can't see what happens in the WAPDA system.

Their mentality can't be changed. Their social relations (*ta'aluqaat*) can't be changed.

They obliged me because I am a WAPDA officer. I could take care of them with their electricity and help them should there be any small problem. They take care of people from government departments (*mehkama*), who can oblige them.[25]

Abbas' experience with the motorway police shows a reciprocal exchange of favors facilitating a systematic subversion of the rules that those departments are supposed to uphold. The motorway police violate the rules of the motorway in exchange for preferential treatment with their electricity supply. Abbas makes no apologies for having the motorway police break their rules for his benefit. His livelihood was at stake, and his reciprocation was not beyond what he would have done for any other public sector organization—many times without as much benefit to himself.

Abbas later told me a story of a run-in between a low-ranking officer of the Federal Investigation Agency (a branch of Pakistani law enforcement) and the LESCO officer who caught him stealing electricity. The conflict resulted in several arrests and raids on LESCO equipment stores when the LESCO officers insisted that the law enforcement official pay the fine for stealing electricity. I related the story to Maqsood sahib, who was working in a Pakistan Electric Power Comany (PEPCO)[26] headquarters. He nodded along and then gave his own example:

> A Hyderabad excise man was caught stealing electricity. The SE [Superintendent Engineer, two levels in the hierarchy above an SDO] who caught him was very hardline and insisted on the fine being paid per the procedures. The excise man explained that he was with customs and excise and asked that the SE let him off. The SE refused.

> The very next day the excise man impounded every single HESCO vehicle in Hyderabad. None of them had paid tax. None of them ran according to the rules. If you try and hold any of them [government departments] to the rules then they will get you back!

Relations between public sector organizations in Pakistan are as informal as those of the dealings with private consumers. There is an expectation among public sector organizations that the rules do not apply to them, nor are payments between them real money. Should these norms be violated in an attempt to apply these rules, then conflict arises, even overtly, with state sector employees using the power of their positions to attack their rivals.[27]

The list of powerful consumers includes both public sector entities and private consumers. Their distinguishing feature is in the response that they get from the staff of IESCO, who find ways to accommodate their needs. There is a shared expectation between powerful consumers and IESCO staff that failure to satisfy such a consumer will lead to negative consequences.

The codified rules of IESCO are, in true Weberian (Weber, Gerth, & Mills, 1991 [1925]) fashion, legalistic, impersonal, and rational. The rules apply to everyone, are to be implemented without reference to the personal standing of the official or the consumer, and publicly stated in advance. The rules of IESCO's bureaucracy are thus in conflict with a social setting in which it is expected that powerful consumers must be accommodated. These shared expectations are underpinned by a power structure in which resources are unequally distributed. The work that IESCO employees do in serving powerful consumers heads off destructive conflicts where they would probably come out worse.

Violence

Conflict between IESCO employees and private consumers can escalate from verbal abuse to physical attacks. In the office of one of the less wealthy subdivisions of Islamabad, a fight broke out in the hallway while I was there. A customer had hit an IESCO officer (Qasim, the line superintendent handling disconnections and reconnections) after an argument over a disconnected meter:

> Qasim describes the customer's case to me. An ERO (Equipment Removal Order) was issued on the 6th of January. His meter was removed on Feb 1st. The ERO affected letter was issued on Feb 26. On March 31st (today) the customer has come to say that the bill was paid, but didn't have the bill with a payment stamp. He demanded that Qasim complete the RCO (Reconnection Order) process for him. Qasim told

> me: "He had a beard so I only said 'Step away'" [after the customer started to get aggressive].
>
> The customer then demanded that Qasim issue a statement on stamp paper[28] saying that he had paid. When Qasim refused, he then slapped Qasim in the face. This led shortly to the commotion which drew out all of Qasim's colleagues and ended the confrontation.[29]

Once the letter reporting the ERO has been issued, the customer must go through the lengthy RCO process to get their meter reconnected. Prior to that letter being issued a customer need only settle the bill. Qasim deviates from procedure (strictly speaking, the letter should be issued immediately upon removal of the meter) because the disconnection of the meter frequently prompts a customer to settle their bill quickly. In this case the customer claims to have paid the bill between the meter's physical removal and the issuance of the letter but has no receipt to back up his words. Qasim's mention of the man's beard is a reference to the perceived piety in keeping a beard—he doesn't want to fight with a pious person. Qasim was saved from having to fight back himself by the intervention of his colleagues. After the disturbance everyone returned to their offices and work in less than two minutes. The altercation that had just taken place was an unusual occurrence, but one that Qasim's colleague Jaffar could relate to:

> Jaffar said that if that had been him he would have hit the customer. Jaffar tells me the story of someone doing that with him. Jaffar said that he listened to a few threats from a man who had identified himself as the subordinate of an SP [Superintendent of Police]. Then he took both him and the SP and 'threw them both outside.' Jaffar laughs softly. 'I punched him very hard.' [Jaffar is tall and broad shouldered. Qasim is short and rotund.][30]

Violence is certainly not part of the job description of IESCO employees, but it is part of the experience of the job.

Babur (a line superintendent responsible for new connections) regularly has to deal with Cheema sahib, a frequent visitor to the subdivision office who submits and follows up on applications he handles for others. Cheema sahib is about 5′6″ tall, slightly built, with a trimmed mustache and a pointed nose and is typically dressed in a kurta shalwar and tweed jacket. When I asked Cheema sahib how he gets work done at IESCO, he answered "*Bas, darra key*" ('By intimidation'). But Cheema sahib insists that he's never given any money to the IESCO staff and involves two nearby IESCO staff into our discussion to back him up. They affirm that he's never given them any money beyond some money for petrol, though one adds that 'All pay their respects to the court you come from' ("*Jiss darbaar sey aap aatay haiN, wahaaN tau saaray salaam kartey haiN*").[31] The court (*darbaar*) being referred to here is akin to the royal court of the Mughal emperors. He means that Cheema is the representative of a higher power whom all must acknowledge and bow down to in a similar manner to how members of the royal court were once treated. Later on, when Cheema has gone, the same IESCO staff member tells me that Cheema has some connection to the Ministry of Water and Power but doesn't specify to whom. On only one of the dozen or so times that I saw Cheema sahib at the subdivision office did he encounter any resistance to his demands. Cheema had approached Babur regarding a request for a new connection:

> Babur responds saying that 'if the need is for more than 20 meters [of cable] then' "I am very sorry." [for the last part Babur switches from Urdu to English]
> Cheema: [rapid response] 'Don't start your English with me, *behnchod*'[32] and insists that Babur 'do the work.'
> Babur doesn't say anything more.[33]

Babur's use of English is an attempt to reach for a more powerful register with which to resist Cheema sahib's demands. The bureaucratic regulations and paperwork of IESCO are all in English even though the IESCO employees and customers employ either Urdu or one of the regional languages. The harsh vulgarity of Cheema sahib's response shows the disregard of any rules that might apply—Babur's English—and reinforces his superior position. The above exchange is exceptional because Babur tried to resist a powerful customer.

The exchange between Cheema sahib and Babur brings together multiple strands of individual identity and resources that all factor into the contests which belong to the first face of power. Money is not directly mentioned in this exchange—and the staff seem to back Cheema's claim that he doesn't pay them off—but the reference is instead toward the powerful figures whom Cheema claims to represent. Cheema is a fixer for these people who stay in the background but weigh heavily on the front stage activities nonetheless. This secondary claim to power is conveyed through Cheema's generally abrasive personal style, which led to him being widely disliked among the IESCO staff.[34] Babur's response is to reach for the abstract formality of the rules of business expressed in a foreign tongue. The use of English is a sign of education and standing, but it has little effect on Cheema, who proceeds to lash Babur into submission verbally.

Discussion and Conclusions

The everyday experience of securing service delivery in Islamabad reveals how the cultural norms and expectations of behavior in state service delivery leave little room for the operation of formal rules—rules that are neither possible nor desirable to observe. Based on the interviews and observations of my fieldwork, I show how the rules of the game in service delivery are shaped by language, power, rents, and violence as much as they are by the codified rules supposedly governing service delivery. Neither the rulebook nor social reality on their own define the rules of the game, which are instead mutually constituted by the interaction of the two.

If governance reforms are intended to achieve superior development outcomes by changing the rules of the game, then they need to be based on an accurate understanding of what those rules actually are. The unwritten aspects of the rules are just as important as the written, though they may be harder to change. A technocratic mindset and a top-down administration lend themselves well to changing written rules, but in Pakistan, as in many developing countries, internal administrative mechanisms are ineffective and an important cause of poor service delivery. Bureaucratic commands are simply not fulfilled, though the paperwork may suggest compliance. Because behavior in public service is not effectively governed by the formal rules, changes in those rules are unlikely to bring about the desired changes in behavior.

Recognizing the role of culture in constituting the institutional field of governance—along with codified rules—can form a basis for governance reforms that are attentive to a specific situational context. In the Pakistani case, a focus on the formal representations of the state as they are codified and reported would doom reforms from the start, as they would not engage with the reasons behind the inefficiencies of the institutional field as it stands. If development is to be achieved through the institutional reforms of governance, reforms must be based on the state, as its citizens must engage with it for service delivery and not as the state would see itself.

Electricity consumers in Islamabad secure service delivery by showing up in person, by paying IESCO employees for their assistance with improper and proper work, by enforcing their will, and by subverting official procedures or even fighting for what they want. The formal edifice of codified rules can only be accessed and navigated through informal channels and in person. When the rules of the game are understood to incorporate culture and power, then helping citizens navigate the rules of the game becomes an inherently relational exercise rather than a rule-based one. In such a context, instead of reform focused on codified rules, reform must focus on information, collective bargaining, and the avenues available for getting the state to respond that are specific to the context in question.

8

Conclusion

This book started by identifying a key puzzle of the Pakistani power sector, which is not that Pakistan doesn't produce enough electricity, or that its economy keeps getting mired in loadshedding and circular debt, but that these problems persist despite there being a broad understanding of the power sector's key shortcomings, a good sense of what an effective power sector looks like, and no lack of attention from the highest levels of government. The book sets out a theoretical framework to understand better Pakistani state capacity from the ground up (rather than with reference to an ideal-typical institution), and the substantive chapters drive the analysis from the national level down to the city and the individual. Through this exercise of following the material infrastructure of electricity across the breadth of the national territory and down to the lives of ordinary citizens, the goal has been to show how national level issues of circular debt and loadshedding are connected to behaviors at lower levels, as well as to explore how unevenness of state capacity at every level is produced. Each of the national, city, and individual levels of analysis constitutes fields in which there is a struggle over electrical power, with outcomes from below influencing the major challenges at the national level.

This conclusion has several objectives. The first is to summarize the key points of the book by building up from the individual level of analysis to the national challenges. Second, I bring the apex field of national power into the picture of this book's study of the state in Pakistan. Third, I provide some ideas of my own toward addressing key challenges of the power sector. Finally, I also discuss on the recent influx of Chinese investments in the Pakistani power sector as part of the China–Pakistan Economic Corridor (CPEC), which is the flagship effort leading the rollout of the Belt and Road Initiative.

Access to Power. Ijlal Naqvi, Oxford University Press. © Oxford University Press 2022.
DOI: 10.1093/oso/9780197540954.003.0008

Summary of the Book

In Pakistan, an individual's encounter with the front-line state is shaped by money, violence, and connections. The rules of the game for access to electrical power are co-produced between individual citizens in their capacity as power consumers and the street-level bureaucrats with whom they must engage. In the background lurk more powerful figures and organizations who can tilt the field one way or the other to influence the outcome. In this field, power is very much relational, and the formal rules are but one factor among several dictating who gets what, when, and where.

The governance compromises that emerge from the field of front-line state show the operation of formal rules, both in the citizen's struggle to access services and in the street-level bureaucrats' limited ability to enforce them. The steel mill operator paid off street-level bureaucrats simply to access his rights rather than to exceed them. Such compromises reveal the limitations of state capacity, even in the locations where it is supposedly strongest. When the process for appointing a chairman of the National Electric Power Regulatory Authority (NEPRA) was subverted, a senate resolution and media attention weren't sufficient to prevent it. The compromises also show how uneven the state's presence is from neighborhood to neighborhood, even when these areas are served by the same material infrastructure and the same staff at the same office.

The discretion of state officials in the application of rules for service delivery is unavoidable, but such discretion isn't always detrimental. Allowing *katchi abadi* residents to have a communal meter in advance of regularization is hardly magnanimous, but it is at least better than denying them electricity or forcing them to steal. The way in which this discretion is employed—to favor the powerful, serve the needy, or secure personal profit—is influenced by the constraints of organizational culture and a degree of embeddedness in the social context. These social constraints are stronger at the street level and offer less by way of a check or guide at the national level.

The city is revealed as a site of pervasive predation across different types of people, all struggling with some version of the individual's challenge in engaging with the front-line state. Although predation is a concern for all, there is a substantial difference of experience among those who have a formal claim to make and those who don't. The *katchi abadi* manages its informality through collective claim making with a moral valence. However, the transition to a more formal claim making is sometimes problematic for the *katchi abadi* dwellers because formal claim making is inherently an individual effort, and they can't always negotiate that challenge on their own. The rules do not on their own offer respite from this environment of pervasive predation, which residents invoke with the phrase "this is Pakistan."

I treat losses as an indicator of state capacity, associating greater state capacity with lower losses. My modeling strategy explores variation within and across subdivisions to ask whether it is identity of the administrative that drives losses or the social characteristics of the population being served by a given feeder. The models show that the administrative identity of a feeder has relatively little contribution to explaining losses, whereas over half the variation in losses can be explained by the consumer profile of the feeder itself.

Taking a quantitative look across the entire city, the distribution of losses reveals a pattern of state capacity that is more influenced by the social formations specific to a location than by the administration that controls them. Even within a single subdivision, you can find a range of high and low loss feeders, suggesting that specific administrators have little influence on controlling losses. The bureaucrat is just another contestant in field of struggle over access to electrical power, and they are more focused on surviving the influence of powerful actors than in bringing them to heel.

In attempting to penetrate power sector performance we see that governance reforms have failed, that they have failed repeatedly, and that there is a tired set of ideas at their heart that have been recycled across the decades and the world. Most especially, there is only one approach being proposed here, and it involves a kind of governance reform by fiat, and hence a fixation on political will—which is always deemed insufficient or absent—at enforcing the changes in formal institutions that convey the reform in question. These national reform efforts have not attempted to work from below, at the feeder level, of the ways in which citizens engage with the state.

The spatial unevenness of electricity across the entire country of Pakistan is an indicator of the limitations of the reach of the state, or infrastructural power. However, the variations should not be understood as an absence of the state in areas of higher losses, but a manifestation of a sustained historical strategy that has seen the state maintain a primarily extractive relationship with some parts of its territory while making a fuller effort to serve its citizens in other parts of its territory. The state has produced this inequality by design, meaning that this unevenness of the state's presence is a direct result of its chosen mode of operation in these different regions of its territory.

Over the longer history of Pakistan's electrical power sector, we see patterns that are being repeated. There are underlying fault lines that can provoke a crisis under certain conditions. The federal government's fiscal exposure to the power sector through subsidies and the foreign exchange requirements of imported fuels is a source of vulnerability linked to the economy's growth rate, export earnings generating foreign exchange reserves, or the state's overall ability to raise tax revenues. These vulnerabilities are exacerbated by losses, which simply increase the amount that the state must ultimately pay into the power sector to keep it running, and so long as the state is unable to secure timely and complete payments it will continue to be vulnerable.

As Thomas Hughes argued, "electric power systems . . . are both causes and effects of social change" (Hughes, 1983, p. 2). Reformers and analysts will occasionally bemoan the lack of underlying social change that would make power sector management easier. I ask instead if electrical power couldn't be the thin edge of the wedge opening a space for a more responsive state policymaking, which embraces the co-production of local capacity allied to a politics of local service delivery.

A Monist National Identity

Bourdieu termed the apex field where dominant actors from various fields take their relative positions as the field of power.[1] It is in this arena where the most powerful claims to national legitimacy are made, and it is by conditioning the field of power itself that the Pakistani army's influence comes to bear on the national-level field of electrical power. With a track record of four coups and direct military rule over 27 years, the Pakistani state of martial rule (Jalal, 1990) is a central pillar of Pakistani politics. And, as Ayesha Siddiqa has documented, the army's vast commercial interests extend into many domains from agriculture to residential real estate (Siddiqa, 2017).[2]

As could be expected from the approach of using the electrical power sector as a lens on the state, it is rare that the army comes directly into view in this study. There are a few exceptions, particularly in the interprovincial political economy of electrical power, but also in the largely forgotten episode where the army took over direct management of electrical power distribution from 1998 to 2001.[3] Mostly the army is behind the scenes of the electrical power sector rather than a direct influence. Chapter 2 argued that the sub-national variation in electricity governance is both the product of internal provincial politics and the product of the province's relations with the federal center, in which the army has a substantial influence. Part of the bargain that binds the provinces of the federation together is the policy of shared pricing for all Pakistani electricity consumers, whence the tariff differential subsidy is born. This common pricing structure follows from a centralized administration of electricity and fits with a singular and unified national identity for Pakistan in which minority voices are suppressed.

The monist national identity (Berlin, 2002) that the Pakistani state propagates is championed in no small part by the army, whose constitutionally designated role as guardian of Pakistan's external borders has been used as a justification for its domestic interventions. Coups aside, the army has heavily shaped the boundaries of acceptable speech in Pakistan and the politics of "common sense."[4] The monist knows a singular truth and that singular vision is the unitary identity to which all must belong. By contrast, a pluralist approach allows for differences, such as ethnicities, that are both commonplace and perhaps inevitable. These questions of nationalism animate certain approaches to policy.[5] The monist national identity underlies the common generation pool and the tariff differential subsidy. This entails all the fiscal exposures that come with them, but so long as losses and the practices of governing remain local as they are, and political as they are, the state will forever struggle to implement governance reforms in this paradigm.

This not to say that the pluralist approach is guaranteed success, but there is at least a pathway that leads from local-level action to national policies in the pluralist approach. The key is connecting politicians from the provincial level and below to serving their people, in a "deepening of democracy" in which its symbolic, procedural, and substantive aspects all reinforce each other (Fung & Wright, 2003; Heller, 2000). However, democracy can't be deepened if the national security apparatus is interfering in domestic politics, disbursing patronage, and guiding the same usual suspects into cabinet time and again. Not only does space have to be made for a programmatic politics to emerge, but decentralizing the administrative controls (and more political responsibility) to provincial and local levels can also serve to defuse the ethnicization of politics in terms of the rivalry between the federal center and the provinces. In such a set up the Council of Common Interests—which is structurally geared to give provinces a strong voice—would become even more important as a coordinating instrument, and thus there would need to be investment in developing the capacity of that institutional body. Pursuing the initiatives described under transparency and decentralization in the previous section would reinforce such a move.

But this book never sought to reimagine Pakistan or to advocate for an alternate vision of national identity. Instead, my goal was to use the approach of the infrastructural state to build an understanding of the state from the ground up, connecting the lived experience of individual citizens and firms to national issues. The ideas for policy interventions are based on a desire to work with the state and the society as they actually are, rather than attempt a radical reshaping of the national field of power. Thus, the policy suggestions just discussed do not depend on a movement toward the adoption of a pluralist national identity, though they are compatible with it. Nonetheless, I hold that the monist view of national identity championed by the army—and its many supporters—is an obstacle to Pakistan's development, as demonstrated by its centrality to Pakistan's extended history of civil conflicts (Butt, 2017).

Ideas for Power Sector Interventions

Increased Transparency

The Pakistani power sector suffers from a lack of transparency around its administration, both internally and in its relationships with civil society. The transparency I envision is enabled by combining a granular level of operating data with maps of the service areas of the distribution companies. The maps should be oriented toward the commercial and administrative side of the distribution company rather than its engineering functions, but they will spatially represent key aspects of operating data for both internal users (i.e., the leadership of the distribution company) and external users, which could involve a variety of civil society, academic, and political actors.[6] Alongside the spatial representation of operating information, externally oriented services delivered through simple mobile phone services involving SMS messaging could provide loadshedding schedules and other useful information to any user.

The provision of useful and comprehensible information to end users will create the possibility of a feedback loop that enables citizens to put pressure on distribution companies. The primitive version of this concept is the protests and riots that occur all too often around electricity shortages. It is possible for social mobilization to provide the necessary pressure, as Evans (2009) argues is the case in Kerala for health provision, but a more systematic approach is for civil society groups to take up the mantle of serving as an array of sensors to guide policy development and implementation in a 21st-century developmental state (Evans & Heller, 2015).

Within the state bureaucracy, an improved degree of insight within the distribution company can be allied to initiatives such as the citizen feedback model in the Punjab, wherein mid-level bureaucrats increase their oversight over street-level bureaucrats by connecting directly with end users to gain insight into state performance (Masud, 2014). The citizen feedback model is an indigenous innovation that successfully increased the performance monitoring of state services such as healthcare and land revenue.

Decentralize the Management of Subsidies and Circular Debt

Political commitments from the federal center to specific constituencies and subunits make substantial contributions to circular debt.[7] Each of these concessions has its own justification in the history of center–province relations. Taken together, these concessions have a substantial bearing on the federal budget. These include tube well subsidies in Balochistan and subsidized electricity pricing in Azad Jammu and Kashmir (AJK), but there is a broader sense in which circular debt accumulates as distribution companies (primarily those outside the Punjab) accrue arrears and exceed their stipulated targets for losses. Beyond these factors, the federal government can often fall behind on meeting its commitment to the tariff differential subsidy. There is a fundamental disconnection between the federal center, which bears the costs, and the prospects for enforcement, which lie with local state capacity at the provincial level and below.

One possible approach to resolving this impasse is to devolve energy subsidy budgets to the province level or below. Until and unless responsibility and accountability for electricity losses are at an appropriate level of the administrative hierarchy, center–province politics will continue to get in the way, and the central state's orientation toward patronage and neo-patrimonial politics of disorder (at the expense of programmatic politics) will remain an obstacle. Decentralization to the level of the province and below creates an opportunity to foster a programmatic politics of local service delivery and improved governance. Ideally, a dynamic would be enabled whereby provincial and local politicians could compete over the effectiveness of administering service provision to their constituents. The high profile of electricity problems on the political stage suggests that politicians would love to be able to claim that they have delivered improved electricity supply to their constituents.

The suggestions to increase transparency and push decentralization are geared toward producing the interaction of feedback loops that serve programmatic politics. A powerful description of such an effort can be found in the provision of primary healthcare in Ceara, Brazil (Tendler, 1997). The outcome can change the calculus of politics so that a service delivery agenda is more appealing to politicians seeking votes, but this result will only be produced if the level at which information and administrative action are taken can be matched to the appropriately decentralized level of elected official. However, the danger with such efforts to change political incentives is that they can provoke responses from the federal center. The response from the center will be especially likely to overcome any decentralizing reforms if these responses are backed by the army, which seeks pliable politicians ready to give their votes in exchange for opportunities to provide patronage to their supporters.

Strengthen Organizational Culture

In an environment where informality is rife and discretion is widespread, relying on formal rules and punitive action to control abuse of public office is a one-dimensional approach with a demonstrated track record of failure. In such a setting, both Piore (2011) and Zaloznaya (2017) encourage looking to organizational culture as a constraint against abuses and as a way of channeling discretion toward more constructive ends. Pakistan has had constructive experience with organizational culture as an enabler of pockets of institutional excellence, with the motorway police being the best-known case (Ayub & Hussain, 2016; Noor, 2009). The motorway police are widely regarded as being one of the least corrupt institutions in the country, and their example suggests that strengthening organizational culture can be very effective. While their salaries are 50%–75% higher than those of comparable bureaucrats, Noor attributes their superior performance to social disapproval and expectations of fair dealings within the organization rather than the salaries alone.

End Collective Punishment through Loadshedding

Although Karachi Electric has improved its overall performance with respect to losses by selectively allocating loadshedding to high-loss areas, this policy has questionable ethical foundations and should be reversed. The policy represents a form of collective punishment because it affects all residents of poor neighborhoods, not just those who don't pay. It also institutionalizes the dynamic whereby a better class of service is provided to the wealthy. Moreover, it turns the state away from the task of extending its reach to areas that are currently high loss but are also neglected from the perspective of state service delivery more generally. Any reduction in aggregate losses achieved through the policy of preferentially allocating electricity to low-loss areas, that is, by loadshedding more in high-loss areas, may simply be the result of redirecting supply. It has not been shown that high-loss areas have changed to become low-loss areas as a result of this strategy. The state needs to meet its responsibility to serve all sectors of the population—not just work within the confines of an unequal citizenship where only those with wealth are considered fully deserving of rights and high-quality service.[8]

Focus on Solar and Wind

There are many valid environmental arguments for focusing on renewables over fossil fuels (in the Pakistan context, see Asif, 2011). I focus on an argument that is more based on accounting and cash flows. A primary source of difficulty for the Pakistani power sector is in the burden it puts on the federal government to make payments in hard currency on a regular basis for the delivery of fossil fuels (particularly furnace oil, but also coal and to a lesser extent liquified natural gas). Not only do wind- and solar-powered plants have remarkably low operating costs, but also their power output is not related to any ongoing requirement for importing expensive foreign fuels. Although the energy output from wind and solar plants fluctuates in a manner that requires appropriate planning, their financing costs (which still fluctuate with exchange rates, although not with fuel prices) won't have an effect on continued power production.

There are other structural and long-term considerations that make wind and solar a good choice. Pakistani cities are already suffering from poor air quality, which will only worsen with the addition of coal-fired power plants.[9] Coal plants also place a demand on water availability that should be considered in addition to their total costs because it has a known effect for irrigation. It should be possible to grow a local capacity to develop, operate, and maintain wind and solar plants, particularly since these are areas where there is Chinese expertise to draw on. Such technical cooperation has not yet been a feature of CPEC, but there is no reason why Pakistani and Chinese universities could not cooperate on developing institutes for training Pakistani engineers within renewable energy technologies. The fact that long-term cost prospects for renewable energies will decline over time makes it even more logical to invest not only in renewable power plants, but also in the skills and organizational capacity to deploy them.

Pakistan's costing for power plants is managed by NEPRA, which will express these costs on a per-unit (i.e., kilowatt hour) basis. Wind and solar plants, however, have such low operating costs that a per-unit cost that reflects the capital costs of their installation is a slight misrepresentation. In a similar but opposite vein, the per-unit costs of hydroelectric power are set at very low levels, dam advocates in Pakistan tout the benefits of cheap power, but dam construction has enormous capital costs that evidence from around the world suggests is almost never justified (Flyvbjerg, 2014; Khagram, 2004; World Commission on Dams, 2000). Unlike hydropower, wind and solar power plants do not rely on a valuable resource such as water, whose timing and availability are hotly contested political commodities.[10] While a single metric such as cost per unit can only do so much work, wind and solar plants offer benefits beyond what their per-unit costs represent. That said, the per-unit costs of solar power in particular have declined to a degree whereby they are now cost competitive with coal, which leaves even less reason not to pursue them. Moreover, it is one more way to lessen Pakistan's reliance on international energy markets, including its erstwhile allies in the Persian Gulf.

Stop Monetizing Geopolitics

Pakistan has made a long habit of monetizing geopolitics—of using its strategic position on the Eurasian landmass as a pressure point to extract funds from allies.

As debts from a mismanaged power sector accumulate, this pressure will likely worsen. There are significant costs associated with this approach. Pakistan's dependence on the United States and Saudi Arabia leaves it unable to benefit from the natural gas pipeline with Iran that has already been built out on the Iranian side. Saudi influence leaves Pakistan ever more open to funds that are sent for Islamic welfare but contribute to polarizing sectarian tensions and supporting the growth of conservative religious views. Pakistan is currently positioned for the federal center to use instability in Afghanistan to its advantage, as it is a crucial ally for U.S. involvement in Afghanistan and a key player in the peace talks, but less attention has been given to the advantages of peace in Afghanistan.

Among the many benefits of having a stable and peaceful Afghanistan as a neighbor is the potential to pursue the Turkmenistan-Uzbekistan-Tajikistan-Afghanistan-Pakistan (TUTAP) project. TUTAP proposes to build Afghanistan's electricity transmission infrastructure so that power from cheaper central Asian sources (gas in Turkmenistan, oil in Tajikistan, and hydroelectric power in Kyrgyzstan) could be delivered to Pakistan. Afghanistan would earn sufficient income from the wheeling charges (essentially a toll on the use of its transmission lines) to fund its own power consumption, as well as have a future-ready energy backbone built out, and with the potential for hugely increasing its own electrification. The shared benefits to all parties involved in this project would in effect serve as a peacebuilding exercise, establishing a basis for cooperation and trust among partners who have long suffered without a lot of previous experience of constructive regional cooperation (Huda & Ali, 2017).

The China–Pakistan Economic Corridor

In their scale and unaffordability, the changes to the energy sector under CPEC bear more than a passing resemblance to the private power plants (IPPs) built under the 1994 policy. Once again, there are allegations of corruption as well as attempts by the Government of Pakistan to renegotiate its contractual commitment to purchasing power. At the heart of Pakistan's continuing struggles with the power sector despite the newfound abundance of capacity is—as before with the 1994 IPPs—a question of managing the sector's cash flows in a sustainable manner. The stock of unpaid electricity bills ("arrears") in fiscal year 2020 was Rs. 2,150 billion, an increase of Rs. 538 billion from 2019, a mind-boggling 5% of GDP! The government's Circular Debt Management Plan (CDMP) as presented to the cabinet in March 2021 proposed to reduce the accumulation of circular debt by tariff increases coupled with efficiency gains in distribution. Those tariff increases proved politically infeasible. In the longer run, power prices to the government would be reduced through renegotiating power purchase agreements with IPPs, but these reforms are dependent on ensuring that distribution companies (DISCOs) can manage cash flows adequately. While the CDMP of 2021 doesn't provide details on how to reduce losses and increase collections—nor is it the place for those details—NEPRA's Performance Evaluation Report for Distribution Companies in 2019–2020 laments the continuation of "business as usual" and despairingly calls for privatization as the only viable remedy (National Electric Power Regulatory Authority, 2020, p. 2).

When Tilly (1985, p. 170) claimed that "War makes states," he was referring to the instruments and institutions of the state that were generated, refined, and developed as a result of the imperatives of war making, of the need to raise revenue and the need to channel that revenue into productive capacity and specifically into the instruments of war. John Brewer (1989) called this the sinews of power, referring to the Whitehall clerks who managed the taxation paperwork and administration at the rise of the British Empire. Louis XIV backed the Canal du Midi because it competed with war for its "ambition and symbolic possibility" (Mukerji, 2009, p. 16), but developing the logistics to deliver that project developed state capacities for impersonal rule that underpinned the development of the modern French state.

What the Pakistani government did not attempt, and what CPEC consequently lacks, is the sense of mission to develop such a project domestically, to nurture it through internal contests of politics, to bind domestic actors toward one purpose under a common authority. CPEC, because the use of domestic logistics and resources is so minimal, has not cultivated indigenous state capacity. By abandoning the logistics of infrastructure development, Pakistan hopes to achieve the accoutrements of statehood and state performance without doing the hard work of building state capacity. All of this is being left behind in the insistent rush toward achieving given objectives such as ending loadshedding (no doubt a worthwhile objective). Yet achieving it in this way will be hollow, and perhaps not sustainable, because the most consequential gains of building state capacity organically will have been undermined, which are a symbolic and practical unity of purpose channeled through state instruments toward delivering what the people of Pakistan actually need.

NOTES

Chapter 1

1. "Governance" is a broad term with various meanings. The *Oxford Handbook of Governance* includes a range of meanings for governance as "structure, process, mechanism, and strategy," of which my usage most closely corresponds with governance as process, or "the practices of governing" (Levi-Faur, 2012, pp. 8–9).
2. I thank an anonymous reviewer for suggesting this phrasing.
3. The World Bank's Enterprise Surveys found that 15.6% of firms in 89 countries including Pakistan considered electricity to be the most serious constraint to business operations. The only constraint cited more often—by 15.7% of respondents—was access to finance (World Bank, 2010, p. 3). Of Pakistani firms surveyed in 2007, 78% identified electricity as a major or very severe obstacle, up from 50% in 2002. A 2003 Lahore University of Management Sciences survey of the investment climate found that 80% of small and medium enterprises had deferred investment due to the cost and reliability of electricity (Haq, 2005).
4. The Ministry of Finance (2011) estimate does not contain a great deal of detail, but a more rigorous explanation is provided by the Institute of Public Policy at Beaconhouse National University (2010). Some of the underlying research behind the determination of key parameters for this estimate are, however, quite dated (Pasha, Ghaus, & Malik, 1989).
5. *The Daily Times*, March 30, 2008.
6. See Husain (2018) for a brief summary and comment.
7. In 2015, $37 billion worth of Memoranda of Understanding were signed for CPEC energy projects when Chinese Premier Xi Jinping visited Pakistan (Haider, 2015). Exactly which projects should be considered as part of CPEC is a contested and fluctuating issue. The official CPEC website now features approximately $17 billion worth of "priority" energy projects: http://cpec.gov.pk/energy (last accessed December 10, 2020).
8. A *nazim* is the head of local government and comparable to a mayor.
9. See Timothy Mitchell's *Carbon Democracy* (2011) on the materiality of energy production and the implications for democracy. Mitchell's analysis is international in scope, encompassing the colonial era and its aftermath. The approach of this book is centered on Pakistan, but still part of and subject to the international dynamics of energy politics.
10. One reason why economists may have come to occupy this space is a disciplinary willingness to make prescriptive suggestions when other social scientists will typically reserve judgement behind scholarly caveats and nuance (Fourcade, Ollion, & Algan, 2015).
11. However, scholars often restrict themselves to the formal rules even when building on North's formulation of institutions. Daron Acemoglu et al.'s (2001) widely cited paper linking the strength of current institutions in the Global South to European settler mortality uses a commercially developed risk of expropriation as a measure of the strength of formal institutions. The details of the "cluster of institutions" that the authors are interested in include "constraints

on government expropriation, independent judiciary, property rights enforcement, and institutions providing equal access to education and ensuring civil liberties, that are important to encourage investment and growth" (Acemoglu et al., 2001, pp. 1370–1371, footnote 1373). Despite the breadth of the authors' interests across legal, political, economic, and social institutions, the variable employed is a "Risk of Expropriations" as a proxy for institutions, an indicator developed by a company that provides political risk assessments for international business. The operation of institutions is thus reduced to a single black box (Acemoglu et al., 2001, p. 1396), a situation not remedied by a later paper unbundling the effects of property rights institutions (Acemoglu & Johnson, 2005, p. 988), which still asks how institutions have their effect.

12. For an overview of this substantial and influential literature, see Haggard (2018).
13. da Cruz et al. (2019, p. 9) are unimpressed by the long and indeterminate causal chains of new institutionalism: "But being at the center of a feedback loop—institutions 'somehow' influence policy outcomes that may 'somehow' lead to institutional reform—and contingent on so many aspects, such as the policy sectors in question, how should political leaders engage with their design?"
14. The field is a flexible enough sociological concept to have been applied to numerous empirical cases ranging from the forms of British and U.S. imperialism (Go, 2008) to 19-century French gastronomy (P. P. Ferguson, 1998), the exclusion of Ahmedis in Pakistan (Saeed, 2017), and women's protest movements in India (Ray, 1999). Swartz's (2013) summation and commentary on Bourdieu's political sociology serve as an excellent reference on fields.
15. Some prominent recent treatments of emergence span organizational theory (Padgett & Powell, 2012) and critical realism (Gorski, 2016). Moreover, Giddens' (1984) structuration theory, in which social structures both shape and are constantly being shaped by individual actions, is a broadly influential theoretical position in the social sciences that has emergent processes at its core.
16. For an overview of how complexity science can inform development thinking, see Ramalingam (2013).
17. The original statement of the key Washington Consensus policies was provided by Williamson (1990).
18. For a view of some of the scholarship in this field inspired by Hughes, see the edited volume *Technologies of Power* (Hecht & Allen, 2001).
19. See Manu Goswami's (2004, p. 104) description of colonial-era rail travel and its legacies in India, where civil servants were required to take a rail journey across the country as part of their orientation process: "As a privileged vector of colonial state space, railways not only enabled the masses and unprecedented circulation of peoples and commodities within the boundaries of colonial India. They were also key sites for the institution of the colonial political economy of difference, the refashioning of everyday experience and collective self-understandings, and the shaping of a range of categories of practice."
20. See Anand (2017) and Bjorkman (2015) for studies of water and citizenship in Mumbai. Earlier, Robert Wade (1982, p. 287) studied irrigation systems in South India both to learn about irrigation and "to illuminate more general features of Indian government and society."
21. For a fuller discussion, see the special issue of *Studies in Comparative International Development* edited by Soifer and vom Hau (2008). More recently, a special issue of *Revista* (Altman & Luna, 2012) has explored infrastructural power in Latin America. Soifer's (2015) book urges a context-specific set of measures attentive to the local context and elaborates this idea through an empirical engagement with state-building in Latin America.
22. O'Donnell's statement on uneven stateness shaped the views of many, including Centeno et al. (2017, p. 16): "We also need to understand that the state is not a solid mass equally present throughout a territory, but a fluid variable that is more and less present and one part or another."
23. Unlike Foucauldian bio-power, however, what Ferguson saw in Lesotho did not amount to the imposition of a single rationality analogous to the disciplining and optimization of the body. State actors in Lesotho—and across the Global South—might aspire to such a role, but it lies beyond their capacity.

24. Tariq Ali (1983) questioned whether Pakistan could survive, and Pakistan scores poorly in indices of state fragility and failure, ranking 20th in the world (Fund for Peace, 2018). However, as Lieven (2012) notes, reports of Pakistan's demise may be premature. For other broader recent works on Pakistan, see (Jalal, 2014; Shaikh, 2009; Talbot, 2009). In a study of Karachi under the rule of the Muttahida Qaumi Movement (a situation that has since changed), Gayer (2014) described a condition of "ordered disorder" in which the violence of local politics destabilized opponents while reinforcing the MQM's dominant position.
25. Lieven's original title for *Pakistan: A Hard Country* was "How Pakistan Works," with a goal of showing that "it has actually worked according to its own imperfect functional patterns" (Lieven, 2012, p. 19). In my use of the phrase "Pakistan works," and as is evident from the discussion of Chabal and Daloz (Chabal & Daloz, 1999), I focus on who Pakistan works for as well as question the degree to which the patterns of its workings should be described as developmental.
26. A more extensive critique of methodological nationalism can be found in the agenda of *Global Historical Sociology*, which adopts instead the position of methodological relationalism, examining "the ways in which entities in motion are historically constituted and reconstituted via their interactions with other actors" (Go & Lawson, 2017, p. 27). I am sympathetic to the relationalist position described by Go and Lawson (and their allied contributors), but this book reorients their approach by being less historical. The first substantive chapter will address the historical constitution of the Pakistani electrical power sector, but the book thereafter is more oriented toward the present-day inequalities and unevenness within the Pakistani infrastructural state.
27. The name "Farid" is a pseudonym, as are all the names of my informants. *Sahib* is an Urdu word that roughly translates as "mister" and is used as a polite (though not overly deferential) honorific.

Chapter 2

1. The 10 distribution companies in Pakistan are known as DISCOs. They are named for the areas (and typically the largest city) that they serve: Islamabad, IESCO; Lahore, LESCO; Faisalabad, FESCO; Gujranwala, GEPCO; Peshawar, PESCO; Hyderabad, HESCO; Multan, MEPCO; Sukkur, SEPCO; Quetta, QESCO; the Federally Administered Tribal Areas (now incorporated into Khyber Pukhtunkhwa), TESCO.
2. See the research of Naomi Hossain and collaborators on energy riots in fragile contexts (Hossain et al., 2018).
3. See Naqvi et al. (2021) for a review of electricity losses in economistic and humanistic academic literature.
4. Field notes, April 6, 2009.
5. Note that even the economic development initiatives conceived of for Balochistan, such as the Reko Diq mining project, are primarily extractive and do not entail investment in the local population.
6. The data for this chart is taken from *Power System Statistics, 43rd Edition* (National Transmission and Despatch Company, 2019, pp. 42–43).
7. The declining capability of the Pakistani state apparatus over time is an idea supported by many scholars and offered as a partial explanation for poor governance outcomes in Pakistan. Ilhan Niaz (2010) takes the view that the inheritance of the Indian Civil Service (the "steel frame" of the raj) was diluted over time, resulting in a diminished capacity. Prime Minister Zulfiqar Ali Bhutto's mass dismissal of 2,000 civil servants in March 1972 is a key turning point toward personalization and politicization of governance, after which directives from the prime minister replaced "resource-allocation decisions based on multi-year planning made by technocrats in the Planning Commissions" (LaPorte, 1991, p. 117). Ishrat Husain gives a broader context to the decline of the civil service: "The top-down nature of the administrative fabric, the control mind set of the decisionmakers, and the centrally-commanded ways of doing things are major factors accentuating this fragility" (I. Husain, 2000, p. 401). The decline in achievement of planning targets suggests some support for these views.

However, not all observers are so favorable about the early days of the bureaucracy in Pakistan. Hamza Alavi condemned the senior officers for a mentality born of clerking for "White masters," a primary concern with their own survival, and having "neither the will nor the ability to take responsibility" for innovation (Alavi, 2003, italics added). Hamza Alavi's view that Pakistani bureaucrats are risk averse to the point of inaction has been repeated to me in interviews with serving and retired bureaucrats who identify the imbalance between potential punishment for doing something versus limited rewards for innovation.

8. Victor and Heller's (2007) comparative study came to this conclusion.
9. This technical audit was based on a survey of five feeders.
10. The audit report was for an investigation of the Kasur circle, which is one of eight such circles in LESCO. For the Kasur circle alone, a cumulative amount of Rs. 627 million was written off between 2009 and 2011 as a "credit adjustment" rather than recovered (K. Husain, 2012).
11. In 2012–2013, the World Bank determined that the Tariff Differential Subsidy comprised 96% of total electricity subsidies (World Bank, 2017).
12. NEPRA presentation on Power Sector Regulation, October 4, 2010.
13. Total Government Revenues for FY2009–2010 were Rs. 2,590 billion according to the Ministry of Finance's State of the Economy Report (Ministry of Finance, 2010).
14. Bulk supply consumers are those who take 11 kV or more directly from the distribution company. One example is Bahria Town, a private real estate developer that builds housing societies (similar to a suburban subdivisions in the United States) and manages the electricity metering and distribution itself for the residents. The distribution company then only has to serve one bulk consumer rather than many individuals.
15. No data was available for this study that would allow us to break down the difference between technical and nontechnical losses. While the causes of the two are different, it is reasonable to assume that they covary as maintenance of electricity distribution infrastructure is likely to decline in poorer areas where higher losses are typically found.
16. A major premise of this and later chapters is the viability of using electricity losses to study variations in state capacity. Taxes are in many senses a more classic focus for such a study, and the field of fiscal sociology examines the topic in great detail (see, e.g., I. W. Martin, Mehrotra, & Prasad, 2009). While developing the ideas that led this research project, I considered studying taxes but saw little prospect for gaining entry to the tax bureaucracy. Further, while electricity is a common feature of everyday life in Pakistan that connects almost everyone to the state, a much smaller percentage of the population pays direct income taxes. A mere 2.178 million individuals and companies were listed by the Federal Board of Revenue as active taxpayers in 2021.
17. Field notes, April 6, 2009.
18. In the concluding statement its staff mission issued in November 2021, the IMF reported progress toward implementation "[d]espite a difficult environment," highlighting achievements such as the amendment of the NEPRA Act, higher power tariffs, and payments of arrears to IPPs (International Monetary Fund, 2021).
19. See Table G-3 in *Electricity Marketing Data* (National Transmission and Despatch Company, 2010, p. 5).
20. There are several reasons why the simple sum of power plant–installed capacities is a misleading measure of what the national system can produce. Firstly, every power plant must be maintained, with annual maintenance typically taking up perhaps one month in every year when that power plant will be unavailable. Secondly, system reliability is ensured through spinning reserves—capacity that is reserved as backup in the event of a failure in other parts of the system. In times of power shortages such as most of the period from 2006 to 2015, however, reliability from maintaining spinning reserves is typically foregone, and that capacity is committed to generation instead. Thirdly, wear and tear on the machinery is reflected in what is called the "derated capacity"—what the power plant can produce at the current time as opposed to the date of its installation. Lastly, breakdowns of the equipment and the availability of fuel are reflected in the dependable capacity, which is what the power system can be relied upon to produce on any given day. Installed capacity is the sum of derated capacities of individual power plants and is widely reported, but dependable capacity—the more accurate measure—is never reported because it fluctuates too often. These inaccuracies

notwithstanding, installed capacity is the upper limit of what is available, and it is still indicative of the total power generation capacity in the system as a whole.

21. The data for this figure is taken from the Planning Commission's Five Year Plans and Medium Term Development Framework as well as the National Transmission and Despatch Company's Power System Statistics. The data on installed capacity at the start of the plan and planned additions is drawn from the plan in question. For the first four plans, only figures for public utilities are included. Targets and capacities of power plants in Bangladesh as well as industrial facilities are excluded. IPPs added after 1994 are included. Data on the achieved gain in installed capacity is taken from the next five-year plan, unless noted otherwise. All years here refer to fiscal years ending on June 30.
22. On the Planning Commission website (www.planningcommisison.gov.pk) where all five-year plans are, the Fourth Five-Year plan is labeled "The Non-Plan Years." The Fourth Plan is included here out of completeness as—even less than the other plans—it ceased to provide a guiding framework after 1971.
23. The *Medium Term Development Framework* is a plan produced by the Planning Commission to guide the Government of Pakistan through the period of 2005–2010. It is not, however, one of the numbered five-year plans, though there is no significant difference in approach or content between the MTDF and a five-year plan.
24. The Ninth and Tenth Plans were never published. Preparations for the energy-related sections of the Tenth Five-Year Plan were made by USAID-funded consultants working alongside the Energy wing of the Planning Commission in 2011, but no Tenth Five-Year Plan was ever published. I was able to obtain no records at all of the Ninth Five-Year Plan.
25. Hussain, "Hours of Darkness," *Dawn*, 2018, available at https://www.dawn.com/news/1412587/hours-of-darkness.
26. Field notes, June 2011.
27. The episode was covered in *Dawn* (for example, see AFP, 2011).
28. For a more extended discussion of this contentious topic, see Butt (2017) and Saikia (2011), among many others.
29. Arundhati Roy's account of the popular resistance organized by the Narmada Bachao Andolan against the Sardar Samovar Dam on the Narmada River in India is perhaps the best known of these efforts (Arundhati Roy, 1999). Sanjeev Khagram puts the Narmada Bachao Andolan into a broader cross-national perspective (Khagram, 2004). See Haines (2013) for the heroic rhetoric of empire- and nation-building invoked in hydraulic engineering projects in Sindh.
30. Lal Shahbaz Qalandar is also known as Jhule Lal. Jhule Lal is an incarnation of a Hindu deity whose home is the River Indus itself. For a fuller account of Lal Shahbaz Qalandar and associated practices of worship at his shrine, see Frembgen (2011).
31. See Shams ul Mulk's comments as reported in *Dawn*, May 22, 2012, https://www.dawn.com/news/720405.
32. *Country Analysis Brief: Pakistan*, December 2006, available at www.eia.doe.gov.
33. Dates of previous insurgencies were 1948, 1958–1960, 1962–1969, and 1973–1977. Ahmad (2011) reports 1,600 casualties in 1,850 conflict incidents, of which 50% are civilians, 23% militants, and 22% security forces.
34. Presentation of the QESCO chief executive officer to the Planning Commission Workshop on Power Sector Reforms, October 5, 2010.
35. "Balochistan Timeline," South Asia Terrorism Portal, Institute for Conflict Management, New Delhi. Available at http://www.satp.org/satporgtp/countries/pakistan/Balochistan/timeline/index.html#.
36. Sandor Peto, "Hungary's MOL Says Two Workers Killed in Pakistan," *Reuters*, January 20, 2011. Available at https://www.reuters.com/article/pakistan-killings-idAFLDE70J2AZ20110120.
37. Field notes June 22, 2011.
38. This is a recent development whose full effects won't be seen for some time to come. There are too many uncertainties as to how and when FATA's full integration will be handled to allow me to comment.

39. Veena Das argues that "Because the state project is always an unfinished project, it is best observed at the margins, but these margins are not simply peripheral places—they run into the body of the polity as rivers run through a territory" (Das, 2007, p. 183).
40. Field notes, April 21, 2011. I visited Gomal Zam as a member of a USAID team supporting a press event to commemorate the construction of the dam. I was working as a consultant with the contractor through which USAID support to the construction of the dam was being managed.
41. See Flyvbjerg (2014) for a review of megaprojects across the world that are over time, are over budget, and under-deliver on their promises, time and again.
42. The plant at Port Qasim (in Karachi) with almost identical specifications sells its power to the national grid at a lower cost than the Sahiwal plant. Although they both use imported fuel, the fuel cost component of the Port Qasim plant is 5.5406 Rs/kWh compared with 7.7756 Rs/kWh for the Sahiwal plant. It is reasonable to attribute this differential to the cost of transporting the coal over 1,000 km north to Sahiwal from Karachi. Details on coal tariffs are available from NEPRA at https://nepra.org.pk/tariff/Generation%20IPPs%20Coal.php.
43. Munawar Hasan, "Sahiwal Coal-Fired Power Plants Feared Closure on Non-Payment of Dues," *The News*, April 3, 2018. Available at https://www.thenews.com.pk/print/299722-sahiwal-coal-fired-power-plants-feared-closure-on-non-payment-of-dues. Last accessed March 29, 2019.

Chapter 3

1. DFID merged with the Foreign and Commonwealth Office in 2020 to form the Foreign and Commonwealth Development Office (FCDO).
2. Looking at eight developing countries from 1990 to 2006, Phadke (2009) found that the stated capital costs for independent power producers selected through competitive bidding were 44%–56% lower than those selected without competitive bidding.
3. Field notes, June 14, 2011.
4. In my own capacity as a USAID contractor, I handled requests for such reports and the need to produce success stories at regular intervals.
5. Relatedly, international development initiatives such as the Private Infrastructure Development Group are unapologetically focused on supporting the role of the private sector in infrastructure provision for development impact.
6. See also Rueschemeyer and Evans (1985).
7. The need to have a feedback loop that links state decision-making to its consequences for ordinary people is underlined in Evans and Heller's (2015) reformulation of the classic developmental state paradigm for the 21st century.

Chapter 4

1. For a review, see Smith (2004).
2. NEPRA gives the total transmission losses for the PEPCO system at 2.73% for 2015 (National Electric Power Regulatory Authority, 2016).
3. Collecting on those bills, while in many respects an equally important challenge for managing cash flows, typically gets lets attention than losses.
4. See Rowland and Passoth (2015) for a review of recent science and technology studies (STS) scholarship on the state that highlights a key intellectual antecedent in the question posed by Langdon Winner (1980), "Do artefacts have politics?"
5. Nonetheless, during my fieldwork and in pursuing this data set over several years, I did visit LESCO headquarters and WAPDA House many times for conversations with utility management. I was born in Lahore, and the majority of my immediate family members (as well as a *lot* of extended family) live there. Lahore is the primary location of my personal and familial attachment to Pakistan.
6. The 2017 census summaries are available at: https://www.pbs.gov.pk/content/population-census.

7. These numbers are derived from a list provided by LESCO (personal communication, June 12, 2015). The exact numbers in the descriptive statistics and quantitative modeling are slightly different due to the data cleaning necessary for a statistical analysis. For reference, the LESCO website in 2021 identifies eight circles, 39 divisions, and 199 subdivisions (no such definitive statement is currently available for 2015). The term "operational" distinguishes circles used to supply electricity to consumers from the Grid Systems Operations (GSO) circle and the Project Construction circle, which have other responsibilities but use the same administrative nomenclature.
8. In the data set provided by LESCO, the median number of feeders per subdivision is 6, while the modal number is 3. This distribution has an extremely long tail, which skews the mean (7.8) due to there being 80 feeders in the industrial subdivision, which is based on an administrative and thematic grouping rather than on geographic contiguity.
9. The average household size in Lahore per the 2017 census is 6.3.
10. Government effectiveness per the World Governance Indicators website is defined as: "Government effectiveness captures perceptions of the quality of public services, the quality of the civil service and the degree of its independence from political pressures, the quality of policy formulation and implementation, and the credibility of the government's commitment to such policies." Available at http://info.worldbank.org/governance/wgi/. Last Accessed May 18, 2022.
11. There is a discrepancy in Pakistan's level of losses between official government figures from NEPRA and NTDC compared with the World Development Indicators (WDIs), from which the data for this figure is drawn. I use the WDI figures for consistency of comparison across countries. However, even if we use the higher NEPRA figures, Pakistan would still be below the line of best fit.
12. I define medium and heavy Industries in terms of tariff categories B2, B3, and B4. I categorize B1 as light industry. The details of these tariff categories are as follows: B1 is for connections up to 25 kW at 230/400 V; B2 is for 25–500 kW at 400 V; B3 is for up to 5000 kW at 11 or 33 kV; B4 is at 66 or 132 kV, or above (National Electric Power Regulatory Authority, 2016).
13. There is one industrial subdivision that is thematic rather than geographic and serves 80 feeders of entirely medium and heavy industrial consumption, amounting to 21% of all LESCO consumption for this category. Almost all the consumption is for B3 categories. A small amount is in the "Others" category, though this is likely to be bulk supply. Losses for this subdivision are 0.4%.
14. The approximated borders of each subdivision are Thiessen polygons that are drawn based on a single a point location for each subdivision. The reference point is based on the street address of the subdivision office listed the LESCO website. Thiessen polygons are drawn so that the entirety of the area within the polygon is closer to the reference point inside that polygon than any other reference point. This figure was created using the Thiessen feature of the QGIS software v2.18.15.
15. For a similar modeling exercise that does have a spatial component, see Naqvi et al. (2021) for a study of feeder-level losses in Karachi. Feeder-level losses in Karachi are more similar to other feeders that are close to them, suggesting that the model is not capturing aspects of urban life that influence governance outcomes but are instead based on spatial location, such as a neighborhood.
16. For the purpose of this analysis, we exclude feeders with negative losses for the year. These are, to some extent, an administrative anomaly, as billing should not exceed consumption if that billing is supposedly based on consumption. However, the model is robust to the inclusion of feeders with negative losses up to 50%.
17. In the model of feeder-level losses in Karachi (Naqvi et al., 2021), spatial autocorrelation was present at the feeder level rather than at the administrative unit level of the Integrated Business Center (IBC). However, an IBC typically serves some five hundred thousand people and might have 50 feeders, which means we can't compare it with a subdivision.
18. My thanks to Ali Cheema for suggesting this insight.
19. See Naqvi et al. (2021) for a more detailed discussion.

Chapter 5

1. Infrastructural arrangements provide sites for historical power inequalities shaped by policies and political actions initiated by dominant social groups to play out in cities (McFarlane & Rutherford, 2008). Holston and Appadurai (1996, p. 191) cite exclusionary attempts by the propertied to prevent the propertyless from accessing basic services (and thus their associated infrastructures) as one of the contemporary sites of violence where differences in substantive citizenship play out.
2. As Roy (2009) argues, the planning process in India must be understood as the management of resources through the dynamic process of informality, a state of deregulation where the law is an arbitrary tool subject to multiple interpretations and interests. Roy uses Ghertner's (2010) case study of Delhi to illustrate this, where most constructions violate some law, but where only slums inhabited by the urban poor are designated as "nuisance[s]" and their residents a secondary category apart from "normal" private- property-owning citizens due to their violation of an arbitrary urban aesthetic favored by the state.
3. The idea that the poor would be better off with documentation of their tenure was popularized by the Chilean economist Hernando De Soto (2000), who termed the informal properties owned by the poor as "dead capital"—assets that could not be integrated with and circulated easily within the formal economy. In India, this perspective has led to efforts by municipal planning and developmental agencies to partner with private developers to redevelop existing informal settlements and resettle their residents so as to realize the economic value of the occupied land. A prime example of this process is demonstrated by Weinstein (2014) in her account of efforts by developer Mukesh Mehta, who, together with the Municipal Corporation of Greater Mumbai, tried to redevelop Dharavi as a mixed-use, mixed-income township.
4. In Vanessa Watson's (2009, p. 2260) account of planning in the cities of the Global South, there is an inherent conflict resulting from the gap between entrenched or static planning systems—often inherited from colonial governments—and the survival efforts of the poor.
5. James Ferguson (1990) expressed this very Foucauldian depiction of the state in his study of the Thaba Tseka development project in Botswana. The state "is not the name of an actor, it is the name of a way of tying together, multiplying and coordinating power relations, a kind of knotting or congealing of networks of power" (p. 273).
6. Timothy Mitchell (1991, p. 78) argues that the distinction between state and society "must not be taken as the boundary between two discrete entities, but as a line drawn internally within the network of institutional mechanisms through which a social and political order is maintained." This manifests itself through the distinctions made between everyday categories such as the informal and the formal that mark various infrastructures used by city residents to access services. Thus, "infrastructures are lived as contingent, power-laden, processes" (Graham & McFarlane, 2014, p. 12) that also provide the means for multiple forms of informal and formal claim making across multiple levels (Larkin, 2013). While the state has significant power in determining the distinction between the formal and the informal, everyday practices of governance are determined by the intersections between and contestations over these domains.
7. Graham and Marvin (2001) use the term "splintering urbanism" to underscore the various manners in which infrastructures fragment how various individuals and groups experience the city. Often, these fragmented experiences are cruelly juxtaposed; for example, as if to highlight inequalities in living standards, squatter settlements are often located immediately next to areas where those rights are more secure (Perlman, 1976).
8. Interpreting Chatterjee's political society as a strategic space of action, Subadevan and Naqvi (2017) demonstrate how the urban poor use various means of state engagement in response to the prevailing context and environment. Their analysis bands together various methods of state engagement that had previously been presented as discrete strategies.
9. See DiMaggio and Powell (DiMaggio & Powell, 1983) as well as Pritchett et al. (2013).
10. For some of the literature on informality and the everyday state, see Blundo and Olivier de Sardan (2006), Fuller and Harriss (2000), and Roitman (2004).
11. Analyses of infrastructure go beyond the technical, to reflect the ambient experiences and affective registers that are mobilized through people's interactions of infrastructure (Larkin, 2013). Such analyses enable moving beyond the immediate and individual to make sense

of seemingly disparate social developments and large-scale social change (Angelo & Hentschel, 2015).

12. See Gazdar and Mallah (2013) on political violence in Karachi. See Verkaaik (2004) for political violence as a source of fun for Karachi's youth population. Islamabad's planning history is described in Chapter 1 of Matthew Hull's (2012) *Government of Paper*.
13. A *katchi abadi* is a squatter settlement. All individual and place names used here are pseudonyms.
14. The criteria for regularization under the act is that they had more than 40 households before March 23, 1985.
15. Christians constitute 1.59% of the total population of Pakistan. *Katchi abadis* in Islamabad are both Christian and Muslim. Without making any claims of representativeness, the analysis in this article proceeds on the basis that the processes and power relations at work in 44 Quarter are not an artifact of the residents' belonging to a religious minority. That view has been validated through fieldwork and accepted at presentations of this research at academic conferences in Pakistan and elsewhere. However, Pakistani Christians are undoubtedly a persecuted minority.
16. While *kunda* literally means a hook or clasp, referring to a metal wire hooked onto a live electricity transmission cable, it is more broadly used for all undocumented electricity connections, irrespective of the specific modality.
17. Field notes, March 19, 2010.
18. Field notes, March 19, 2010.
19. Field notes, July 28, 2010.
20. While the distribution company's responsibilities always end at the consumer's meter, it is not usual for there to be anything other than household wiring at the other side.
21. Field notes, July 28, 2010.
22. Field notes, July 28, 2010.
23. Field notes, July 28, 2010.
24. Field notes, March 10, 2008.
25. Field notes, March 19, 2010.
26. Field notes, March 19, 2010.
27. Field notes, April 9, 2010.
28. A distribution box is a junction point at which the electricity meter serving a home can be connected to the underground electric cables supplying a street. Islamabad is unique in Pakistan for its underground electricity supply.
29. Field notes, July 6, 2010.
30. Field notes, June 8, 2010.
31. James Holston (2008) developed the concept of insurgent citizenship to describe struggles for substantive citizenship in São Paolo, Brazil, that involve the poor using informal or paralegal means for their own ends, and thereby unsettling the existing citizenship regime.

Chapter 6

1. A division typically contains 6–10 subdivisions and might serve up to 500,000 people.
2. Field notes, September 8, 2008.
3. Field notes, October 2, 2009.
4. Field notes, February 24, 2009.
5. Available at http://www.iesco.com.pk/downloads/Consumer%20Service%20Manual-2010.pdf. Last accessed on May 2, 2011. I cannot verify when the Customer Service Manual 2010 was posted, but the document's properties indicate that it was created on May 12, 2010. No earlier version of this document was posted online.
6. While living in Islamabad I drove a Honda Civic that belonged to my parents. I was enormously grateful for this support, as my income as a graduate student was limited, but it did mean that I would drive to my fieldwork in (by Pakistani standards) a nice car that clearly marked my social class. More to the point, when joining my IESCO informants on their travels around the city for their work, they would sometimes ask if we could take my car rather than their conveyance. I always declined this request because I felt that a key part of the

fieldwork was to experience their mode of transport as well as observe their duties. However, this stance created some awkwardness, as transport was a real burden for them, and I was obviously in a position to do them a favor by giving them a ride.

7. Field notes, April 7, 2010.
8. "An Act to Provide for the Regulation of Generation, Transmission, and Distribution of Electric Power," *The Gazette of Pakistan, Extraordinary*, December 16, 1997. Available at https://nepra.org.pk/Legal.php.
9. "Khalid Saeed Retained as NEPRA Chairman," *Business Recorder*, January 7, 2009. Available at https://fp.brecorder.com/2009/01/20090107861371/.
10. Parliament had been dissolved prior to the 2008 elections originally scheduled for January 8, 2008, but delayed to February 18, 2008, due to the assassination of Benazir Bhutto.
11. "Senate Resolve against Appointment of Khalid Saeed as Chairman NEPRA," Associated Press of Pakistan, February 26, 2008. Available at http://app.com.pk/en_/index.php?option=com_content&task=view&id=29955.
12. "PS to Soomro Quits as Senate Passes Resolution," *The News*, February 27, 2008. Available at https://web.archive.org/web/20080227051928/http://www.thenews.com.pk/top_story_detail.asp.
13. "Appointment of Nepra Chief Challenged in LHC," *OnePakistan News*, February 11, 2010. Available at http://www.onepakistan.com/news/national/32834-Appointment-Nepra-chief-challenged-LHC.html.
14. As the dates of the newspaper articles cited above show, there was ample media coverage of what was happening with the NEPRA chairmanship as events unfolded.

Chapter 7

1. *Tum* and *aap* are, respectively, the casual and formal second-person pronouns of Urdu and Hindi.
2. This study is not a workplace ethnography, nor can it be classified as participant observation, although I was present for extended periods at the IESCO offices while I observed their work being done. I never had an official position at the IESCO offices. Once I helped secure a rope that was holding up a pylon on which maintenance was being performed. Another time an IESCO staff member asked me to help him draft a personal letter unrelated to his official duties. Those two instances are the sum of my useful contribution to their lives. My time at their offices was overwhelmingly spent chatting and drinking tea, which it was nigh on impossible to refuse, and for which I was also never allowed to pay when it was usually ordered from a nearby tea stall.
3. Sudhir Venkatesh (2002) has described this mutual construction of ethnographer and subjects.
4. Javier Auyero (2012) examines the politics of waiting for public service in Argentina from the perspective of the citizen, who is subjected—with Kafkaesque indifference—to an arbitrary and always exceptional state apparatus. Less has been written about the public servants who simply sit around and wait for an occasional task, as always seems to be the case in the Pakistani government offices I have observed.
5. For a more direct look at the experience of everyday governance in South Asia with an explicit focus on gender, see Poulami Roychowdhury's (2021) account of how politics and violence shape governance in West Bengal.
6. I have attempted to describe this office in generic terms in order not to make it identifiable.
7. Although Salman is an IESCO employee, he regularly uses WAPDA—the Water and Power Development Authority—to refer to his employer. WAPDA was disaggregated in 1997, with IESCO being formed as one of its successor organizations. Despite the passage of 13 years, it is far more common to refer to WAPDA than IESCO (or the other successor companies) among both state employees and private citizens.
8. Field notes, January 6, 2009.
9. Field notes, September 30, 2009.
10. 1 *lakh* rupees, Rs. 100,000, is approximately US$1200.
11. Field notes, January 6, 2009.
12. Field notes, October 20, 2009.

13. From 1998 to 2002 the Pakistan army took administrative charge of IESCO and all other distribution companies in a move distinct from General Musharraf's coup of 1999. The then-elected Prime Minister, Nawaz Sharif, invited the army in to clean up the corruption in the distribution companies.
14. Field notes, February 10, 2009.
15. Field notes, January 23, 2009.
16. Hajji sahib's response to the Hajj is consistent with the findings of Clingingsmith et al.'s (2009) study of Hajj participants who return with a broadened worldview toward other ethnicities, peace, and gender equality. The study benefits from the Pakistani lottery for Hajj visas in attributing these changes in attitudes specifically to the pilgrimage experience.
17. Field notes, January 23, 2009.
18. Field notes, October 2, 2009.
19. Field notes, May 7, 2010.
20. *Daily Times*, November 15, 2009.
21. When I asked a higher education official who complained to me of high electricity bills why he simply didn't pay, he responded that 'the universities can't play that kind of game.' Field notes, May 7, 2010.
22. Field notes, July 13, 2010.
23. Field notes, July 13, 2010.
24. The motorway police are widely regarded as being one of the few non-corrupt institutions in the country. Their salaries are 50%–75% higher than those of comparable bureaucrats, but Noor (2009) attributes their superior performance to social disapproval and expectations of fair dealings within the organization.
25. Field notes, March 24, 2010.
26. PEPCO is the parent company of regional distribution companies such as IESCO and LESCO.
27. Disagreements and rivalries among state organizations are by no means unique to Pakistan. Graham Allison's *Essence of Decision* (1971) had a model of bureaucratic decision-making as politics—time bound, personalistic, and rivalrous. Nor was Robert Moses, the driving force behind so many New York City public works, any stranger to working outside the rules (Caro, 1974).
28. A notarized statement.
29. Field notes, March 31, 2010.
30. Field notes, March 31, 2010.
31. Field notes, February 10, 2009.
32. A literal translation of this swear word is 'sister fucker.' Although there are many uses for this word—the interested reader can introduce themselves to its semiotics through *Maximum City* (Mehta, 2004, pp. 9–10)—it was used here to intimidate and convey a threat.
33. Field notes, January 13, 2009.
34. I rapidly came to share this dislike, and I would not be surprised if the reader has picked up this fact already. While I strive for some sense of objectivity in my depiction of the fieldwork, this individual's personal conduct and style are those with which I had little sympathy. For a discussion of this and other failings of ethnographers, see Gary Allen Fine's (1993) "Ten Lies of Ethnography."

Chapter 8

1. In an interview with Loic Wacquant, Bourdieu defines the field of power as "the system of positions occupied by the holders of the diverse forms of capital which circulate in the relatively autonomous fields which make up an advanced society" (Wacquant, 1993, p. 20).
2. For a more detailed treatment of the Pakistani army, see Nawaz (2008) and Shah (2014), as well as Chapter 3 of Cohen (2004).
3. Unfortunately, documentation of that episode proved difficult to obtain, and I had to abandon my interest in writing about it. I've no doubt that the enterprising scholar who can get access to the right archives that speak to that issue will have a fascinating story to tell.
4. Common sense is here used in the sense of Akhtar's (2018) Gramscian analysis of hegemony in Pakistan.

5. For the implications on language policy, see Rahman (1996).
6. It is possible that Pakistani security sensitivities might lead to objections to such a mapping exercise. However, the fact that the mapping is of administrative boundaries rather than engineering equipment (such as locations of transformers or transmission lines) means that it should be possible to have such a spatial representation that does not create new security vulnerabilities.
7. This overtly political quality is what distinguishes the unevenness of the infrastructural state in Pakistan from the phenomenon of forbearance in Latin American municipalities described by Alisha Holland (2017). Forbearance is revokable and hidden from legislative oversight, whereas the unevenness of the infrastructural state in Pakistan is documented and difficult to undo.
8. Paul Farmer makes a related argument about healthcare provision in poor countries (Farmer, 2010).
9. A citizen-driven initiative for monitoring air quality can be found online at https://www.airvisual.com/pakistan/punjab/lahore. The air quality in Lahore and Faisalabad for 2018 (measured using $PM_{2.5}$ concentration) puts them both among the top 10 most of the world's most polluted cities.
10. Pakistan's looming water crisis is becoming more of a concern (Daanish Mustafa et al., 2013). By 2025 Pakistan's water problems could become more acute, with less than 1,000 liters of fresh water available per person per year. See https://www.iisd.org/library/making-every-drop-count-pakistan-s-growing-water-scarcity-challenge.

REFERENCES

Acemoglu, Daron, & Johnson, Simon. (2005). Unbundling Institutions. *Journal of Political Economy, 113*(5), 949–995.

Acemoglu, Daron, Johnson, Simon, & Robinson, James. (2001). The Colonial Origins of Comparative Development: An Empirical Investigation. *American Economic Review, 91*(5), 1369–1401.

Acemoglu, Daron, & Robinson, James A. (2012). *Why Nations Fail: The Origins of Power, Prosperity, and Poverty.* New York: Crown Books.

Adelman, Jeremy. (2013). *Worldly Philosopher: The Odyssey of Albert O. Hirschman.* Princeton, NJ: Princeton University Press.

AFP. (2011). MQM Announces Return to Government. *Dawn.* January 7, 2011. Retrieved from https://web.archive.org/web/20110110185303/http://www.dawn.com/2011/01/07/pm-reaches-nine-zero.html.

Ahmad, Munir. (2011). *The Battle for Pakistan: Militancy and Conflict in Balochistan.* Washington, DC: New America Foundation.

Akhtar, Aasim Sajjad. (2018). *The Politics of Common Sense: State, Society and Culture in Pakistan.* New Delhi: Cambridge University Press.

Akhter, Majed. (2015). Infrastructure nation: State space, hegemony, and hydraulic regionalism in Pakistan. *Antipode,* 47(4), 849–870.

Alavi, Hamza. (1988). Pakistan and Islam: Ethnicity and Ideology. In Fred Halliday & Hamza Alavi (Eds.), *State and Ideology in the Middle East and Pakistan* (pp. 64–111). London: Palgrave.

Alavi, Hamza. (2003). Fragment of a Life. Retrieved from https://www.himalmag.com/hamza-alavi-a-life/.

Alexander, Christopher. (1964). *Notes on the Synthesis of Form.* Cambridge, MA: Harvard University Press.

Ali, Tariq. (1983). *Can Pakistan Survive?: The Death of a State.* New York: Penguin Books.

Allison, Graham T., & Zelikow, Philip. (1999). *Essence of Decision: Explaining the Cuban Missile Crisis.* New York: Longman.

Altman, David, & Luna, Juan Pablo. (2012). Introduction: The Latin American State in its Labyrinth. *Revista de Ciencia Política,* 32(3), 521–543.

Anand, Nikhil. (2017). *Hydraulic City: Water and the Infrastructures of Citizenship in Mumbai.* Durham, NC: Duke University Press.

Andrews, Matt. (2013). *The Limits of Institutional Reform in Development: Changing Rules for Realistic Solutions.* Cambridge: Cambridge University Press.

Ang, Yuen Yuen. (2016). *How China Escaped the Poverty Trap.* Ithaca, NY: Cornell University Press.

Angelo, Hillary, & Hentschel, Christine. (2015). Interactions with Infrastructure as Windows into Social Worlds: A Method for Critical Urban Studies: Introduction. *City, 19*, 306–312. doi:10.1080/13604813.2015.1015275.

Arthur, W. Brian. (1990). Positive Feedbacks in the Economy. *Scientific American, 262*(2), 92–99.

Asian Development Bank. (2005). *Project Completion Report: PAK 26409. Ghazi Barotha Hydropower Project (Loan 1424-PAK) in Pakistan*. Retrieved from https://www.adb.org/sites/default/files/project-document/69136/pcr-pak-26409.pdf.

Asif, Muhammad. (2011). *Energy Crisis in Pakistan: Origins, Challenges and Sustainable Solutions*. Karachi: Oxford University Press.

Auyero, Javier. (2012). *Patients of the State: The Politics of Waiting in Argentina*. Durham, NC: Duke University Press.

Axelrod, Robert M. (1997). *The Complexity of Cooperation: Agent-Based Models of Competition and Collaboration*. Princeton, NJ: Princeton University Press.

Ayub, Mahmood Ali, & Hussain, Syed Turab. (2016). *Candles in the Dark: Successful Organizations in Pakistan's Weak Institutional Environment*. Karachi, Pakistan: Oxford University Press.

Bardach, Eugene, & Kagan, Robert A. (1982). *Going by the Book: The Problem of Regulatory Unreasonableness*. Philadelphia: Temple University Press.

Bardhan, Pranab K. (1984). *The Political Economy of Development in India*. New Delhi: Oxford University Press.

Bates, Robert H. (1995). Social Dilemmas and Rational Individuals: An Assessment of the New Institutionalism. In John Harriss, Janet Hunter, & Colin Lewis (Eds.), *The New Institutional Economics and Third World Development* (pp. 27–48). London: Routledge.

Bayart, Jean Francois. (1993). *The State in Africa: The Politics of the Belly*. London: Longman.

Bayat, Asef. (2013). *Life as Politics: How Ordinary People Change the Middle East*. Standford, CA: Stanford University Press.

Benjamin, Solomon. (2008). Occupancy Urbanism: Radicalizing Politics and Economy beyond Policy and Programs. *International Journal of Urban and Regional Research, 32*(3), 719–729.

Berlin, Isaiah. (2002). *Liberty: Incorporating Four Essays on Liberty*. Oxford: Oxford University Press.

Birdsall, Nancy. (2010). *U.S. Development Assistance to Pakistan's Energy Sector (Third open letter to Ambassador Richard Holbrooke)*. Retrieved from http://www.cgdev.org/sites/default/files/1424170_file_Open_Letter_3_Pakistan_s_Energy_Sector_0.pdf.

Birdsall, Nancy, Elhai, Wren, & Kinder, Molly. (2010). *Beyond Bullets and Bombs: Fixing the U.S. Approach to Development in Pakistan*. Retrieved from http://www.cgdev.org/files/1425136_file_CGD_Pakistan_FINAL_web.pdf.

Birdsall, Nancy, Malik, Adeel, & Vaishnav, Milan. (2005). *Poverty and the Social Sectors: The World Bank in Pakistan 1990–2003*. Retrieved from http://www.cgdev.org/blog/poverty-and-social-sectors-world-bank-pakistan-1990-2003.

Björkman, Lisa. (2015). *Pipe Politics, Contested Waters: Embedded Infrastructures of Millennial Mumbai*. Durham, NC: Duke University Press.

Blundo, Giorgio, & Olivier de Sardan, Jean-Pierre. (2006). *Everyday Corruption and the State: Citizens and Public Officials in Africa*. London: Zed Books.

Boone, Catherine. (2012). Territorial Politics and the Reach of the State: Unevenness by Design. *Revista de Ciencia Política, 32*(3), 623–641.

Boone, Catherine. (2014). *Property and Political Order in Africa: Land Rights and the Structure of Politics*. New York: Cambridge University Press.

Booth, David, & Unsworth, Sue. (2014). *Politically Smart, Locally Led Development*. Retrieved from London: http://www.odi.org/publications/8800-politically-smart-locally-led.

Bourdieu, Pierre. (1999). State/Culture: State-Formation after the Cultural Turn. In George Steinmetz (Ed.), (pp. 53–75). Ithaca, NY: Cornell University Press.

Brass, Paul R. (1997). *Theft of an Idol: Text and Context in the Representation of Collective Violence*. Princeton, NJ: Princeton University Press.

Brenner, Neil. (2004). *New State Spaces: Urban Governance and the Rescaling of Statehood*. New York: Oxford University Press.

Brewer, John. (1989). *The Sinews of Power: War, Money, and the English State 1688–1783.* New York: Knopf.

Brown, David, & Mobarak, Ahmad. (2009). The Transforming Power of Democracy: Regime Type and the Distribution of Electricity. *American Political Science Review, 103,* 193–203.

Butt, Ahsan. (2017). *Secession and Security: Explaining State Strategy against Separatists.* Ithaca, NY: Cornell University Press.

Caro, Robert A. (1974). *The Power Broker: Robert Moses and the Fall of New York.* New York: Knopf.

Centeno, Miguel A., Kohli, Atul, Yashar, Deborah J., & Mistree, Dinsha. (2017). *States in the Developing World.* Cambridge: Cambridge University Press.

Chabal, Patrick, & Daloz, Jean-Pascal. (1999). *Africa Works: Disorder as Political Instrument.* Oxford: James Currey.

Chatterjee, Partha. (2004). *The Politics of the Governed.* New York: Columbia University Press.

Clingingsmith, David, Khwaja, Asim Ijaz, & Kremer, Michael. (2009). Estimating the Impact of the Hajj: Religion and Rolerance in Islam's Global Gathering. *The Quarterly Journal of Economics, 124*(3), 1133–1170.

Cohen, Stephen. (2004). *The Idea of Pakistan.* New Delhi, India: Oxford University Press.

Colander, David C., & Kupers, Roland. (2014). *Complexity and the Art of Public Policy: Solving Society's Problems from the Bottom Up.* Princeton, NJ: Princeton University Press.

da Cruz, Nuno F., Rode, Philipp, & McQuarrie, Michael. (2019). New Urban Governance: A Review of Current Themes and Future Priorities. *Journal of Urban Affairs, 41*(1), 1–19.

Das, Veena. (2007). Life and Words: Violence and the Descent into the Ordinary. Berkeley: University of California Press.

Davidson, Jamie S. (2015). *Indonesia's Changing Political Economy: Governing the Roads.* Cambridge: Cambridge University Press.

Davis, Kenneth Culp. (1969). *Discretionary Justice; a Preliminary Inquiry.* Baton Rouge: Louisiana State University Press.

Delbourgo, James. (2006). *A Most Amazing Scene of Wonders: Electricity and Enlightenment in Early America.* Cambridge, MA: Harvard University Press.

de Soto, Hernando. (2000). *The Mystery of Capital: Why Capitalism Triumphs in the West and Fails Everywhere Else.* New York: Basic Books.

DiMaggio, P. J., & Powell, W. W. (1983). The Iron Cage Revisited - Institutional Isomorphism and Collective Rationality in Organizational Fields. *American Sociological Review, 48*(2), 147–160. doi:10.2307/2095101.

Disch, Arne, Vigeland, Endre, & Sundet, Geir. (2009). *Anti-Corruption Approaches: A Literature Review.* Retrieved from http://www.sida.se/contentassets/3f5c8afd51a6414d9f6c8f8425fb935b/anti-corruption-approaches-a-literature-review_3153.pdf.

Dobbin, Frank. (1994). *Forging Industrial Policy: The United States, Britain, and France in the railway age.* New York: Cambridge University Press.

Edge, David. (2001). Reinventing the Wheel. In Sheila Jasanoff, Gerald E. Markle, James C. Peterson, & Trevor J. Pinch (Eds.), *Handbook of Science and Technology Studies* (pp. 3–23). Thousand Oaks, CA: SAGE Publications.

Evans, Peter. (1995). *Embedded Autonomy: States and Industrial Transformation.* Princeton, NJ: Princeton University Press.

Evans, Peter. (2009). Population Health and Development: An Institutional-Cultural Approach to Capability Expansion. In Peter Hall & Michele Lamont (Eds.), *Successful Societies: How Institutions and Culture Affect Health* (pp. 104–127). New York: University of Cambridge Press.

Evans, Peter, & Heller, Patrick. (2015). Human Development, State Transformation and the Politics of the Developmental State. In Stephan Leibfried, Evelyn Huber, Matthew Lange, Jonah Levy, Frank Nullmeier, & John Stephens (Eds.), *The Oxford Handbook of Transformations of the State* (pp. 691–713). Oxford University Press.

Eyben, R. (2010). Hiding Relations: The Irony of "Effective Aid." *European Journal of Development Research, 22*(3), 382–397.

Farmer, Paul. (2010). *Partner to the Poor: A Paul Farmer Reader* (Vol. 23). Berkeley: University of California Press.

Fatima, Umbreen, & Nasim, Anjum. (2013). Inter-Provincial Differences in Power Sector Subsidies and Implications for the NFC Award. *The Pakistan Development Review, 52*(4), 421–436.

Feldman, Martha. (1992). Social Limits to Discretion: An Organizational Perspective. In Keith Hawkins (Ed.), *The Uses of Discretion* (pp. 163–184). Oxford: Oxford University Press.

Ferguson, James. (1990). *The Anti-Politics Machine: "Development," Depoliticization, and Bureaucratic Power in Lesotho*. Cambridge; New York: Cambridge University Press.

Ferguson, Priscilla Parkhurst. (1998). A Cultural Field in the Making: Gastronomy in 19th-Century France. *American Journal of Sociology, 104*(3), 597–641.

Fine, Gary Alan. (1993). Ten Lies of Ethnography: Moral Dilemmas of Field Research. *Journal of Contemporary Ethnography, 22*(3), 267–294.

Fligstein, Neil, & McAdam, Doug. (2012). *A Theory of Fields*. New York: Oxford University Press.

Flyvbjerg, Bent. (2014). What You Should Know about Megaprojects and Why: An Overview. *Project Management Journal, 45*(2), 6–19.

Fourcade, Marion, Ollion, Etienne, & Algan, Yann. (2015). The Superiority of Economists. *Journal of Economic Perspectives, 29*(1), 89–114.

Fraser, Julia. (2005). *Lessons from the Independent Private Power Experience in Pakistan*. Retrieved from http://documents.worldbank.org/curated/en/2005/05/6330936/lessons-independent-private-power-experience-pakistan.

Frembgen, Jürgen Wasim. (2011). *At the Shrine of the Red Sufi: Five Days and Nights on Pilgrimage in Pakistan*. Karachi: Oxford University Press.

Friends of Democratic Pakistan. (2010). *Integrated Energy Sector Recovery Report & Plan*. Retrieved from http://www.adb.org/publications/integrated-energy-sector-recovery-report-and-plan.

Fuller, C. J., & Harriss, John. (2000). For an Anthropology of the Modern Indian State. In C. J. Fuller & Véronique Bénéï (Eds.), *The Everyday State and Society in Modern India* (pp. 1–30). New Delhi: Social Science Press.

Fund for Peace. (2018). Fragile States Index. Retrieved from http://fundforpeace.org/fsi/data/.

Fung, Archon, & Wright, Erik Olin. (2003). *Deepening Democracy: Institutional Innovations in Empowered Participatory Governance* (Vol. 4). London: Verso.

Gayer, Laurent. (2014). *Karachi: Ordered Disorder and the Struggle for the City*. Oxford: Oxford University Press.

Gazdar, Haris, & Mallah, Hussain Bux. (2013). Informality and Political Violence in Karachi. *Urban Studies, 50*, 3099–3115. doi:10.1177/0042098013487778.

Ghertner, D. Asher. (2010). Calculating without Numbers: Aesthetic Governmentality in Delhi's Slums. *Economy and Society, 39*(2), 185–217.

Giddens, Anthony. (1984). *The Constitution of Society*. Berkeley: University of California Press.

Giridharadas, Anand. (2011). *India Calling: An Intimate Portrait of a Nation's Remaking* (1st ed.). New York: Times Books/Henry Holt and Co.

Glen, Jack. (1992). *Private Sector Electricity in Developing Countries: Supply and Demand*. Retrieved from http://documents.worldbank.org/curated/en/1992/09/440459/private-sector-electricity-developing-countries-supply-demand.

Go, Julian. (2008). Global Fields and Imperial Forms: Field Theory and the British and American Empires. *Sociological Theory, 26*(3), 201–229.

Go, Julian, & Lawson, George. (2017). *Global Historical Sociology*. New York: Cambridge University Press.

Gorski, Philip S. (2016). The Matter of Emergence: Material Artifacts and Social Structure. *Qualitative Sociology, 39*(2), 211–215.

Goswami, Manu. (2004). *Producing India: From Colonial Economy to National space*. Chicago: University of Chicago Press.

Government of Pakistan. (1994). *Report of Prime Minister's Task Force on Energy*. Islamabad, Pakistan.

Government of Pakistan. (2010). *Prime Minister's Vision Statement for Accelerated Development of Pakistan's Power Sector for Sustained Economic Growth*. Islamabad, Pakistan.

Government of Pakistan. (2020). *Federal Budget 2021: Budget in Brief*. Retrieved from https://www.finance.gov.pk/fb_2020_21.html.

Govt Agencies to Manage Flood Aid, Donors Told. (2010). *Dawn*. December 22, 2010. Retrieved from http://www.dawn.com/news/853909/govt-agencies-to-manage-flood-aid-donors-told.

Graham, Stephen, & Marvin, Simon. (2001). *Splintering Urbanism: Networked Infrastructures, Technological Mobilities and the Urban Condition*. London; New York: Routledge.

Graham, Stephen, & McFarlane, Colin. (2014). *Infrastructural Lives: Urban Infrastructure in Context*. New York: Routledge.

Gravois, John. (2005). The De Soto Delusion. Retrieved from http://www.slate.com/articles/news_and_politics/hey_wait_a_minute/2005/01/the_de_soto_delusion.html.

Green, Duncan. (2014). Thinking and Working Politically Update: Where Have Aid Agencies, Consultants etc Got to? Retrieved from https://oxfamapps.org/fp2p/thinking-and-working-politically-update-where-have-aid-agencies-consultants-etc-got-to/.

Guldi, Jo. (2012). *Roads to Power: Britain Invents the Infrastructure State*. Cambridge, MA: Harvard University Press.

Haggard, Stephan. (2018). *Developmental S tates*. Cambridge: Cambridge University Press.

Haider, Irfan. (2015). Details of Agreements Signed during Xi's Visit to Pakistan. *Dawn*. April 20, 2015. Retrieved from https://www.dawn.com/news/1177129.

Haines, Daniel. (2013). *Building the Empire, Building the Nation: Development, Legitimacy and Hydro-Politics in Sind, 1919–1969*. Karachi, Pakistan: Oxford University Press.

Hall, Peter A., & Taylor, Rosemary C. R. (1996). Political Science and the Three New Institutionalisms. *Political Studies, 44*(5), 936–957.

Haq, M. (2005). Entrepreneurship, Private Investment, Economic Growth. *The Lahore Journal of Economics, 10*, 27–44.

Hasan, Arif. (2009). *The Unplanned Revolution: Observations on the Processes of Socio-Economic Change in Pakistan*. Karachi, Pakistan: Oxford University Press.

Hecht, Gabrielle, & Allen, Michael Thad. (2001). Technologies of Power. Cambridge, MA: MIT Press.

Heller, Patrick. (2000). Degrees of Democracy: Some Comparative Lessons from India. *World Politics, 52*(4), 484–519.

Henisz, Witold J., Zelner, Bennet A., & Guillén, Mauro F. (2005). The Worldwide Diffusion of Market-Oriented Infrastructure Reform, 1977–1999. *American Sociological Review, 70*, 871–897.

Herbst, Jeffrey Ira. (2000). States and Power in Africa: Comparative Lessons in Authority and Control. Princeton, NJ: Princeton University Press.

Hetherington, Kregg. (2011). *Guerrilla Auditors: The Politics of Transparency in Neoliberal Paraguay*. Durham, NC: Duke University Press.

Hirschman, Albert O. (1967). *Development Projects Observed*. Washington, DC: Brookings Institution.

Holland, Alisha C. (2017). *Forbearance as Redistribution: The Politics of Informal Welfare in Latin America*. New York: Cambridge University Press.

Holland, John. (1992). Complex Adaptive Systems. *Daedalus, 121*(1), 17–30.

Holston, J., & Appadurai, A. (1996). Cities and Citizenship. *Public Culture, 8*(2), 187–204.

Holston, James. (2008). *Insurgent Citizenship: Disjunctions of Democracy and Modernity in Brazil*. Princeton, NJ: Princeton University Press.

Hood, Christopher, & Dixon, Ruth. (2015). *A Government That Worked Better and Cost Less?: Evaluating Three Decades of Reform and Change in UK Central Government*. Oxford: Oxford University Press.

Hossain, Naomi, Aremu, Fatai, Buschmann, Andy, Chaimite, Egidio, Gukurume, Simbarashe, Javed, Umair, . . . Marston, Olivia. (2018). *Energy Protests in Fragile Settings: The Unruly Politics of Provisions in Egypt, Myanmar, Mozambique, Nigeria, Pakistan, and Zimbabwe, 2007–2017.* IDS Working Paper 513. Brighton, UK: IDS.

Huda, Mirza Sadaqat, & Ali, Saleem H. (2017). Energy Diplomacy in South Asia: Beyond the Security Paradigm in Accessing the TAPI Pipeline Project. *Energy Research & Social Science, 34*, 202–213.

Hughes, Thomas Parke. (1983). *Networks of Power: Electrification in Western Society, 1880–1930.* Baltimore: Johns Hopkins University Press.

Hull, Matthew S. (2012). *Government of Paper: The Materiality of Bureaucracy in Urban Pakistan.* Berkeley: University of California Press.

Human Rights Commission of Pakistan. (2010). *State of Human Rights in 2009*. Lahore, Pakistan: Human Rights Commission of Pakistan.

Husain, Ishrat. (2000). *Pakistan: The Economy of an Elitist State.* Karachi, Pakistan: Oxford University Press.

Husain, Khurram. (2012). The Ghost in the Machine. *Dawn.* June 13, 2012. Retrieved from https://www.dawn.com/news/726295/the-ghost-in-the-machine.

Husain, Khurram. (2018). Hours of Darkness. *Dawn.* June 7, 2018. Retrieved from https://www.dawn.com/news/1412587/hours-of-darkness.

IGI Securities. (2010). *Financial Sector and Market Perception of Pakistan's Power Sector.* Retrieved from

Institute of Development Studies. (2010). *An Upside-Down View of Governance.* Retrieved from https://archive.ids.ac.uk/gdr/cfs/pdfs/AnUpside-downViewofGovernance.pdf.

Institute of Public Policy at Beaconhouse National University. (2010). *State of the Economy: Pulling Back from the Abyss.* Lahore, Pakistan.

International Monetary Fund. (2021). *Pakistan: Staff Concluding Statement of the 2021 Article IV Mission and Staff-Level Agreement on the Sixth Review under the Extended Fund Facility.* Retrieved from https://www.imf.org/en/News/Articles/2021/11/19/mcs-pakistan-staff-concluding-statement-2021-art-iv-staff-level-agreement-6th-review-eff.

International Resources Group, Putnam Hayes & Bartlett, & Hunton & Williams. (1992). *WAPDA's Strategic Plan for the Privatization of the Pakistan Power Sector (Prepared for USAID/Islamabad).* Washington, DC.

Islamabad Electric Supply Company. (2010). *Consumer Services Manual.* Retrieved from http://www.iesco.com.pk/downloads/Consumer%20Service%20Manual-2010.pdf.

Jalal, Ayesha. (1990). *State of Martial Rule: The Origins of Pakistan's Political Economy of Defence.* Cambridge: Cambridge University Press.

Jalal, Ayesha. (1995). Conjuring Pakistan: History as Official Imagining. *International Journal of Middle East Studies,* 27(1), 73–89.

Jalal, Ayesha. (2014). *The Struggle for Pakistan: A Muslim Homeland and Global Politics.* Cambridge, MA: Harvard University Press.

Jamali, Hafeez Ahmed. (2014). *A Harbor in the Tempest: Megaprojects, Identity, and the Politics of Place in Gwadar, Pakistan.* Austin: University of Texas at Austin.

Javed, Umair. (2019). Refusing to Learn. *Dawn.* February 11, 2019. Retrieved from https://www.dawn.com/news/1463124.

Jervis, Robert. (1997). *System Effects: Complexity in Political and Social Life.* Princeton, NJ: Princeton University Press.

Jinnah, Muhammad Ali. (1948). Address by Muhammad Ali Jinnah, Governor General of Pakistan, in Dacca, East Pakistan; March 21st, 1948. Retrieved from http://www.columbia.edu/itc/mealac/pritchett/00islamlinks/txt_jinnah_dacca_1948.html.

Joseph, K. L. (2010). The Politics of Power: Electricity Reform in India *Energy Policy, 38*, 503–511.

Kale, Sunila. (2004). Current Reforms: The Politics of Policy Change in India's Electricity Sector. *Pacific Affairs,* 77(3), 467–491.

Kauffman, Daniel, Kraay, Aart, & Mastruzzi, Massimo. (2009). *Governance Matters VIII: Aggregate and Individual Governance Indicators, 1996–2008*. Retrieved from http://info.worldbank.org/governance/wgi/.

Kelsall, Tim, & vom Hau, Matthias. (2020). Beyond Institutions: Political Settlements Analysis and Development. Barecelona, Spain: Institute Barcelona Estudis Internacionals.

Kenny, Charles. (2007). *Infrastructure Governance and Corruption: Where Next?* Retrieved from

Khagram, Sanjeev. (2004). *Dams and Development: Transnational Struggles for Water and Power.* Ithaca, NY: Cornell University Press.

Khan, Iftikhar. (2018). Plan to Hike Power Tariff through Ordinance Assailed. *Dawn*. March 21, 2021. Retrieved from https://www.dawn.com/news/1613732.

Khan, Mushtaq H. (2018). Political Settlements and the Analysis of Institutions. *African Affairs, 117*(469), 636–655. doi:10.1093/afraf/adx044.

Kiani, Khaliq. (2014). IPPs Suspend Notices Calling Sovereign Guarantees. Dawn. December 12, 2014. Retrieved from http://www.dawn.com/news/1150322.

Kinder, Molly. (2010). Pakistan's Energy Sector: Groundhog Day for USA? Center for Global Development, blog post, June 4, 2010. Retrieved from http://www.cgdev.org/blog/pakistan%E2%80%99s-energy-sector-groundhog-day-usa.

Krause, Philipp. (2013). *Of Institutions and Butterflies: Is Isomorphism in Developing Countries Necessarily a Bad Thing?* Retrieved from https://odi.org/en/publications/of-institutions-and-butterflies-is-isomorphism-in-developing-countries-necessarily-a-bad-thing/.

Kurtz, C. F., & Snowden, D. J. (2003). The New Dynamics of Strategy: Sense-Making in a Complex and Complicated World. *IBM Systems Journal, 42*(3), 462–483.

LaPorte, Robert, Jr. (1991). Administrative Restructuring During the Zia Period. In Shahid Javed Burki & Craig Baxter (Eds.) *Pakistan under the Military: Eleven Years of Zia ul-Haq* (pp. 137–154). Boulder, CO: Westview Press.

Larkin, Brian. (2013). The Politics and Poetics of Infrastructure. *Annual Review of Anthropology, 42*, 327–343.

Lee, Ching Kwan. (2017). *The Specter of Global China: Politics, Labor, and Foreign Investment in Africa*. Chicago: University of Chicago Press.

Lefebvre, Henri. (2009). Space and the State. In Neil Brenner & Stuart Elden (Eds.), *State, Space, World: Selected Essays* (pp. 223–253). Minneapolis: University of Minnesota Press.

Levi-Faur, David. (2012). *The Oxford Handbook of Governance*: Oxford University Press.

Levy, Adrian, & Scott-Clark, Catherine. (2007). *Deception: Pakistan, the United States, and the Secret Trade in Nuclear Weapons*. London: Atlantic Books.

Lieven, Anatol. (2012). *Pakistan: A Hard Country.* New York: PublicAffairs.

Lipsky, Michael. (2010[1980]). *Streel-Level Bureaucracy: Dilemmas of the Individual in Public Services*. New York: Russell Sage Foundation.

Lukes, Steven. (1974). *Power: A Radical Review.* London: MacMillan.

Mahadevan, Subadevan, & Naqvi, Ijlal. (2017). Contesting Urban Citizenship: The Urban Poor's Strategies of State Engagement in Chennai, India. *International Development Planning Review, 39*(1), 77–95.

Mamdani, Mahmood. (1996). *Citizen and Subject: Contemporary Africa and the Legacy of Late Colonialism.* Princeton, NJ: Princeton University Press.

Mann, Michael. (1984). The Autonomous Power of the State: Its Origins, Mechanisms and Results. *European Journal of Sociology/Archives européennes de sociologie, 25*(2), 185–213.

Mann, Michael. (1986). *The Sources of Social Power*. Cambridge; New York: Cambridge University Press.

Martin, Isaac William, Mehrotra, Ajay K., & Prasad, Monica. (2009). *The New Fiscal Sociology: Taxation in Comparative and Historical Perspective.* Cambridge; New York: Cambridge University Press.

Martin, John Levi. (2003). What Is Field Theory? *American Journal of Sociology, 109*(1), 1–49.

Masud, Muhammad Omar. (2014). Calling Citizens, Improving the State: Pakistan's Citizen Feedback Monitoring Program, 2008–14. Innovations for Successful Societies, Princeton

University. Retrieved from https://successfulsocieties.princeton.edu/publications/calling-citizens-improving-state-pakistan%E2%80%99s-citizen-feedback-monitoring-program-2008-%E2%80%93.

Mathur, Nayanika. (2017). *Paper Tiger: Law, Bureaucracy and the Developmental State in Himalayan India*. Cambridge: Cambridge University Press.

Mbembe, Achille. (2000). *On the Postcolony*. Berkeley: University of California Press.

McDonnell, Erin Metz. (2017). Patchwork Leviathan: How Pockets of Bureaucratic Governance Flourish within Institutionally Diverse Developing States. *American Sociological Review, 82*(3), 476–510.

McFarlane, Colin, & Rutherford, Jonathan. (2008). Political Infrastructures: Governing and Experiencing the Fabric of the City. *International Journal of Urban and Regional Research, 32*, 363–374. doi:10.1111/j.1468-2427.2008.00792.x.

Mehta, Suketu. (2004). *Maximum City: Bombay Lost and Found* (1st ed.). New York: Alfred A. Knopf.

Meyer, John, & Rowan, Brian. (1977). Institutional Organizations: Formal Structure as Myth and Ceremony. *American Journal of Sociology, 83*, 340–363.

Miller, John H., & Page, Scott E. (2007). *Complex Adaptive Systems: An Introduction to Computational Models of Social Life*. Princeton, NJ: Princeton University Press.

Min, Brian. (2015). *Power and the Vote: Elections and Electricity in the Developing World*. New York: Cambridge University Press.

Min, Brian, & Golden, Miriam. (2014). Electoral Cycles in Electricity Losses in India. *Energy Policy, 65*, 619–625.

Ministry of Finance. (2011). *Pakistan Economic Survey 2010–2011*. Retrieved from https://www.finance.gov.pk/survey_1011.html.

Ministry of Water and Power. (1997). *Report of the Committee Constituted by the Ministry of Water and Power for Corporatization of WAPDA (Power Wing)*. Islamabad, Pakistan.

Mitchell, Melanie. (2009). *Complexity: A guided Tour*. New York: Oxford University Press.

Mitchell, Timothy. (1991). The Limits of the State: Beyond Statist Approaches and Their Critics. *American Political Science Review, 85*(1), 77–96.

Mitchell, Timothy. (2011). *Carbon Democracy: Political Power in the Age of Oil*. London: Verso Books.

Mukerji, Chandra. (2009). *Impossible Engineering: Technology and Territoriality on the Canal du Midi*. Princeton, NJ: Princeton University Press.

Mustafa, Daanish, Akhter, Majed, & Nasrallah, Natalie. (2013). *Understanding Pakistan's Water-Security Nexus*. Washington, DC: United States Institute of Peace.

Mustafa, D., Gioli, G., Karner, M., & Khan, I. (2017). *Contested Waters: The Sub-National Scale of Water and Conflict in Pakistan*. Washington, DC: United States Institute for Peace, USIP.

MWP-USAID Power Distribution Improvement Program. (2011). *Islamabad Electric Supply Company (IESCO) Operational Audit Report*. Islamabad, Pakistan

Naqvi, Ijlal, Poorthuis, Ate, & Govind, Anirudh. (2021). Urban Governance and Electricity Losses: An Exploration of Spatial Unevenness in Karachi, Pakistan. *Energy Research & Social Science, 79*, https://doi.org/10.1016/j.erss.2021.102166.

Naseemullah, Adnan. (2016). The Contested Capacity of the Indian State. *India Review, 15*(4), 407–432.

National Electric Power Regulatory Authority. (2016). *State of the Industry Report 2015*. Islamabad, Pakistan.

National Electric Power Regulatory Authority. (2020). *2019–2020 Performance Evaluation Report: Distribution Companies*. Retrieved from https://nepra.org.pk/publications/Performance%20Reports.php.

National Transmission and Despatch Company. (2017). *Power System Statistics, 41st Edition*. Lahore, Pakistan.

National Transmission and Despatch Company. (2019). *Power System Statistics, 43rd Edition*. Lahore, Pakistan.

Natsios, Andrew. (2010). *The Clash of the Counter-Bureaucracy and Development*. Center for Global Development. July 1, 2010. Retrieved from http://www.cgdev.org/publication/clash-counter-bureaucracy-and-development.

Nawaz, Shuja. (2008). *Crossed Swords: Pakistan, Its Army, and the Wars Within*. New York: Oxford University Press.

Needham, Andrew. (2014). *Power Lines: Phoenix and the Making of the Modern Southwest*. Princeton, NJ: Princeton University Press.

Niaz, Ilhan. (2010). *The Culture of Power and Governance of Pakistan 1947–2008*. Oxford: Oxford University Press.

Niazi, Tarique. (2018). Contesting Instrumental Knowledge with Communicative Action: Why Kalabagh Dam (Pakistan) Remains Unbuilt. *Organization & Environment*, 32(4), 441–465.

Noor, Muhammad Tahir. (2009). *Institutional Dynamics of Governance and Corruption in Developing World: The Case of Pakistan*. Ph.D. dissertation, Ruprecht-Karls-Universität, Heidelberg.

North, Douglass. (1990). *Institutions, Institutional Change, and Economic Performance*. New York: Cambridge University Press.

Nye, David E. (1990). *Electrifying America: Social Meanings of a New Technology, 1880–1940*. Cambridge, MA: MIT Press.

O'Donnell, Guillermo. (1993). On the State, Democratization and Some Conceptual Problems: A Latin American View with Glances at Some Postcommunist Countries. *World Development*, *21*(8), 1355–1369.

Padgett, John Frederick, & Powell, Walter W. (2012). *The Emergence of Organizations and Markets*. Princeton, NJ: Princeton University Press.

Pasha, Hafiz, Ghaus, Aisha, & Malik, Salman. (1989). The Economic Cost of Power Outages in the Industrial Sector of Pakistan. *Energy Economics*, *11*(4), 301–318.

Perlman, Janice. (1976). *The Myth of Marginality*. Berkeley: University of California Press.

Phadke, Amol. (2009). How Many Enrons? Mark-Ups in the Stated Capital Cost of Independent Power Producers' (IPPs') Power Projects in Developing Countries. *Energy*, 34(11), 1917–1924. doi:https://doi.org/10.1016/j.energy.2009.07.043.

Piore, M. J. (2011). Beyond Markets: Sociology, Street-Level Bureaucracy, and the Management of the Public Sector. *Regulation & Governance*, 5(1), 145–164. doi:10.1111/j.1748-5991.2010.01098.x.

Planning Commission. (1955). *First Five Year Plan*. Islamabad, Pakistan: Government of Pakistan.

Planning Commission. (1965). *Third Five Year Plan*. Islamabad, Pakistan: Government of Pakistan.

Planning Commission. (1970). *Fourth Five Year Plan*. Islamabad, Pakistan: Government of Pakistan.

Planning Commission. (1983). *Sixth Five Year Plan*. Islamabad, Pakistan: Government of Pakistan.

Planning Commission. (1988). *Seventh Five Year Plan*. Islamabad, Pakistan: Government of Pakistan.

Planning Commission. (2005). *Medium Term Development Framework*. Islamabad, Pakistan: Government of Pakistan.

Planning Commission. (2013). *Eleventh Five Year Plan*. Islamabad, Pakistan: Government of Pakistan.

Polanyi, Karl. (2001). *The Great Transformation: The Political and Economic Origins of Our Time*. Boston: Beacon Press.

Prasad, Monica. (2021). *Problem-Solving Sociology: A Guide for Students*. New York: Oxford University Press.

Pritchett, L., & Woolcock, M. (2004). Solutions when the Solution Is the Problem: Arraying the Disarray in Development. *World Development*, 32(2), 191–212. doi:10.1016/j.worlddev.2003.08.009.

Pritchett, Lant, Woolcock, Michael, & Andrews, Matt. (2013). Looking like a State: Techniques of Persistent Failure in State Capability for Implementation. *Journal of Development Studies*, 49(1), 1–18. doi:10.1080/00220388.2012.709614.

Private Power and Infrastructure Board. (2001). *Status Report: Power Policy, 1994*. Islamabad, Pakistan

Radaelli, Claudio M., Dente, Bruno, & Dossi, Samuele. (2012). Recasting Institutionalism: Institutional Analysis and Public Policy. *European Political Science, 11*(4), 537–550.

Rahman, Tariq. (1996). *Language and Politics in Pakistan*. Karachi, Pakistan: Oxford University Press.

Rahman, Tariq. (2006). West Pakistan Perceptions of the Bengali Language Movement with Special Reference to the Quaid-I-Azam. In Ahmad Salim (Ed.), *It Is My mother's Face: Selected Readings from Bengali Language Movement* (pp. 219–236). Lahore, Pakistan: Sanjh.

Ramalingam, Ben. (2013). *Aid on the Edge of Chaos: Rethinking International Cooperation in a Complex World*. Oxford: Oxford University Press.

Rana, Shahbaz. (2012). Power Sector Dues: Govt Defaults on Sovereign Guarantees. *Express Tribune*, May 9, 2012. Retrieved from http://tribune.com.pk/story/376152/power-sector-dues-govt-defaults-on-sovereign-guarantees/.

Ranganathan, Malini. (2014). Paying for Pipes, Claiming Citizenship: Political Agency and Water Reforms at the Urban Periphery. *International Journal of Urban and Regional Research, 38*(2), 590–608.

Rao, Ursula. (2010). Making the Global City: Urban Citizenship at the Margins of Delhi. *Ethnos, 75*(4), 402–424. doi:10.1080/00141844.2010.532227.

Rashid, Ahmed. (2008). *Descent into Chaos: The United States and the Failure of Nation Building in Pakistan, Afghanistan, and Central Asia*. New York: Viking.

Rasool, Tasadduq. (2010). *Shelter for the Poor*. Islamabad, Pakistan: Akhtar Hameed Khan Resource Center.

Raudenbush, Stephen W., & Bryk, Anthony S. (2002). *Hierarchical Linear Models: Applications and Data Analysis Methods* (Vol. 1). Sage.

Ray, Raka. (1999). *Fields of Protest: Women's Movements in India*. Minneapolis: University of Minnesota Press.

Rifai, Salahuddin. (2009). Economic Despatch in National Transmission and Despatch Company (NTDC) - Pakistan. *Electronic Forum, 5* (January-March), 1–4.

Rodrik, Dani. (2007). *One Economics, Many Recipes: Globalization, Institutions and Economic Growth*. Princeton, NJ: Princeton University Press.

Roitman, Janet. (2004). *Fiscal Disobedience: An Anthropology of Economic Regulation in Central Africa*. Princeton, NJ: Princeton University Press.

Rowland, Nicholas J., & Passoth, Jan-Hendrik. (2015). Infrastructure and the State in Science and Technology Studies. *Social Studies of Science, 45*(1), 137–145. doi:10.1177/0306312714537566.

Roy, Ananya. (2009). Strangely Familiar: Planning and the Worlds of Insurgence and Informality. *Planning Theory, 8*(1), 7–11.

Roy, Ananya. (2015). Governing the Postcolonial Suburbs. In Pierre Hamel & Roger Keil (Eds.), *Suburban Governance: A Global View* (pp. 337–346). Toronto: University of Toronto Press.

Roy, Arundhati. (1999). *The Cost of Living*. New York: Modern Library.

Roychowdhury, Poulami. (2021). Incorporation: Governing Gendered Violence in a State of Disempowerment. *American Journal of Sociology, 126*(4), 852–888.

Rueschemeyer, Dietrich, & Evans, Peter. (1985). The state and economic transformation: toward an analysis of the conditions underlying effective intervention. In Peter Evans, Theda Skocpol, & Dietrich Rueschemeyer (Eds.), *Bringing the State Back In* (pp. 44–76). Cambridge: Cambridge University Press.

Saeed, Sadia. (2017). *Politics of Desecularization: Law and the Minority Question in Pakistan*. Cambridge: Cambridge University Press.

Saikia, Yasmin. (2011). *Women, War, and the Making of Bangladesh*. Durham, NC: Duke University Press.

Schrank, A. (2013). Rewarding Regulation in Latin America. *Politics & Society, 41*(4), 487–495. doi:10.1177/0032329213507549.

Shah, Aqil. (2014). *The Army and Democracy*. Cambridge, MA: Harvard University Press.

Shaikh, Farzana. (2009). *Making Sense of Pakistan*. New York: Columbia University Press.

Siddiqa, Ayesha. (2017). *Military Inc.: Inside Pakistan's Military Economy*. Penguin Random House India.

Silbey, S. S. (2011). The Sociological Citizen: Pragmatic and Relational Regulation in Law and Organizations. *Regulation & Governance*, *5*(1), 1–13. doi:10.1111/j.1748-5991.2011.01106.x.

Smith, Thomas. (2004). Electricity Theft: A Comparative Analysis. *Energy Policy*, *32*, 2067–2076.

Snyder, Richard. (2001). Scaling Down: The Subnational Comparative Method. *Studies in Comparative International Development*, *36*, 93–110.

Soifer, Hillel David. (2015). *State Building in Latin America*. New York: Cambridge University Press.

Soifer, Hillel, & Vom Hau, Matthias. (2008). Unpacking the Strength of the State: The Utility of State Infrastructural Power. *Studies in Comparative International Development*, *43*(3–4), 219.

Swartz, David L. (2013). *Symbolic Power, Politics, and Intellectuals: The Political Sociology of Pierre Bourdieu*. Chicago: University of Chicago Press.

Swartz, David L. (2014). Theorizing Fields. *Theory and Society*, *43*(6), 675–682.

Talbot, Ian. (2009). *Pakistan: A Modern History*. London: Hurst.

Taylor, Charles. (2002). Modern Social Imaginaries. *Public Culture*, *14*(1), 91–124.

Tendler, Judith. (1997). *Good Government in the Tropics*. Baltimore: Johns Hopkins University Press.

Tilly, Charles. (1985). War Making and State Making as Organized Crime. In Peter Evans, Dietrich Rueschemeyer, & Theda Skocpol (Eds.), *Bringing the State Back In* (pp. 169–187). Cambridge: Cambridge University Press.

Tonkiss, Fran. (2013). *Cities by Design: The Social Life of Urban Form*. Cambridge: Polity.

United States Agency for International Development. (2010). *Terms of Reference: Pakistan Power Distribution Companies (DISCOs) Performance Improvement Program*.

United States Agency for International Development. (2014). *Local Systems: A Framework for Supporting Sustained Development*. Washington, DC. Retrieved from http://www.usaid.gov/policy/local-systems-framework.

Venkatesh, Sudhir. (2002). Doin' the Hustle: Constructing the Ethnographer in the American Ghetto. *Ethnography*, *3*(1), 91–111.

Verkaaik, Oskar. (2004). *Migrants and Militants: Fun and Urban Violence in Pakistan*. Princeton, NJ: Princeton University Press.

Victor, David G., & Heller, Thomas C. (2007). *The Political Economy of Power Sector Reform: The Experiences of Five Major Developing Countries*. New York: Cambridge University Press.

Wacquant, Loïc J. D. (1993). From Ruling Class to Field of Power: An Interview with Pierre Bourdieu on La Noblesse d'Etat. *Theory, Culture & Society*, *10*(3), 19–44.

Wade, R. (1982). The System of Administrative and Political Corruption - Canal Irrigation in South-India. *Journal of Development Studies*, *18*(3), 287–328. doi:10.1080/00220388208421833.

Water and Power Development Authority. (1986). *Power Development Plan for Elimination of Loadshedding by January 1990*. Lahore, Pakistan.

Watson, Vanessa. (2009). Seeing from the South: Refocusing Urban Planning on the Globe's Central Urban Issues. *Urban Studies*, *46*, 2259–2275. doi:10.1177/0042098009342598.

Weber, Max, Gerth, H. H., & Mills, C. Wright. (1991 [1925]). *From Max Weber: Essays in Sociology*. London: Routledge.

Wedeen, Lisa. (2003). Seeing like a Citizen, Acting like a State: Exemplary Events in Unified Yemen. *Comparative Studies in Social History*, *45*, 680–713.

Weinstein, Liza. (2014). *The Durable Slum: Dharavi and the Right to Stay Put in Globalizing Mumbai*. Minneapolis: University of Minnesota Press.

Wells, Louis T., & Ahmad, Rafiq. (2007). *Making Foreign Investment Safe: Property Rights and National Sovereignty*. Oxford: Oxford University Press.

Williams, J. H., & Dubash, N. K. (2004). Asian Electricity Reform in Historical Perspective. *Pacific Affairs*, *77*(3), 411–436.

Williams, J. H., & Ghanadan, R. (2006). Electricity Reform in Developing and Transition Countries: A Reappraisal. *Energy*, *31*(6–7), 815–844.

Williamson, John. (1990). What Washington Means by Policy Reform. In John Williamson (Ed.), Latin American Adjustment: How Much Has Happened? (Vol. 1, pp. 90–120). Washington, DC: Peterson Institute for International Economics.

Wilson, James Q. (1989). *Bureaucracy: What Government Agencies Do and Why They Do It.* New York: Basic Books.

Winner, Langdon. (1980). Do Artifacts Have Politics? *Daedalus (Cambridge, Mass.), 109*(1), 121–136.

Wirsing, Robert. (2008). *Baloch Nationalism and the Geopolitics of Energy Resources: The Changing Context of Separatism in Pakistan.* Retrieved from

Woodhouse, Erik. (2006). The Obsolescing Bargain Redux: Foreign Investment in the Electric Power Sector in Developing Countries. *N.Y.U. Journal of International Law and Politics, 38,* 121–246.

World Bank. (1993). *Power Supply in Developing Countries: Will Reform Work? Proceedings of a Roundtable Co-Sponsored by the World Bank and Electricité de France.* Retrieved from http://www-wds.worldbank.org/servlet/WDSContentServer/IW3P/IB/1999/09/10/000009265_3980513111708/Rendered/PDF/multi_page.pdf.

World Bank. (2001). *Implementation Completion Report (03370; 29820) on a Loan in the Amount of US$150 Million to the Islamic Republic of Pakistan for a Private Sector Energy Development Project.* Retrieved from http://www-wds.worldbank.org/servlet/WDSContentServer/IW3P/IB/2001/06/23/000094946_01061204004242/Rendered/PDF/multi0page.pdf.

World Bank. (2004). *Implementation Completion Report (SCL-39650) on a Loan in the Amount of US$350.0 MILLION to The Islamic Republic of Pakistan for a Ghazi Barotha Hydropower Project.* Retrieved from http://documents.worldbank.org/curated/en/539771468774911654/Pakistan-Ghazi-Barotha-Hydropower-Project.

World Bank. (2008). *Public Sector Reform: What Works and Why? An IEG evaluation of World Bank Support.* Retrieved from http://hdl.handle.net/10986/6484.

World Bank. (2010). *Getting Electricity: A Pilot Indicator Set from the Doing Business Project.* Retrieved from

World Bank. (2017). *Residential Electricity Subsidies in Pakistan: Targeting, Welfare Impacts, and Options for Reform.* Retrieved from http://hdl.handle.net/10986/29196.

World Commission on Dams. (2000). *Dams and Development: A New Framework for Decision-Making: The Report of the World Commission on Dams.* London: Earthscan.

World Governance Indicators. (2017). Retrieved from http://info.worldbank.org/governance/wgi/.

Yakubovich, V., Granovetter, M., & McGuire, P. (2005). Electric Charges: The Social Construction of Rate Systems. *Theory and Society, 34*(5–6), 579–612.

Zaloznaya, Marina. (2017). *The Politics of Bureaucratic Corruption in Post-Transitional Eastern Europe.* New York: Cambridge University Press.

INDEX

For the benefit of digital users, indexed terms that span two pages (e.g., 52–53) may, on occasion, appear on only one of those pages.